D0484546

Creating a Learning

Strategy, Technology, and Practice

Creating a Learning Culture features insightful essays from industry observers and revealing case studies of prominent corporations. Each chapter revolves around creating an environment where learning takes place each day, all day, fundamentally changing the way we think about how, what, and when we learn, and how we can apply learning to practice. Three sections address key aspects of a learning culture: the modern business context and the importance of learning at every juncture; the organic and adaptive approaches organizational leaders can take to design enduring success; and the expanding role of individuals within organizations and the implications for business leaders, educators, technologists, and learners. Identifying the steps companies must take to remain competitive for years to come, this book explains how learning strategies applied to all aspects of every job can provide swift returns and lasting results.

Marcia L. Conner is Managing Director of Ageless Learner, a think-tank and advisory services practice, and a Fellow of the Batten Institute, Darden Graduate School of Business Administration, University of Virginia. She is the author of *Learn More Now: 10 Simple Steps to Learning Better, Smarter, and Faster*.

James G. Clawson is Professor of Business Administration, Area Coordinator for Leadership and Organizational Behavior, and Chair of the First Year MBA Program Committee at the Darden Graduate School of Business Administration, University of Virginia. He is also a consultant and the author of *Level Three Leadership: Getting Below the Surface* and co-author of *Self-Assessment and Career Development* and *An MBA's Guide to Self-Assessment and Career Development*.

"Quite simply the best book I have read on all that matters for getting better at getting better . . . Should be mandatory reading for educators and organization leaders everywhere. A superb synthesis of perspectives and intelligence from individuals who have demonstrated an extraordinary understanding of what matters most in learning and excelling. Read it to learn how to create excellence and success around you."

Kantha Shelke, scientist, and founder of Corvus Blue LLC

"As organizations take learning to the next phase, to meet the learning challenge at the global level, they will benefit from the insights and lessons presented in this excellent book. *Creating a Learning Culture* will help them cost-effectively provide learning resources and interactive learning environments to employees anywhere in the world."

Eilif Trondsen, Director, Learning on Demand, SRI Consulting Business Intelligence

"Organizations that excel at learning will be the only ones that survive in the 21st century. This book points the way for those who realize that this is not just another 'management fad.' Continuous, accelerated organizational learning represents the key discriminator between 'winners' and 'losers.' I strongly recommend this book to those who want to be counted amongst the 'winners!'"

Richard Bozoian, Director of Learning and Organizational Development, BAE Systems

"You will want to have *Creating a Learning Culture* within your grasp at all times. One of the great things about this collection is that you can spend a second flipping open to almost any page, or take a whole sabbatical to really absorb it all, and in either case your time will be amply rewarded with new insights, inspiration, and ideas."

Wayne Hodgins, Strategic Futurist, Director of Worldwide Learning Strategies, Director of Strategic Executive Services, Autodesk Inc.

"*Creating a Learning Culture* takes a deep dive into a topic that no business leader can afford to ignore – or delegate to HR. We've all been told that learning is *the* source of competitive advantage – but how do we get there? . . . From technology to metrics, from trust to tools – it's all here, with frameworks, philosophies, *and* plenty of real life stories. There's something of interest for anyone ready to take learning from talk to action."

Jeanne Liedtka, former Chief Learning Officer, United Technologies Corporation

"I would suggest the traffic warning 'Read Slowly: Curve Ahead.' Each essay develops learning culture from a different perspective. In the world's current change-acceleration mode, we had better learn about learning from all angles."

John Sall, Co-founder and Executive Vice President, SAS Institute

Creating a Learning Culture

Strategy, Technology, and Practice

EDITED BY MARCIA L. CONNER

AND JAMES G. CLAWSON

CAMBRIDGE
UNIVERSITY PRESS

PUBLISHED BY THE PRESS SYNDICATE OF THE UNIVERSITY OF CAMBRIDGE
The Pitt Building, Trumpington Street, Cambridge, United Kingdom

CAMBRIDGE UNIVERSITY PRESS
The Edinburgh Building, Cambridge, CB2 2RU, UK
40 West 20th Street, New York, NY 10011–4211, USA
477 Williamstown Road, Port Melbourne, VIC 3207, Australia
Ruiz de Alarcón 13, 28014 Madrid, Spain
Dock House, The Waterfront, Cape Town 8001, South Africa

http://www.cambridge.org

First published 2004

Printed in the United Kingdom at the University Press, Cambridge

Typeface Sabon 10/13 pt.   *System* LATEX 2_ε [TB]

A catalogue record for this book is available from the British Library

Library of Congress Cataloguing in Publication data
Creating a learning culture: strategy, technology, and practice / edited by Marcia L.
Conner and James G. Clawson.
    p.   cm.   Includes bibliographical references and index.
ISBN 0 521 83017 6 (hb) – ISBN 0 521 53717 7 (pb)
1. Learning – Case studies.   2. Organizational learning – Case studies.
3. Employees – Training of – Case studies.   I. Conner, Marcia L., 1965–
II. Clawson, James G., 1947–
LB1060.C75   2004
658.3'124 – dc22   2003056854

ISBN 0 521 83017 6 hardback
ISBN 0 521 53717 7 paperback

Contents

Contributors

Lisa Abrams is a research consultant at IBM's Institute for Knowledge-Based Organizations in Cambridge, Massachusetts. Most of her projects have focused on social capital, knowledge-sharing, trust on the Internet, and the links between trust and project performance. She has spoken frequently on the topic of social capital and has written several articles, including "Translation Technology Considerations for Global Organizations" (KOPF White Paper Series, June 2003), "Best of Both Worlds: Combining Knowledge Management and Learning and Development" (KOPF White Paper Series, April 2003), "Trust and Knowledge Sharing: A Critical Combination" (IKM White Paper Series, June 2002), and "Why Should I Trust You? The Antecedents of Trust in a Knowledge Transfer Context" (IKM White Paper Series, March 2002). Abrams received an AB from Brown University, an MBA from MIT's Sloan School of Management, and an MPA from Columbia University's School of International and Public Affairs.

Laurie Bassi is the chief executive officer and a founding partner of McBassi & Company, Inc. She also serves as the chairwoman of the board of Knowledge Asset Management, Inc., an investment company that invests in companies that invest in their employees. From 1996 to 1999, she was vice-president for research at the American Society for Training and Development, and from 1982 to 1995 she was a tenured professor of economics and public policy at Georgetown University. Bassi has served as co-chair of the National Academy of Science's Board on Testing and Assessment, and chair of the human capital subcommittee of the Brookings Institution's taskforce on intangible assets. She has written more than fifty books and papers. Bassi holds a BS in mathematics from Illinois State University, an MS in industrial and labor relations from Cornell University, and a PhD in economics from Princeton University.

John Seely Brown was chief scientist of Xerox and director of its Palo Alto Research Center (PARC), where he was responsible for guiding one of the most famous technology think-tanks in the world and leading one of the most celebrated and far-ranging corporate research efforts. His current areas of interest include growing up in the digital age, organizational learning, nurturing radical innovation, rich media and the gaming world, and the direction of information technology. Brown is co-author, with Paul Duguid, of *The Social Life of Information* (Harvard Business School Press, 2000) and editor of *Seeing Differently: Insights on Innovation* (Harvard Business School Press, 1997). He is a Batten Fellow at the University of Virginia's Darden Graduate School of Business Administration and a visiting scholar at the Annenberg Center and Annenberg School of Communication at the University of Southern California. Brown has an AB from Brown University and a PhD in computer and communication sciences from the University of Michigan.

Gunnar Brückner is a coach, consultant, strategist, and expert in organizational learning and staff development. He is chief executive officer of coachingplatform Inc., a company specializing in providing a broad range of learning-related services, including a proprietary online collaboration software. Brückner is the former chief learning officer of the United Nations Development Programme, where he conceived and implemented innovative strategies for staff learning and development on a global scale. He has presented at numerous professional conferences and serves on several advisory boards. He holds an MA in sociology from the Free University in Berlin and a certificate in organizational development from New York University.

James G. Clawson is a professor at the University of Virginia's Darden Graduate School of Business Administration, where he has taught since 1981. He was a visiting professor at the International University of Japan in 1991 and taught at Harvard Business School before moving to Virginia. Clawson has consulted with corporations and organizations on issues of organizational design, management development, career management, change management, leadership development, and human resource management. He has designed and led or taught in a number of Darden School executive education programs, including "Power and Leadership." He has written hundreds of cases on management and career issues and several books, including *Level Three*

Leadership (Prentice Hall, 1998). He received a bachelor's degree in Japanese language and literature from Stanford University, an MBA from Brigham Young University, and a DBA in organizational behavior from Harvard Business School.

Eileen Clegg is a senior consultant for Global Learning Resource, a research affiliate with the Institute for the Future (IFTF), and associate of the group graphics firm The Grove. Her recent research at IFTF has focused on K-12, university, and corporate education. She has also developed a graphic recording method for "public listening" and "visual speaking," which provides immediate synthesis of content and an alternative record of the event. Clegg was a newspaper journalist for twenty years, most of those at the *Santa Rosa Press Democrat*, where she developed several award-winning projects, including "What if It Happened Here," a look at oil spill clean-up infrastructure in California, which won a Scripps-Howard National Journalism Award (second place in the United States, 1990). Clegg has published three books and many articles. Her most recent book is *Claiming Your Creative Self* (New Harbinger Publications, 1999). She has a BA from the University of California at Berkeley.

Harlan Cleveland, political scientist and public executive, is president emeritus of the World Academy of Art and Science. He has served as a United Nations relief administrator in Italy and China, a Marshall Plan executive, a magazine editor and publisher, assistant secretary of state, and US ambassador to NATO. As an academic leader he has twice been an academic dean and once a university president (at the University of Hawaii). He has written hundreds of magazine and journal articles, and is author or co-author of twelve books on executive leadership and international affairs. His most recent book is *Nobody in Charge: Essays on the Future of Leadership* (Jossey-Bass, 2002). He earned his bachelor's degree from Princeton University and was a Rhodes Scholar.

Wendy L. Coles is acting director of Alternatives For Girls, a not-for-profit organization in Detroit, Michigan, dedicated to helping at-risk girls and young women. As director of corporate strategy and knowledge development at General Motors, Coles was dedicated to transforming GM into a knowledge-based enterprise. Her twenty-four years with GM also included serving as director of organization and employee development within numerous units. She has done extensive work with W. Edwards Deming and Russell Ackoff, world leaders in quality and systems thinking. Her publications can be found in the *Knowledge Management Review*, the *1999 Handbook of Business Strategy*, and the Michigan state publication *What's What in Jackson County*. Coles has a BA from the University of Waterloo in Ontario, Canada, an MA from Central Michigan University, and a PhD in adult and continuing education from Michigan State University. She is also a graduate of Indiana University's Executive Development Program and MIT's Leading Learning Communities.

Marcia L. Conner is managing director of Ageless Learner, a think-tank and advisory services practice focused on learning and adapting across the life span, and co-founder of the Learnativity Alliance, bringing people together to work at the intersection of learning, productivity, activity, and creativity. She is a frequent keynote speaker and provocateur in adult education, human capital development, innovative leadership, organizational change, and learning culture. She serves as senior counsel and executive coach to leaders around the globe. She is a Fellow of the Batten Institute at the Darden Graduate School of Business Administration at the University of Virginia. She was vice-president of education and information futurist for PeopleSoft and senior manager of worldwide training at Microsoft. She has studied, lived, and worked on three continents. She has published many articles and has authored *Learn More Now: 10 Simple Steps to Learning Better, Smarter, and Faster* (John Wiley & Sons, 2004).

Rob Cross is an assistant professor of management at the University of Virginia's McIntire School of Commerce. He also directs the social network research program for IBM's Institute for Knowledge-Based Organizations in Cambridge, Massachusetts, where he has worked with more than fifty well-known companies and government agencies in applying network concepts to critical business issues. His work on social networks has been published in *Harvard Business Review, Sloan Management Review, California Management Review, Organizational Dynamics*, and *Business Horizons*. He is also the author of two books, *Networks in the Knowledge Economy* (Oxford University Press, 2003) and *The Hidden Power of Social Networks: Understanding How Work Really Gets Done in Organizations* (Harvard Business School Press, 2004). Cross holds a BS and an MBA from the University of Virginia and a PhD from Boston University.

Dori Digenti works with corporate, community, and academic groups to assist them in building collaborative networks to face complex challenges. She is currently senior research associate and director of the Community, Science & Environment Program at Mount Holyoke College in Massachusetts. She is also founder of Learning Mastery, a consultancy, and the C3 LearnNet corporate learning network. Digenti has held positions as director of training and special executive programs at MIT, and as Far East regional manager for a high-tech firm. She is webmaster of www.edschein.com and www.communityscience.net. Her publications include *The Collaborative Learning Guidebook* (1999), *Creating Virtual Teams that Learn* (with Lisa Kimball, 2001), and articles in leading journals such as *Systems Thinker* and *Reflections: The SoL Journal*. Digenti has a BA from Cornell University and an MS in organization development from American University.

Cliff Figallo is an independent consultant and expert in the field of online community, collaboration, and knowledge-sharing. He is a founding veteran of The Farm, the largest intentional self-sustaining community established during the 1970s, and was director of The WELL – called "the world's most influential online community" by *Wired* magazine – during its early years. Figallo has continued to pioneer productive applications of group interaction through electronic networks. He has consulted for AOL, Genentech, IBM, and Cisco Systems, among many other organizations. He has authored *Hosting Web Communities* (John Wiley & Sons, 1998), co-authored, with Nancy Rhine, *Building the Knowledge Management Network* (John Wiley & Sons, 2002), and has written many articles for print and Internet publications. Figallo has a BA from the University of Maryland.

David Grebow consults on learning strategies and is an expert on emerging learning technologies. He was a director of e-learning strategy for IBM and co-founder of the IBM Institute of Advanced Learning (IAL) in Zurich. He also held executive positions at PeopleSoft, Global Knowledge, and Digital Equipment, developing corporate strategies and leading major programs focused on communications, learning, and technology. He was the creator and director of the worldwide EPSS program for Digital and researched the effects on learning of storytelling, simulation, and collaboration at IBM's IAL. He has written, spoken, and been interviewed numerous times on the past, present, and future intersection of education and technology. Grebow holds a BS from Boston University.

Karen Kocher is vice-president of the CIGNA Technology Institute, where she is responsible for career management and employee development for the CIGNA systems community and for the company's technology-related education and technology-enabled learning. Before joining CIGNA, Kocher worked at IBM's Mindspan Solutions organization, where she defined e-learning strategies, solutions, and offerings. She was also the offering executive of advanced and emerging technologies education within IBM Learning Services. Before joining IBM, Kocher was a vice-president of education for IKON. She speaks regularly at major events on issues surrounding corporate learning and business management, and she is frequently recognized by the technology training industry. Kocher was presented with a *Service News* magazine award as one of the most innovative IT service leaders of the year, and she earned the Chartered Property Casualty Underwriter designation in 1995.

Brook Manville heads the Center for Community Leadership for the United Way of America, where he is responsible for organizational development, leadership, knowledge management, and learning across the organization. Prior to taking on this role, he was chief learning officer at Saba Software. He was a partner and member of the leadership team of the organizational practices at McKinsey & Company and served as McKinsey's first director of knowledge management. He has also been a professor of classics and history at Northwestern University. Manville has published widely on topics related to organization, knowledge management, and workplace learning in such venues as *Fast Company, Leader to Leader, Sloan Management Review*, and *Harvard Business Review*. Manville is co-author, with Josiah Ober, of *A Company of Citizens: What the World's First Democracy Can Teach Leaders About Building Great Organizations* (Harvard Business School Press, 2003). Manville received a BA from Yale University, an MA from Oxford University, and a PhD in history from Yale University.

Karen L. McGraw is a founding partner at McBassi & Company, Inc. She was a co-developer of the Human Capital Capability Scorecard and has been responsible for the implementation of the Scorecard in client organizations and for the continual refinement of the scorecard toolset. McGraw is also the president of Cognitive Technologies Group, a firm that specializes in improving workforce performance through the re-engineering of training delivery, the implementation of learning and knowledge management systems, and better job design. Previously, she served in leadership positions in the area of human performance engineering and improvement for firms including Saba, RWD, and Loral. She has been an adjunct research associate and professor at the University of Texas and the University of Maryland, and is the author of numerous texts and articles. McGraw received her PhD from Texas Tech University, where she specialized in the cognitive impact of instructional technology.

Dan McMurrer is the vice-president for research at McBassi & Company, Inc. He is also the chief research officer at Knowledge Asset Management, Inc., an investment firm that invests in companies that invest in their people. Much of his recent research has focused on the relationship between organizations' human capital investments and organizational results, such as financial and market performance. He is the author of numerous articles and two books, *Workplace Training for Low-Wage Workers* (with Amanda Ahlstrand and Laurie Bassi, Upjohn Institute Press, 2003) and *Getting Ahead: Economic and Social Mobility in America* (with Isabel Sawhill, Urban Institute Press, 1998). McMurrer holds a BA from Princeton University and an MPP from Georgetown University.

Andrew Parker is an independent consultant and researcher. He has employed social network analysis techniques to map important knowledge relationships between people and departments in more than fifty well-known organizations. Through his research, which examines the flow of knowledge within top-level executive teams, functional departments, communities of practice, and recently merged companies, organizations have gained insight into critical knowledge creation and sharing activities. Parker is a co-author of two books, *Networks in the Knowledge Economy* (Oxford University Press, 2003) and *The Adaptable Organization: Creating Networks for Strategic Success* (Harvard Business School Press, 2004), and more than ten articles and white papers. His articles have appeared in *Sloan Management Review,*

Organizational Dynamics, and *California Management Review*. He holds a MSc from the London School of Economics and is currently studying for a PhD in sociology at Stanford University.

Clark N. Quinn is executive director of OtterSurf Laboratories, a cognitive design consultancy. In his work he applies what is known about how people think and learn to the design of systems. His achievements include innovative and award-winning interactive applications as well as publications and presentations on such topics as learning objects, game design, and meta- and mobile-learning. He led the design and development of an intelligently adaptive online learning system for Knowledge Universe/Knowledge Planet, designed and programmed educational computer games with DesignWare, and spent several years researching interaction and learning experience design at the University of New South Wales. He also assisted two Australian government-sponsored initiatives in online learning and new media. Quinn has a PhD from the University of California, San Diego.

Mitch Ratcliffe is president of Internet/Media Strategies Inc., a seven-year-old media consultancy. He is also editorial director for Innova-tionWORLD, a foreign direct investment research company, which he co-founded. Ratcliffe was editor and publisher of the newsletter *Digital Media* in the mid 1990s, has developed and run a number of websites for ZD Net, and was chief content officer at ON24, the first streaming media news network. He worked as an investment banker specializing in media and as a venture investor, representing Softbank Ventures on the board of dating service Match.com. He is also the co-founder of Correspondences.org, a civic journalism project and creator of several well-trafficked weblogs at www.ratcliffeblog.com. A widely published author and commentator, his books include *PowerBook: The Digital Nomad's Guide* (Random House, 1994) and *Newton Solutions: Taking the Apple PDA from Toy to Tool* (Academic Press, 1996). Ratcliffe holds a bachelor's degree in political science from Washington State University.

Garry O. Ridge is president and chief executive officer of the WD-40 Company in San Diego, California. He has been with WD-40 since 1987 and has worked with WD-40 in forty-eight countries, with a focus on the Pacific Rim and Asia. A native of Australia, Ridge has served as national vice-president of the Australian Marketing Institute and the Australian Automotive Aftermarket Association, which awarded him its Outstanding Service to Industry Award in 1999. He hosts a website focused on learning culture at www.thelearningmoment.net. Ridge received his diploma in retail/wholesale distribution from the Sydney Technical College and his MS in executive leadership from the University of San Diego.

Marc J. Rosenberg is an independent consultant, educator, and expert in training, organizational learning, e-learning, knowledge management, and performance improvement. He is the author of *E-Learning: Strategies for Delivering Knowledge in the Digital Age* (McGraw-Hill, 2001). He has spoken at the White House and at numerous professional and business conferences, and is a frequently quoted expert in business and trade publications. Rosenberg is a past president of the International Society for Performance Improvement (ISPI) and holds degrees in communications and marketing and a PhD in instructional design from Kent State University.

Edgar H. Schein has taught at the MIT Sloan School of Management since 1956 and was named the Sloan Fellows Professor of Management in 1978. He is currently professor emeritus and senior lecturer. He is the author of many articles and books, most recently *Process Consultation Revisited* (Addison-Wesley, 1998), *The Corporate Culture Survival Guide* (Jossey-Bass, 1999), and *DEC Is Dead, Long Live DEC* (Berrett-Koehler, 2003). He has consulted with many organizations in the United States and overseas on organizational culture, organization development, process consultation, and career dynamics. Schein has a master's degree in psychology from Stanford University and a PhD in social psychology from Harvard University.

Douglas K. Smith is a consultant, speaker, and executive concerned with performance, change, strategy, innovation, and ethics. He is named in *The Guru Guide* as one of the world's top hundred consultants and has worked for clients, large and small, across the private, nonprofit, and governmental sectors. In addition, he has taught high school, practiced law, and co invented new technology in entertainment and education. He is the author of several articles and books, including the business classic *The Wisdom of Teams* (HarperCollins, 1994), and his newest book *On Value and Values: Thinking Differently About We in an Age of Me* (Prentice Hall, 2004).

William M. Snyder is the founder of Social Capital Group, a research-consulting group that helps civic leaders organize community-based approaches to social and economic development. He is a co-founder, with Etienne Wenger, of CPsquare, a cross-organizational, cross-sector community of practice on communities of practice. He has consulted for twenty years on large-scale organizational change efforts in the private and public sectors, and worked at McKinsey & Company on strategic knowledge initiatives for the firm and its clients. His work focuses on community-of-practice applications in the civic domain – both within cities and across cities at national and international levels. His publications include "Communities of Practice: The Organizational Frontier" (*Harvard Business Review*, 2000), *Cultivating Communities of Practice* (Harvard Business School Press, 2002), and "Communities of Practice: A New Tool for Managers" (IBM Foundation for the Business of Government, 2003). Snyder holds AB and EdM degrees from Harvard and a PhD in business administration from the University of Southern California.

Estee Solomon Gray is founding partner of Congruity, where she focuses on the design and use of next-generation knowledge systems that capitalize on the emergent properties of work, organizations, and Internet technologies. She is a consultant and thought leader on cultivating corporate communities of practice and "social computing" approaches to human- and social-capital management. She has worked with *Fortune* 100 executive teams, start-up management teams, and nonprofit boards, and has held key positions in marketing, customer support, and product development, most recently as chief e-learning officer and vice-president of marketing for InterWise. Solomon Gray was a founding member of Regis McKenna's technology marketing practice, and she has worked closely with top management teams at Xerox, HP, Silicon Graphics, National Semiconductor, Raychem, and others. Her work has been featured in *Fast Company*, *Release 1.0*, and in several books on knowledge management. She holds a BS in neurophysiology and biomechanics from Yale University and an MBA and an MSEE in computer architecture from Stanford University.

Etienne Wenger is an independent consultant and thought leader in the field of communities of practice. He was featured by *Training Magazine* in its series "A New Breed of Visionary." A pioneer of community-of-practice research, he is the author and co-author of seminal books on the topic, including *Situated Learning* (Cambridge University Press, 1991), *Communities of Practice: Learning, Meaning, and Identity* (Cambridge University Press, 1998), and *Cultivating Communities of Practice* (Harvard Business School Press, 2002). Wenger's work is influencing a growing number of organizations in the private and public sectors. He is co-founder of CPsquare, a cross-organizational, cross-sector community of practice on communities of practice. He holds a PhD from the University of California at Irvine.

Brenda Wilkins is president of Big Sky Learning Institute and has been a leadership and organizational strategist for fifteen years. Wilkins is recognized as one of the seminal researchers in the area of executive coaching. She has consulted to a wide array of organizations, including Boeing, the Department of Public Health and Human Services for Montana, the community group Zonta International, the family business Galko Homes, and the small enterprise Don's Rubber Stamps. She also serves as the development director for Missoula Children's Theatre (MCT), the largest touring theatre company of its kind. Wilkins has an EdD in educational leadership and counseling from the University of Montana.

Foreword

Welcome!

You have opened a wonderful collection of essays. So, let me congratulate you. You must be a learner!

I hope you do not feel alone and scared. I hope you are not sneaking into some janitorial closet for a furtive glimpse at the wisdom and insight of some of the world's most thoughtful learners and learning advisers. I hope you do not feel like a criminal or a thief, stealing company time for learning.

I hope, instead, you have this book open at your desk – for all the world to see that you are a learner and that you know learning matters to your organization as much as it does to yourself.

Sometimes, I know, taking time at work to learn can feel odd. It can feel somehow taboo – an activity that must be justified by more than its own rewards. Sometimes it feels that our lives in organizations do not quite make sense. We know in our hearts and souls, and, increasingly, from our experience, that our work is impossible without learning. We know that any number of critical, recurring challenges – from customer service and quality to innovation, technology, and values – cannot be met without learning. But, still, we act as if learning is something to be done in private time instead of organizational time, and with strict, clear, complete, and overwhelming justification by the bottom line.

Somehow we act as if learning is a fad, some new-fangled form of empowerment and feel-good human relations management that is nice to have as long as it does not bust any budgets. Somehow we have not quite come clean that learning and work are actually two peas in the same pod.

Somehow we act as if we actually know CEOs, presidents, division heads, functional heads, middle managers, or others who scream at the top of their voices: "Stop learning! Learners are not welcome. Anyone caught learning will immediately be shown the door. There is no place or time in this company for learning."

After a quarter-century of leading and consulting to organizations, and writing about organizational change and performance, I have yet to meet such people. I have never – *never* – heard any executive wholly and witheringly denounce learning and take action to stamp out and eradicate learning of any sort.

Yes, I have witnessed plenty of people *behave* in ways that discouraged learning or ignored the inevitable, inescapable links among learning, work, and performance. I have seen, as have you, leaders who demand demonstrable results from learning or who question the resources dedicated to it. But however difficult and challenging, those behaviors are not the same as declarations against learning itself.

Such behaviors, however, do need to change. People like you – people who are learners, workers, and organizational performers – must address the contribution learning makes to organizations and those who participate in them. You must work hard and learn much to match the best possible combination of understanding about learning to the purposes and people of organizations.

Learners never stop learning. Learners never stop performing. Learners about learning cultures never stop rising to threats and opportunities. People like you care about individual learning because you are learners. And you care about organizational learning because you care about your organization.

You care about learning more about how learning happens among people and in organizations; how learning cultures might best be understood, designed, and implemented; how various tools (technological or otherwise) contribute to learning; how leaders are responsible for learning; and what the case is for more or better learning.

This book is a treasure for learners like you, a feast of offerings on these and other topics. As you continue to learn from it, I have only one suggestion: Don't box with shadows that are not there; don't fear a leadership that is anti-learning – because no such leadership exists. Yes, respect the complex, messy, and very human challenges of leadership and learning inside organizations. But remember this: human beings cannot be "against" learning.

The days are long gone when learning was solely a form of leisure, and leisure was traded off against labor. That kind of either/or no longer makes much sense. Perhaps it did in the gritty world of nineteenth- and early twentieth-century industrialization, the movement that so often seemed bent on converting men into machines and women into housewives. In that world, perhaps, learning was a hobby for the very rich, the very bored, and the very disengaged.

But you do not live in that world. It is unlikely that you work in brutal coal mines or slavish cotton fields, or on mindless automobile assembly lines. You may work in industries having to do with coal, cotton, or cars, but you do not have jobs that divide thinking from doing or learning from working.

Today, you cannot avoid human questions like these: What must I learn next? What do I need to be learning in order to be more productive? What does my organization need to be learning in order to compete more effectively? How can we learn best? How can we learn how to retain what we learn so we do not have to learn it again? What are we doing *now* that enhances our personal and organizational learning?

Don't ignore these questions. Embrace them.

So, welcome again. As you learn more about learning, share your wisdom with others. Bring them into the party. Quit acting as though the nineteenth century is not long gone. Stop assuming that learning is more about leisure than labor. And stay out of janitors' closets – especially those of your own making.

Douglas K. Smith

Introduction

JOHN SEELY BROWN AND
ESTEE SOLOMON GRAY

T H E success of a volume like this can be measured by its power to compel us to browse through its pages (thank goodness for paper!), to take excursions into its texts (praised be prose!), to create or extend relationships with its authors (thank G-d for friends!), to sense the shape of the landscape by hovering over its table of contents (some structure is good!), and, finally, to settle back, lengthen our focal point, and take the time to reflect on critical questions (time, oh precious time!). How did we get here? What, if anything, is being said here that could not have been said before? And why are we saying it now?

The contributors to this volume and the diverse participants at a Darden Graduate School of Business Administration colloquium in spring 2002, which set this book in motion, pose these questions even more pointedly: How have we – the practitioners and stakeholders in the art of creating learning cultures – learned what we know? What do we need to learn next? Beyond articulating these essential questions, the contributors to this volume offer some answers.

It takes twenty years

It was in 1990, with Peter Senge's *The Fifth Discipline: The Art and Practice of the Learning Organization*, that learning was first catapulted from the peripheral corporate domains of training and development departments to a place much closer to the center of business discourse. E-mail was still a creature of early adopters and large institutions, and PowerPoint (or its aptly named predecessor, Persuasion) was just coming onto desktops and into conference rooms across the world.

We are indebted to Teddy Zmrhal for his help on this chapter and more generally to Paul Duguid for his continual contributions to our understanding of social practice.

Because each technology purported to change the way people communicate rather than what they think, neither was considered particularly relevant to learning. In contrast, the five disciplines – personal mastery, mental models, shared vision, team learning, and systems thinking – appeared as tools to change the organization precisely by changing its thinking (and its thinking about thinking) and were easily recognized as valuable management tools for a knowledge-based, competitive era.

For those paying attention, the management conversation about learning had begun almost two decades earlier, when Chris Argyris and Donald Schön published *Theory in Practice*. They challenged organizations to recognize the limitations of "single-loop learning," familiar from the quality movement, which fosters the ability to detect and correct errors within the frame of current assumptions and policies, and to aspire instead to "double-loop learning," the ability to detect, determine, and perhaps even modify the organization's underlying norms, policies, and objectives.[1] The first type of learning implies *assimilation*, the domain of experience curves, which is relatively straightforward – both for people and for organizations. The second, considerably harder, implies *accommodation* – altering one's frame of reference or basic assumptions about the world. Double-loop learning involves changing the kinds of stories we construct to make sense of the world and, using the terms of gestalt therapy, requires a fresh, unbiased hearing of the "other." It is the ultimate goal of any learning culture. In corporations, double-loop learning is also the domain of strategic shifts. When Senge's five disciplines showed up on management's radar screens, they provided instant utility to the many organizations then engaged in strategic efforts to reframe existing markets and envision new business models. Yet Argyris's Model II learning organizations remain rare to this day.

Meanwhile, in the mid 1980s, from a more personal perspective, a community of researchers at and around Xerox PARC (Palo Alto Research Center) resolved to crack the learning problem by coming at it with multifocal conceptual lenses. One result was the founding in 1987 of the independent Institute for Research on Learning (IRL), a multidisciplinary community that undertook research to explore

---

[1] See C. Argyris and D. Schön, *Theory in Practice: Increasing Professional Effectiveness* (San Francisco: Jossey-Bass, 1974). For additional information on Argyris, see http://www.infed.org/thinkers/argyris.htm.

"everyday learning." Merging the practices of diverse fields – cognitive science, computer science, social linguistics, educational technology, and ethnography – proved painful but instructive. By the early 1990s, IRL began to inject a new, more social constructivist voice into the business conversations cascading from the learning organization work.[2] Amplified on one flank by workplace practitioners who worked with companies to enact new products, markets, and business models and on its other flank by educational practitioners who were elaborating new means to teach secondary school physics and mathematics, IRL put forth two fundamental understandings. First, that learning is fundamentally social and, second, that learning *about* is quite different from learning *to be*, which is a process of enculturation.

Building on observations in workplace, school, and craft settings, IRL researchers noted that successful learning happens with and through other people and that what we choose to learn depends on who we are, who we want to become, what we care about, and which communities we wish to join. In this frame, learning is also a matter of changing identity, not just acquiring knowledge. Learning of this nature occurs primarily through the process of gaining membership in a community of practice and is critically enabled by what Jean Lave and Etienne Wenger described as "legitimate peripheral participation" – the essence of classical apprenticeship. By this measure, a marketing manager has learned enough about wireless networking to drive his or her company's participation in that market when and only when he or she can understand the goings-on at an insider's wireless conference or have a mutually satisfying conversation with a committed member of the wireless community. Practice is not merely the measure of learning but the medium of it. In communities that arise less through organizational fiat (the authorized infrastructure of work) and more through pursuit of common work by the ecology of crafts, disciplines, and personalities needed to accomplish that work (the emergent infrastructure of work) practice is invented – and learning captured – each step of the way.[3] Members in such communities are co-constructing knowledge, which is literally embodied in their practice. Practice is not the stuff in

[2] For a complete list of IRL's Seven Principles of Learning, see http://www.linezine.com/6.2/articles/phuwnes.htm and http://www.newhorizons.org/trans/abbott.htm.

[3] Our colleague at IRL, Susan Stucky, first put forth the idea of "authorized" and "emergent" as parallel types of organization.

libraries but *knowing in action*. Words, books, simulations, tool-kits, and the like are artifacts deliberately crafted to transfer knowledge by evoking practice in the participant; they are not the knowledge itself.

In 1995, twenty years after Argyris and Schön, five years after *The Fifth Discipline*, and a year after the extended IRL community's first corporate client retreat, a pair of former *Harvard Business Review* editors launched *Fast Company*, a "handbook of the business revolution" targeted at readers "old enough to make a difference and young enough to be different." Readers were enjoined to "leap into the loop" by using e-mail to interact with the editors – a novel thought at the time – and to watch for a website yet to be constructed. By this time, PowerPoint was fully established as the first-language tool of business. Conference rooms were filled with people engaged in shoulder-to-shoulder knowledge-sharing, literally returning to the ancients' practice of reading and writing knowledge on the walls, although this time with beams of light instead of charcoal, chalk, or pigment.

Learning was so central to the new rules of business that an article by the two of us entitled "The People Are the Company" anchored the core Big Idea section of *Fast Company*'s first issue. "Work Is Personal . . . Computing Is Social . . . Knowledge Is Power" blared the cover art. "Learning is about work, work is about learning, and both are social," we wrote. In one of the most-cited articles in the publication's history, we asserted that the community of practice is the "critical building block of a knowledge-based company," the place where peers in the execution of real work create and carry the competences of the corporation. Veterans of numerous internal change initiatives, we quietly faced down the tanks of prevailing workplace ideology by proclaiming, "Processes don't do work, people do." We pointed out that "the real genius of organizations is the informal, impromptu, often inspired ways that real people solve real problems in ways that formal processes can't anticipate. When you're competing on knowledge, the name of the game is improvisation, not rote standardization." We also took on the sister shibboleths behind the traditional corporate approach to learning and knowledge; namely, that learning means individual mastery and that everything knowable can be made explicit. We did so in the way we knew would work: by telling stories. We told stories about Xerox field reps using radios and an "electronic knowledge refinery" called Eureka, and about how National Semiconductor's PLL ("phase locked loop," a specialized kind of circuit) designers coalesced almost instantly into a powerful, strategic, and ultimately much emulated presence in the company simply by being given the language, the license, and, eventually, the funding to organize. On one hand, these stories about the tacit and collective dimensions of learning and work eased quite naturally into readers' experiences. On the other hand, partly by design, the words *emerge* and *social* seemed to jump off the pages into people's faces – simple and familiar yet mysterious and somehow uncomfortable.

A decade distilled

Internet-time was upon us. The knowledge economy roared in, reshaping mainstream and management culture. It inflated. Burst. Rolled on. Contributors to this volume were deeply engaged in these formative years of the knowledge culture, as individuals and as professionals. As a result, things are being said within these pages that could not have been said before. Here we can begin to comprehend the fruits of the first decade of the knowledge economy.

In light of our early work at Xerox and that nascent whiff of learning culture themes in our *Fast Company* article, Marcia Conner and Jim Clawson, the editors of this collection, asked us to introduce the burgeoning learning movement and to assist readers on their journey through these essays. Here is what we glean from this volume and what we would urge readers to consider.

(1) Whether as individuals, as corporate entities, or as smaller productive groups (teams, communities, groups, business units), we all struggled to adapt to the economic, cognitive, and social implications of speed and globalization. We came to understand on a very practical level that learning is the strategic competence for an entity experiencing change. We quickly recognized that becoming a learning organization entails deliberate culture change. With that, we began to abandon our old instincts to reify and broadcast and to develop skills that help us cultivate new business practice. We struggled to honor local differences. And we learned to celebrate the unique power of narrative in conveying knowledge across otherwise formidable epistemic boundaries.

(2) Whether we consider ourselves skeptics or optimists, we are aware that a different model of the human at work is emerging. People need

to be trusted; work and therefore decision-making must be distributed. Relationships among workers – as learners – are key. People need to be given tools, as well as the social and informational spaces to interact as voluntary members of communities and as self-governing citizens. The outcome of investments in learning must be measured in new ways – in actual performance in real work. Thus, to the optimist's eye, the globally teamed workplace is beginning to seem like the norm; authority is naturally reaching down the ladder and closer to the customer, where the real knowledge is anyway. Meanwhile, to the skeptical eye, all this collaboration is a hair's breadth from enforced coordination; members of communities are being manipulated or, worse, exploited in their pursuit of personal and professional goals. But the signs of change are unmistakable.

(3) Whether our early professional identities are rooted in the sciences or the arts and humanities, we are busily incorporating new metaphors and intuitions drawn from the theory and practice of adaptive systems, ecologies, and other biological models. We are elaborating new approaches to organizational design and to civic activity. We are recrafting the standard tools of the learning trade – such as technology, classrooms, and coaching – and integrating the lessons of first-generation online communities. We are more articulate and deliberate about the social systems underlying learning. We are slowly but surely deploying systems that enable and honor learning – *in situ*.

Reflecting upon the learning trajectory of the last decade, captured so well in this volume, the days when *learning* usually meant *training*, *knowledge* meant *information*, and "content was king" seem to be fading. Community of practice is now a common term in business language and a sanctioned, funded approach to global knowledge-sharing and postmerger competence integration in leading companies. Learning is clearly no longer synonymous with individual mastery. It is now tacitly expressed in practice that not everything knowable can or should be made explicit, that content must be delivered in context to be effective. High-performance workscapes are built less through training and more through creating opportunities for collaboration and continual renewal, usually through teams, communities, networks, or forums. The words *social* and *emergent* no longer crimp business conversations about learning cultures but spark them.

Creating learning cultures: what's next?

So, what do practitioners and stakeholders in the art and practice of creating learning cultures need to learn next? Not surprisingly, our response begins with a critique of current practice – individual and collective. For all we have learned and for all that learning cultures have ostensibly changed, there is surely more learning and changing ahead of us.

• **We, as corporate practitioners, are still not taking advantage of authentic practice, and until we do so, we cannot master the dual art of knowledge-sharing and innovation.** The key to spreading actionable knowledge is understanding how shared practice provides the rails on which knowledge travels. Shared practice (which usually reflects shared roots) carries with it a shared worldview, which, in turn, enables people to trust the meaning of one another's words and actions. Without shared practice, knowledge tends to resist transfer, or "stick." The documents, tools, and instructions intended to convey actionable knowledge across organizations are quietly ignored, judged inapplicable, misapplied, or otherwise fail because, without shared practice, their recipients can neither decode their true meaning nor recode that meaning into appropriate local practice. Conversely, communities of practice are powerful learning venues and knowledge creation loci precisely because knowledge flows (or "leaks") so easily within their boundaries. Similarly, the looser (but sometimes equally durable) networks of practice to which many professionals now belong provide somewhat thinner rails on which knowledge can travel quite well between practitioners in distant parts of an organization or in different companies. As a rule, knowledge leaks in the direction of shared practice and sticks where practice is not shared.[4] Very often, sharing knowledge across an enterprise requires leaving the rails of a shared practice and jumping between two different practices (marketing/sales and research, or materials science and production engineering, for example) or organizational cultures. In these cases, we must literally find ways to bridge different practices. Bridging practices is never easy, even (or especially!) when accompanied by process-imposing tools like

---

[4] J. S. Brown and P. Duguid, "Knowledge and Organization: A Social-Practice Perspective," *Organization Science*, July 2000, p. 14.

Lotus Notes or enterprise systems like those from SAP, PeopleSoft, or Oracle. Bridging requires nuanced knowledge brokers, people who can span practices and speak multiple languages at the same time. It requires intentional boundary objects – documents, prototypes, phase gates of a process, and the like, around which a negotiation-in-practice can be afforded. It is in reflection upon this negotiation that the second loop of learning occurs – the ability to accommodate, to change under-lying models, methods, and our own view of others. Yet few strategies or technologies honor the role of practice – of action on the ground and meaning negotiated in the crucible of work, among people. And too many focus, instead, on the warm friendly notion of communities.

The common corporate goal of sharing best practices is related to but distinct from the challenge of having actionable knowledge jump across distinct communities of practice. In this case, it is crucial to realize that every best practice emerged in a highly situated way; it was grown and honed in a particular context. In order for it to travel, it must first be disassembled from that context and then re-embedded in a new context (that is, in a different part of an organization or in a different organization entirely). The process of re-embedding is highly problematic since the best practice must be viewed as a seed that is allowed to germinate in its new context and sprout in a form that honors the nuances of this new context. It takes time and a willingness to let the people influenced by the new best practice do their part to shape it and grow it, preserving its essence but also modifying it to fit its new circumstances.

Practice does not come in discrete pieces like Lego toys but in clumps and clusters of yarn like a knitter's remnant box after a three-year-old child has played in it. To move a strand from one community to another, from one type of product to another, from one country to another means to disentangle, snip, and re-entangle – without consuming the yarn.

• **We have not yet faced up to the imminent and gnarly challenge of "learning to unlearn."** Reframing is clearly the order of the early twenty-first century. But we will continue to cultivate learning cultures that assimilate rather than accommodate unless we take the lead in inventing, adopting, and embedding a repertoire of new practices (tech-niques, technologies, processes, experiences) aimed at learning to see differently. Let us start with a zero-digital-technology example of such a practice that builds directly on knowledge-sharing and innovation. Say you want to transfer a new, hard-earned strategic shift from business unit A, where it was hammered out over eighteen months, to business unit B, which faces a similar set of strategic issues and, furthermore, sits directly up- or downstream from A. Time is of the essence. There is very little shared practice between A and B, although there is significant hand-off and therefore some history of communication. Bridging A and B, we know, will take nuanced brokering, mediating boundary objects, and time – time to negotiate meaning in practice, and time to disembed and re-embed key innovations.

The technique is called *2 x 2 x 2 x 2 x 2*: take two people from group A and two from group B, and bring them together for two meetings, each two hours long, two days apart. Ideally, there is a pre-existing positive professional relationship between one of the As and one of the Bs. Perhaps they are both current or former members of a particular engineering network of practice; perhaps they both served on a corporate change-initiative task force which was related, even tangentially, to the strategic issues on the table; perhaps they have functioned as customer and supplier to one another within the organization's value chain. Equally important is the relationship between the two members of each unit. Within their dyad, they must be able to reflect on and articulate elements of the practice they share; they must be able to share stories, hash out details, follow each other's leads, and refine each other's thoughts. What happens around the table the first day (and it really should be a physical table if possible) is intense. It takes tacit teaming by each side to establish and maintain the conversation – one talking while the other watches body language or searches for the next example. During the two hours, A1 and A2 help B1 and B2 enter into the new way of thinking and doing by describing, showing illustrative artifacts, answering questions, identifying and, if possible, addressing objections, and working with B1 and B2 to map the new way into at least two specific situations or practices under way in B. Each of these situations is explored in depth, often primarily in dialog between the two Bs with, by now, only intermittent interjections by an A. These situations then become the subject of continued exploration and experimentation in practice by the two Bs over the next two days. Success rests on the fact that with two representatives, each side can bring its practice into the room. The second meeting brings all four people back to reflect and to continue to negotiate meaning. Reframing occurs continuously. Repeat the last two steps as necessary. Unlearning alternates with learning throughout as the three sets of dyads (A1A2, B1B2; A1B1, A2B2; A1B2, A2B1) argue, test, witness, internalize, challenge, and change.

Almost every important new point of view or piece of technology, we argue, imposes a burden of unlearning on would-be adopters, often swamping or preventing the better-known learning demands it makes. No more dramatic an example exists today than "naturalized" Internet citizens literally looking at Internet-native genres like MMPOG (massive multiplayer online games). A fundamental act of reframing – learning to swap the periphery for the center – is necessary, we've learned, before one can begin to see the game. This is not an easy shift, unless you have a good guide plus an inclination to see.

In John's case, he realized early on how difficult it was to understand the culture being created by kids who grew up digital. Fortuitously, he met young author J.C. Herz,[5] who offered to be John's "reverse mentor." Over a year's time, J.C. structured a set of experiences that would give John a way in to the practice of this emerging digital culture, help him unlearn certain biases, and slowly construct a new set of conceptual lenses through which he could see, hear, and make sense of the massively multiplayer game world. For John, being reverse mentored also presented an opportunity to hone his ability to listen with humility and through engagement. What unfolded over the year was a realization that until then, John, like most adult game novices, had focused on the actual playing of the game – at the center of the game screen, if you will – while remaining moderately oblivious to the rich social activities transpiring around the edge of the game. There, at the edge, a rich constructivist ecology was evolving – the sharing of tricks and heuristics, the bartering of magical swords, avatars, and other objects of play, the general swapping of stories, and more. Suddenly, he realized that what he thought of as the center was in fact the periphery and that what he initially considered to be periphery (or context) was in fact the center (or content) of the game. The real game, he saw,

---

[5] J. C. Herz, *Joystick Nation* (Boston: Little, Brown and Co., 1997) and *Surfing on the Internet* (Boston: Little, Brown and Co., 1995).

is deeply social. The real action, he understood, lies in the new kind of nonlinear, multiauthored narrative being constructed collectively by the players.

In Estee's case, the guides are her fifteen- and eleven-year-old Internet-native sons. For them, summer vacation begins when – and only when – they are allowed to devote *entire* days in succession to their favorite MMPOG, which this year happens to be Korean Ragnarok Online. Being Mom, Estee worries about eyestrain, their relative lack of fresh air, sunshine, and exercise, and their willingness to forgo physically apprenticing with their father as he constructs an addition to their house. But, armed with a deeply internalized appreciation for the social and situated aspects of learning and prodded periodically by John to follow their experience closely, she does *not* worry about wasted time, social isolation, or (lack of) future memories of joyful togetherness. The boys prefer to play on adjacent computers in what they call the "downstairs computer room," where they are in constant verbal connection with each other. Occasionally, they or a friend are forced to use a third machine upstairs, which means they tie up two phone lines in order to keep up the conversation. Add to this the roughly 200 people with whom each interacts on a good Ragnarok day, in passing, as a close fellow traveler in their current party, as member of their latest guild, as famous personality players, and as buyer or seller of various items. Their ability to multitask is, well, awesome. To them, systems thinking seems natural. Later in the summer, letters from the younger to the older at overnight camp principally feature updates on what John has termed a "new kind of nonlinear, multiauthored narrative." As John learned to see, the narrative is not about kills or game places visited or instances of deploying weapons, spells, or other skills – none of the foreground flora and fauna that capture the adult's eye when faced with the game. Rather, it's about how the game is evolving, what particular players are up to, the latest tidbit from one of the three or four user sites they graze, how the strategies they have been exploring are working out, what stupid or cool thing Gravity (the company that makes the game and runs the main servers) has done lately. "You know what I learned today, Mom?" starts the daily report. And as the eleven-year-old talks, all the cyber-age shifts we talk about are manifest. He freely discovers, links, lurks, tries, asks, borrows, and navigates a complex *n*-dimensional space while his mom internally fights her need to know before acting and wishes for a place to start deducing what to do next. (She's wondering, is there a document, a set of base rules, something?) His digital world is social and constructivist from the get-go. Moreover, he is constantly shifting center and periphery – at will.

• **We have yet to deploy software that honors and energizes the emergent.** The age of desktop computing has not given way to the era of social computing. "Almost without exception, companies applied these technologies to explicit work in the authorized organization; they flattened the formal. New digital technologies will enable companies to engage their employees and energize the emergent," we prophesied eight years ago. "Companies that embrace the emergent can tap the logic of knowledge work and the spirit of community. Those that don't will be left behind."

Enormous stocks of ink, budget, attention, engineering, and marketing elbow grease have certainly been devoted since then to technologies supporting communities, collaboration, and knowledge management. Few of these have engaged or energized their intended users beyond an early (often enforced) usage spike. For a time, unabashedly transaction-oriented marketplaces and exchanges hijacked both the noun *community* and the adjective *collaborative*. Knowledge management is often a synonym for taxonomy-driven content management. So-called collaboration systems are still primarily means for posting, retrieving, and, to a more limited degree, co-producing semistructured content. Even the live-events segment of the collaboration market was sold and purchased largely as a means to broadcast human-delivered presentations or lessons, until demand to replace face-to-face meetings with zero-travel e-meetings skyrocketed after September 11, 2001. New software that honors and activates the emergent has been barely visible.

In the last few months, the term "social software" has arced from the province of bloggers and tech early-adopter conferences to the pages of the *Wall Street Journal* and the *New York Times*. In most of those venues, the focus is on weblog creation tools, including *blogs* – an instant personal publishing technology and practice that has enabled hundreds of thousands of people to find their individual voices over the last two years – and *wikis* – a group voice technology and practice, following on the heels of blogs, but entailing somewhat more structure and shared page ownership.[6] *Social software* also encompasses instant messaging and other emerging forms of presence awareness technology, and hints of tools (still largely academic or researchy in flavor) for tracing, analyzing, and navigating social networks. Some observers include a gaggle of social networking services that interconnect registered individuals (and thereby, theoretically, their social networks) for numerous professional and personal purposes, depending on the service. Whether you believe recent groupware products such as peer-to-peer Groove or contextual collaboration offerings from IBM Lotus also fit the term is left for you, the reader, to decide. Undeniably, most of the Internet-native entries are better classified creatures of the emergent than the authorized. Moreover, the broader software or Web-services market of which they are a fresh part is showing signs of avoiding the tunnel vision that has traditionally excluded social sensibilities from the activities of information technology developers and purchasers. Social software developers and early adopters aspire to a new approach to building adaptive social applications that are easily deployed and can be humanized – not just customized – to support different types of online interaction and different modes of communication. They anticipate a new set of online genres reflecting a tremendous shift in human relationships: from episodic to always-on.[7] Many proudly point out the relative simplicity of blog and wiki technology. But the practice around their use is anything but.

Defined most clinically, social software is designed to be used by three or more people. It is much rarer than it sounds. Most interaction supported by technology is narrowcast (one-to-one), such as telephones and simple e-mail, midcast (one-to-small groups), such as e-mail using distribution lists and small ezines, or broadcast (one-to-many), as in standard publishing and large-scale ezines. Clay Shirky of New York University points out, "Prior to the Internet, the last technology that had any real effect on the way people sat down and talked together was the table. Beyond that, there was no technological mediation for group conversations. The closest we got was the conference call, which never

---

[6] As a point of interest, Eileen Clegg (who created the illuminating images that appear between the parts of this volume) also created visual maps of our dialogs at the Darden colloquium. The term "blogs" appeared on these murals; "wikis" did not.

[7] Lee Bryant and Livio Hughes, London; http://www.headshift.com/moments/archive/sss2.html#_Toc38514168.

really worked right . . ." We interject that a later midcasting technology, the copier, radically affected how people interacted around that table by giving each a copy of shared and sharable documents but agree with Shirky when he continues: "We've had social software for 40 years at most, dated from the Plato Bulletin Board System, and we've only had 10 years or so of widespread availability, so we're just finding out what works."[8]

Designing social software that works is important for creating a culture of learning – inside and outside the corporation. It can, and already does in a few places, complement traditional IT systems designed to support the formal business processes and content stores of an organization but ignore the social fabric where learning and knowledge-sharing happen. But social computing is hard, since we must now understand the emergent properties of groups of people, down to their social- and psychodynamics – both inside the corporation and in society at large. We must learn to distinguish the natural size and activity classes of various groups, communities, networks, and collections, and handle each appropriately. We learn from repeated online experience that by its very self-organizing nature, a community can quickly degenerate into the tyranny of the masses or be hijacked by weirdos, spammers, and the like. Designing social software is much more like designing a constitution than designing an operating system. The constitution needs to exhibit the right balance between supporting dissenting opinions and guaranteeing that the community's real work can get done. It must vary with each community; indeed, it must emerge and evolve along with the community. Borrowing Shirky's language again: "Groups are a run-time effect. You cannot specify in advance what the group will do, and so you can't substantiate in software everything you expect to have happen."

Designing and using social software is therefore like designing and living in ecology; moderators must honor diversity and husband the cross-pollination of opinions and ideas to keep the emergent ever present. There are also business challenges inherent in life on the emergent side of the enterprise in a cost-sensitive era. It can be difficult to garner revenue up front for things that do not yet exist or provide

---

[8] Clay Shirky in a speech at ETech (April 2003) entitled "A Group Is Its Own Worst Enemy," published July 1, 2003, on the *Networks, Economics, and Culture* mailing list.

measurable outcome guarantees. If these design goals and business challenges can be met, social software can act as a true enhancer of our ability to learn from and with each other. We may yet tap the logic of knowledge work and the spirit of community.

A twenty-first-century intuition

It appears in big blue letters encased in a cloud-like form floating toward the top of the Darden colloquium mural: "The 21st century mind is a collective mind." We understand why. Learning is the strategic competence for meeting the economic, cultural, and cognitive implications of increased speed and globalization. A new, more social model of the human at work is emerging as biological metaphors, ecological models, and adaptive system approaches predominate. On a daily basis, twenty-first-century first-world citizens engage in co-production – as consumers, as co-workers, at play and in political life. E-mail is the lifeblood of business. Files that end in .PDF and .PPT are the universal currency of knowledge exchange. While corporate learning practitioners are still not taking advantage of the rails of practice, non-Internet natives are still fundamentally confusing the center and the periphery when looking at genres like MMPOG, and industry has yet to deploy software that honors and energizes the emergent, alongside the authorized, as knowledge workers approach their keyboards with expectations beyond the twentieth-century information highway.

The Cartesian worldview of "I think, therefore I am" seems finally to be giving way. A next step, "We participate, therefore we are," better captures today's ethos, we think.

That next step is strongly in line with the African proverb, "It takes a village to raise a child." It takes a community to change a practice. If double-loop learning were a matter of intrapersonal, interpersonal, or even simple intracommunal learning, we would have seen more of it in the last twenty years. But our experience, our theory, and our intuition suggest that this goal of all learning cultures, and most certainly twenty-first-century ones, is best achieved as an intercommunal dynamic. That is, it may take one working community pushing another in order to reconsider and recast working knowledge. Each center is the other's periphery. What ensues is a creative collision of craft, which – if it can take place in a fabric of trust, with appropriate brokering and cultivation practices – can recreate worlds.

The word "intuition" is purposefully chosen here. However the twenty-first century plays out, none of us today knows how to create a twenty-first-century learning culture. In fact, most of us in charge today of the budget and resources for building tomorrow's learning cultures *know* we do not know how to build them for those coming up behind us. It takes courage to breach the barriers of current practice and head knowingly into the unknown. And it takes intuition to navigate there.

Let us distinguish for the moment between two kinds of intuition. One is the kind of personal intuition that arises from one's own experiences. The other arises from being embedded in a collective. It incorporates learning in the moment, listening with humility, and being able to tap tacitly held beliefs and sensibilities. It is about being able to discern a kind of group resonance. Mystical overtones notwithstanding, some leaders and strategists in the quotidian world already exhibit this ability to make sense at the collective level, but even here it is rarely articulated. As we move forward with the insights in this volume, both types of intuition are necessary.[9]

"I think, therefore I am" has paled. "We participate, therefore we are" is where we are heading. Here is to the next twenty years.

[9] John Seely Brown, in personal communication with Claudia Welss.

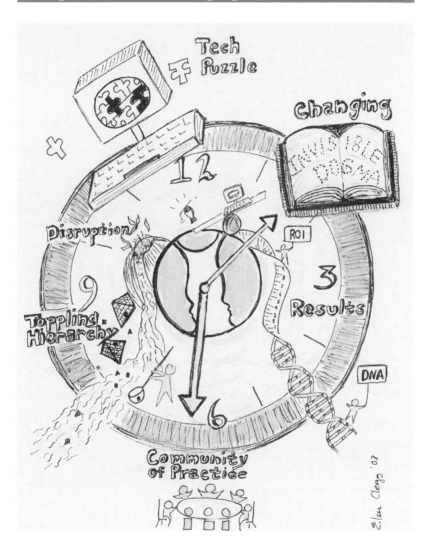

Illustration © Eileen Clegg

1 | *Leading and learning with nobody in charge*

HARLAN CLEVELAND

I F we raise our periscopes for a 360-degree look around, we see that the pyramids and hierarchies of years past are rapidly being replaced with networks and uncentralized systems.

In these systems, larger numbers of people than ever take initiative, make policy, collaborate to point their organizations' ways forward, and work together to release human ingenuity and maximize human choice. These people's actions are not, for the most part, the result of being told what to do. They are the consequence, not of command and control, but of consultation, of relationships that are intermixed, interwoven, and interactive.

This is the state of affairs that led me to describe the most advanced form of human organization as a *nobody-in-charge system*. That phrase, which became a book title, was not wholly tongue-in-cheek; it was a way of describing the style of leadership that was already a strong trend as we moved into the twenty-first century.

In the last quarter of the twentieth century, this trend was driven by the sudden convergence of ever faster, more retentive computers with rapidly spreading, increasingly wider-band telecommunications – a dynamic complexity that gets more dynamic and more complex with each passing year.

It is clear by now, as only a few futurists were forecasting in the 1970s, that information is the world's dominant resource, taking the role that has been played successively in history by such physical resources as labor, stone, bronze, minerals, metals, and energy.

But information – refined by rational thinking into knowledge, converted by both intuition and reasoning into wisdom – is fundamentally different from all its predecessors. Consider these five propositions. Information is not necessarily depletive: it expands as it is used. It is readily transportable, at close to the speed of light – or, by telepathy and prayer, even faster than that. It leaks so easily that it is much harder to hide and to hoard than tangible resources ever were; it cannot be owned (only its delivery service can). The spread of information, converted into knowledge, empowers the many by eroding the influence that once empowered the few who were "in the know." And giving or selling information is not an exchange transaction; it is a sharing transaction.

These deceptively simple propositions, as they sink in around the world and down the generations, require new kinds of learning in every intellectual discipline and the rethinking of every inherited tradition. The same is true, with special emphasis, of future leadership in organizations. Organizations are essentially products of the mind and spirit, expressions of what is thought, imagined, and believed about relationships among people, and thus a rich source of relearning experiences.

A personal note

I came to my own relearning experience from a lifetime as a public executive – in the federal government, magazine publishing, university administration, US diplomacy, and international organizations – and, over the same span of time, as a political scientist trying to capture and record what I was learning from experience about organizations and leadership.

I had often observed, for example, that large organizations needed to be loosely structured in order to work at all. The bosses of totalitarian governance, whether fascist or communist, never came to terms with this axiom; their rigidities seemed to lead to their downfall.

Coming of age in the US government, I often felt like a kind of entrepreneur in the bureaucratic jungle. As I studied its fancies and foibles from inside and outside for half a century, I came to realize that pyramids are not the natural form of organization – as cultures long submissive to monarchs or emperors had evidently come to believe.

Late in the eighteenth century, the leaders of the thirteen American colonies not only declared their independence in human-rights language that reads pretty well in the twenty-first century; they also drafted a constitution that departed dramatically from the pyramids of power and oppression the colonists had learned to despise. Indeed, they created the basis for a nobody-in-charge society – quite literally a unique experiment in uncentralized governance.

The separation of powers with its checks and balances was designed to deny any part of our federal government the chance to make too much yardage at the expense of the other parts – and of the people it was supposed to serve. The federal system itself was designed to create a continuous tussle between the states and the central government. The tussle was intended to be permanent; no part of the system was ever supposed to win.

Looking back on this in 2000, I realized that this way of thinking might well have global implications in the new century. It is not just the durability of their extraordinary invention that testifies to the founders' wisdom. It is clear from the record they left that they – at least, the deepest thinkers among them, James Madison and Thomas Jefferson – knew just how unprecedented was the system they were proposing to build. The people were really *supposed* to be sovereign. Jefferson still believed this even after his eight years of trying, as President from 1801 to 1809, to be their "servant leader." "I know of no safe depository of the ultimate powers of the society but the people themselves," Thomas Jefferson wrote to a friend in 1820, "and if we think them not enlightened enough to exercise their control with a wholesome discretion, the remedy is not to take it from them, but to inform their discretion."

What is truly astonishing is that now, at the beginning of this new century, the practical prospect for a workable world seems to lie in reinventing their nobody-in-charge concept for *global* application.

The real-life management of peace worldwide seems bound to require a Madisonian world of bargains and accommodations among national and functional factions, a world in which people are able to agree on what to do next without feeling the need (or being dragooned by some global government) to agree on religious creeds, economic canons, or political credos. A practical pluralism, not a unitary universalism, is the likely destiny of the human race.

The twilight of hierarchy

In the century to which we recently said goodbye, we learned again and again that complex social systems work badly if they are too centralized. Seismic changes in styles of leadership are shifting social systems nearly everywhere from top-down vertical relationships toward horizontal, consensual, collaborative modes of bringing people together to make something different happen.

The complexities of modern life, and the interconnectedness of every-thing to everything else, mean that in our communities, our nations, and our world, nobody can possibly know enough to be in general charge of anything important or interesting. This state of affairs is becoming more apparent with each passing year. It may be one rea-son why, more and more, the "followers" – especially university stu-dents and educated adults – seem so often to come forth with policy judgments while their established "leaders" are still making up their minds.

That is not the way it was when physical resources were dominant. When the few had access to key resources and the many did not, there never seemed to be enough to go around. This made possible – perhaps even necessary – the development of hierarchies of five kinds: hierar-chies of power based on control (of new weapons, of new transport vehicles, of trade routes, of markets, of communications, and even of knowledge, back when secrets could be secure); hierarchies of influ-ence based on secrecy; hierarchies of class based on ownership; hier-archies of privilege based on early access to particular pieces of land or currently valuable resources; and hierarchies of politics based on geography.

Each of these five bases for hierarchy and discrimination began crum-bling in the waning years of the twentieth century – because the old means of control were of dwindling efficacy, secrets were harder and harder to keep (as the CIA and the White House relearned every few weeks), and ownership, early arrival, and geography were of declin-ing importance in accessing, remembering, analyzing, and using the knowledge and wisdom that are the truly valuable legal tender of our time.

Drift toward uncentralization

The drift toward uncentralized systems began to take hold of our des-tiny in the second half of the twentieth century. Just below the surface in every kind of organization, something important was happening, something very different from the vertical practice – recommendations up, orders down – of both public administration and business man-agement. The "bright future for complexity," foretold in a 1927 *New Yorker* piece by E. B. White, had come to pass, prodded and speeded by the modern miracles of information technology.

This was not a temporary aberration from some centralized norm. It was happening because information had recently become the world's dominant resource. With every generation of information technology – that is, every two or three years – our future becomes more uncentralized. This has to be good news for individual creativity and invention, for personal freedom, for human choice.

The twilight of hierarchy means that we need new kinds of leaders. The new era requires leaders who are nonstop learners and will eagerly share what they learn. It requires leaders who learn, early and often, how to fuse chaos and order in uncentralized systems.

The century just past thus gave rise to a dichotomy between how organizations are described and how they actually work. Many organizations, for instance, still look like pyramids from a distance; but both their internal processes and their external relations feature much less order-giving and much more consultation and consensus. The sheer complexity of what has to get done – by governments and corporations, and by their myriad contractors, subcontractors, and nonprofit critics and cheerleaders – means that huge numbers of people exercise independent judgment and consult with each other and with outsiders; they do not just do as they are told.

Naturally, the search has been on for alternatives to *centralization* as an organizing concept. The first and seemingly obvious candidate was *decentralization*. It turned out, however, that most of the central administrators who opted to decentralize found, to their satisfaction, that this was a new way to preserve hierarchy. If things were becoming so complicated that grandpa could no longer understand it all, he could still subdivide and parcel out the work to be done – while hanging onto central control with more and more creative accounting systems.

Decentralization thus became an aspect, indeed a subhead, of centralization. The real opposite of centralization is of course *uncentralization*. Decentralizing is arranged from the top, by delegation of authority. Uncentralization features, indeed encourages, imaginative initiative and entrepreneurship from all members of an organization, whatever their hierarchical rank. Mao Tse-tung played with this idea for a time; he called it "many flowers blooming." He then pulled back when it became clear that if China's government really permitted the free exercise of opinion and initiative, the Communist Party's central control would be the first casualty.

Despite the trend toward looser, less hierarchical organizational systems, for most twentieth-century people the image of good organization was still a pyramid. In corporations, organization charts were drawn following Max Weber's model of bureaucracy. Nonprofit agencies usually did likewise; they assumed that organizations making a profit must be doing something right. In government, the pyramid's top tier was typically staffed by political executives, with serried ranks of civil servants – servants expected to be civil to politicians – arranged in the lower tiers. Organized religion had likewise developed hierarchical trappings – that's what "organized" was taken to mean. Holy men (and in some denominations, grudgingly, holy women) were in the pulpit; affluent laypersons served as middle managers; parishioners in the pews were expected to be religious but not self-organized. Labor unions, despite their more egalitarian vocabulary, often had the look and feel of pyramids. And so did many social service agencies – though few went so far as the Salvation Army did in using military titles and uniforms.

The marriage of computers and telecommunications multiplied the speed and extended the global range of financial speculation, business transactions, military operations, political dissidence, and humanitarian activity. The widening access to information about what is happening, about who is doing what to whom and when and where, brought into financial markets and business decisions and military strategy and political protest and even humanitarian relief a host of kibitzers, lobbyists, and second-guessers who knew so much – or could readily discover it on the Internet – that they had to be taken into account.

There are still, to be sure, distinctions between organizations where the style of management is looser and more collegial and others where recommendations mostly go up and orders mostly come down. But by the end of the twentieth century, *all kinds* of organizations – from military platoons to urban hospitals – were moving away from vertical administration toward more consultative styles of operation.

The nature of uncentralization

Uncentralized systems feature personal initiative, voluntary cooperation, joint ventures, committee work, and networking. Their workways are reinforced by the rapid progress of information technology and its impact on everything from preschool education to the understanding of our universe.

Very large uncentralized systems, many of them global in scale, based on massive information outputs and widespread feedback, have been developed in the twentieth century. Global information systems unimaginable before the marriage of computers and telecommunications – currency and commodity markets, epidemic controls, automatic banking, worldwide credit cards, airline and hotel reservation systems, global navigation guidance, and the World Weather Watch come readily to mind – already seem normal, almost routine.

It is no accident of history that each of these systems grew from the propensity of ambitious leaders to think hard about how the spread of knowledge could enable more and more people to solve problems by organizing information in imaginative ways – in other words, leading by learning.

In all these cases, there are commonly agreed standards, plus a great deal of uncentralized discretion. The same is true, even more true, of the international foreign exchange market and the Internet, now the world's two most pervasive nobody-in-charge systems. Their common standards so far are mostly technical. Ethical standards for global human behavior await the social inventors of the twenty-first century.

It is in the nature of uncentralized organization that every participant must be continuously in learning mode. It is also natural that those who learn the most, and learn most rapidly, emerge as leaders. And part of what they learn is the necessity to teach their colleagues (regardless of rank) about what they're doing together and how and, especially, why.

What is less certain, and most important as complexity increases, is how we develop our capacity to educate a growing proportion of our population to direct toward human needs and purposes our extraordinary talent for scientific discovery, our unexampled capacity to convert scientific insights into useful technologies, our bent toward doing what has never been done before. We will need a rapidly growing cadre of get-it-all-together professionals, educated in integrative thinking.

Aptitudes and attitudes

The spread of knowledge greatly influences the way people in modern organizations work together – working *with* rather than *for* each other.

The executive leaders of the future will, I think, be marked by a set of attitudes and aptitudes that seem to be necessary for the leadership of equals, the key to the administration of complexity. They will be more reflective practitioners than the executives of the past. They will be low-key people, with soft voices and high boiling points. They will show a talent for consensus and a tolerance for ambiguity. They will have a penchant for unwarranted optimism. And they will find private joy in complexity and change.

The work of executives often consists of meeting a series of unforeseeable obstacles on the road to an objective that can be clearly specified only when it has nearly been met. They try to imagine the unforeseen by posing contingencies and asking themselves how *their* organization systems would adjust if these chances arose. Of course, the planned-for contingency never happens; something else happens instead. The planning therefore does not produce a usable plan but something more precious: people better trained to analyze the unpredicted and to winnow out for the decision-makers (who are almost always plural) the choices that would be too costly to fudge or postpone.

This sort of system requires the participating experts and staff assistants to understand what it is like to be an executive leader, how it feels to frame a decision that will stick. But it also demands that the decision-makers themselves participate in the staff work, try to understand the expert testimony, measure the options, and filter the imagined consequences of each through their best computers, which are their own brains.

Even in collective research or policy-making by committee, the breakthrough ideas often turn out to be the product of one person's advance brooding, reading, consulting, and learning – of someone's sudden inspiration that assembles in a usable pattern the random data and partial reasoning of others. Anyone who has worked with organized systems has to be impressed with the capacity of the human brain to cope with complexity. Viewed as a sensitive computer not limited to quantified bits, the brain is able to take in a wide range of observations, weigh them according to their multiple relevance, store them in a memory of fantastic dimensions, retrieve them with high speed and reasonable accuracy, organize them into options, come up with a practical course of action, and transmit instructions to other parts of the body in a fraction of a second.

An organization system is by definition too ramified for any one executive's mind to encompass. But leaders can focus on the relations among its parts and its people, and they can concentrate their executive energy on the parts that do not fit together and on the relationships that are not working well.

In the information-rich environment of the twenty-first century, the leader must therefore be reflective, not just by training but also by temperament. The leader who is not learning all the time, personally plowing through the analysis and trying to figure out what it means, is not making decisions but merely presiding while others decide. My experience has taught me that the obligation to think hard, fast, and free is the one executive function that can neither be avoided nor delegated.

Your personality, your winning smile, your sexiness, or your attractive voice may seem persuasive leadership assets. But it is by thinking and imagining that you can decide where you want to go and persuade others to come along.

Mutual adjustment

If all organizations are – slowly or rapidly – becoming nobody-in-charge systems, how will anything get done? How will we get everybody in on the act and still get some action?

We will do it, I think, by minimizing, and clearly defining, what everybody must agree on – common norms and standards – and in all other matters maximizing each participant's opportunity and incentive to use his or her common sense, imagination, and persuasive skills to advance the organization's common purpose. This requires learning all the time.

It also requires, of course, that those who are going to pursue an organization's purpose together be openly consulted not only about how they will pursue it but also about the purpose itself. Wisdom about uncentralized systems thus starts with a simple observation: most of what each of us does from day to day does not happen because someone told us to do it but because we know it needs to be done.

When you walk along a city street, you do not collide with other pedestrians; you, and they, instinctively avoid bumping into each other. To generalize: any human system that works is working because nearly all of the people involved in it cooperate to make sure it works.

Political scientist Charles Lindblom called this "mutual adjustment": in a generally understood environment of moral rules, norms, conventions, and mores, very large numbers of people can watch each other, then modify their own behavior just enough to accommodate the differing purposes of others, but not so much that the mutual adjusters lose sight of where they themselves want to go.

Imagine large clumps of people on both sides of a busy downtown intersection, waiting for the traffic light to change before crossing the street. There is macro discipline here. The convention of the red light means the same thing – stop – to all the participants in this complexity, even though there is no physical barrier to violating the norm. Then the light turns green. It would be theoretically possible, with the help of a sizable staff of computer analysts, to chart in a central micro plan the passageway for each pedestrian to enable him or her to get to the other sidewalk without colliding with any other pedestrian. But not even the most totalitarian systems have tried to plan in such detail.

What works is mutual adjustment: somehow those two knots of people march toward each other, and there are no collisions. Each person adjusts to the others, yet all reach their objective – a positive-sum game if there ever was one.

What enables mutual adjustment to work is the wide availability of opportunities to learn from relevant information – so each mutual adjuster can figure out what others might do under varied conditions and give forth useful signals about his or her own behavior.

Perhaps the best current example of mutual adjustment at work is the Internet – at least on a good day. People all over the world are exchanging information, images, music, and voice messages, with so little regulation that their "commerce" is often noncommercial – in effect, a multilateral barter system. Most of their transactions are not essentially exchanges but sharing arrangements. Where there are rules of behavior, they are increasingly arrived at by consensus among the participants, or at least ratified in action by those who will be guided by them.

That does not mean the rule-abiding citizens are serfs, doing some lord's bidding; there's no lord around there. If the rules work, it's because nearly all those who need to abide by them are motivated to comply because the rules make sense to them.

The value of integrative thinking

Civilization is rooted in compromise – between democracy and authority, between a free-market economy and a caring society, between openness and secrecy, between vertical and horizontal relationships, between active and passive citizenship. The required solvent for civilization is respect for differences. The art is to be different together.

Civilization will be built by cooperation and compassion, in a social climate where people of different groups can deal with each other in ways that respect their cultural differences. "Wholeness incorporating diversity" was philosopher John Gardner's succinct formulation. The legend on US currency is even shorter, perhaps because it is in Latin: *E pluribus unum* ("from many, one"). Helping the many think of themselves as one, selling wholeness that can incorporate diversity, will be a central challenge for many different kinds of leaders in the twenty-first century.

When nobody can be in general charge, and some self-selected subset of everybody is partly in charge, the notion of educating for leadership morphs into educating for citizenship. In the upside-down pyramid, where the people ultimately do make the policy, leadership is continuous dialog – not acts but interactions between those who lead and those who follow, the leaders and followers often being different mixes of citizens, depending on what is up for decision.

Learning is thus the drivewheel of organizational transformation in the informatized society. With information now the world's dominant resource, the quality of life in our communities and our leadership in the world depend on how many of us (and which of us) get educated for the new knowledge environment – and how demanding, relevant, continuous, broad, and wise (not merely knowledgeable) that learning is. *Integrative* learning – learning how to get it all together – has to be the essence of education for leadership.

We are born with naturally integrative minds. I suspect that a newborn baby knows from the start, by instinct, that everything is related to everything else. Before the child is exposed to formal education, its curiosity is all-embracing. The child has not yet been told about the parts and so is interested in the whole.

Children and young students are not shocked to learn that everything is related to everything else, that their destiny is somehow mixed up with the fate of the other six billion people (so far) with whom they share a vulnerable planet. It's only later in life, after they have been taught about the world in vertical slices of knowledge, by different experts in separate buildings in unrelated courses of study, that they lose track of how it all fits together.

That is why children ask more "why?" questions than anybody. It is quite possible for even young children to learn to think in systems. They live with interdependence every day – in families and home-rooms and the local public park, which is a very complex ecological system. The ambience of mutual dependence, the ambiguities of personal relations, and the conflicting ambitions of groups are the stuff of socialization from our earliest years. If they are encouraged to practice integrative thinking from their earliest years, the children who become leaders can tackle with less diffidence the Cheshire Cat's first question: "Where do you want to get to?"

Everyone seems to know that "out there in the real world," all the problems are interdisciplinary and all the solutions are interdepartmental, interprofessional, interdependent, and international. But the more we learn, ironically, the less tied together is our learning. It is not situation-as-a-whole thinking, it is the separation of the specialized kinds of knowledge that (like racial prejudice) must be "carefully taught."

Jasmina Wellinghoff, a scientist and writer, wrote about her daughter:

When my six-year-old learned that we heat the house with forced air, she immediately wanted to know who is forcing the air, where natural gas comes from, and how it got stuck underground. After I did my best to explain all this, came the next question: "If we didn't have natural gas, would we die in the winter?" There you have it. Geology, engineering, physics, and biology, all together in a hierarchy of concepts and facts.

She ended up studying the structure of the earth's crust, combustion, hydraulics, and the classification of living beings – all in different years and quarters, neatly separated, tested, and graded.

Our institutions – including schools and colleges – start with a heavy bias against breadth. For a while it was a useful bias: the secret of the scientific revolution's success was not breadth but specialized depth. Chopping up the study of physical reality into vertically sliced puzzles, each to be deciphered separately by different experts using different analytical chains of reasoning ("disciplines"), made possible the modern division and specialization of labor.

But one thing led to another, as E. B. White thought it would ("Have you ever considered," he wrote in the 1920s, "how complicated things can get, what with one thing always leading to another?").

The resulting complexity now makes it imperative that these differing analytical systems be cross-related in interdisciplinary thinking and coordinated action. Those who would lead must therefore learn to think integratively.

A new core curriculum?

The trouble is that schools and colleges, and especially graduate schools, are geared more to categorizing and analyzing the patches of knowledge than to stitching them together – even though the people who learn how to do that stitching will be the leaders of the next generation. What should we be helping them learn, for this purpose, during the years they are full-time learners?

Most of us who are now parents or grandparents were not exposed early and often to a tangle of cultures, currencies, conflicts, and communities. To our schoolchildren from now on, learning about these complexities should be routine. But that will require a new emphasis on integrative thinking in our schools, our higher education, our popular culture, and at that ultimate educational institution, the family dinner table.

What we need now is a theory of general education that is clearly relevant to life and work in a context whose dominant resource is information – a rapidly changing scene in which uncertainty is the main planning factor.

Perhaps, in the alternating current of general and job-oriented education, it is time for a new synthesis, a new "core curriculum" – something very different from Columbia's "World Civilization," Syracuse's "Responsible Citizenship," or Chicago's "Great Books," yet still a central idea about what every educated person should know, and have, and try to be.

Such a curriculum is not going to have much to do with learning facts. It is said that each half hour produces enough new knowledge to fill a twenty-four-volume edition of the *Encyclopaedia Britannica*. But even if that much data could now be put on a single optical disk, that still would make it accessible only to those who already know what they are looking for. Besides, most of the facts children now learn in school are unlikely to be true for as long as they can remember them. The last time I took physics, in the 1930s, I was told the atom could not be split. That information has not served me well in the nuclear era.

What budding leaders need above all are rechargeable batteries of general theory with which they can creatively process the shifting "facts" they encounter in a lifetime of experience. If we think hard about the requirements of the new knowledge environment and consult the instincts and perceptions of our own future-oriented students, I believe we could construct a new core curriculum from such elements as these:

- Education in integrative brainwork: the capacity to synthesize for the solution of real-world problems the analytical methods and insights of conventional academic disciplines. (Exposure to basic science and mathematics, to elementary systems analysis, and to what a computer can and cannot do, are part, but only a part, of this education.)
- Education about social goals, public purposes, the costs and benefits of openness, and the ethics of citizenship to enable each prospective leader to answer for himself or herself two questions: "Apart from the fact that I am expected to do this, is this what I would expect *myself* to do?" and "Does the validity of this action depend on its secrecy?"
- A capacity for self-analysis: the achievement of some fluency in answering the question, "Who am I?" through the study of ethnic heritage, religion and philosophy, art and literature.
- Some practice in real-world negotiation, the psychology of consultation, and the nature of leadership in the knowledge environment.
- A global perspective and an attitude of personal responsibility for the general outcome – passports to citizenship in an interdependent world.

Uncentralized leadership – a checklist

How to conceive, plan, organize, and lead human institutions in ways that best release human ingenuity and maximize human choice is one of the great conundrums of the century ahead. Long-ago philosophy and recent history provide useful hints for leaders – the people who bring other people together in organizations to make something different happen. Here, by way of summary, are some hints from my own experience.

No individual can be truly "in general charge" of anything interesting or important. That means everyone involved is partly in charge. How big a part each participant plays will depend on how responsible he or she feels for the general outcome of the collective effort, and what he or she is willing to do about it.

Broader is better. The more people affected by a decision feel they were consulted about it, the more likely it is that the decision will stick.

Looser is better. The fewer and narrower are the rules that *everyone* must follow, the more room there is for individual discretion and initiative, small-group insights and innovations, regional adaptations, functional variations. Flexibility and informality are good for workers' morale, constituency support, investor enthusiasm, and customer satisfaction.

Planning is not "architecture"; it is more like fluid drive. Real-life planning is improvisation on a general sense of direction, announced by a few perhaps, but only after genuine consultation with the many who will need to improvise on it.

Information is for sharing, not hoarding. Planning staffs, systems analysis units, and others whose full-time assignment is to think should not report only in secret to some boss. Their relevant knowledge has to be shared, sooner rather than later, with all those who might be able to use it to advance the organization's purpose. (Some years ago Japanese auto companies – advised by a genius engineer from Michigan – started sharing much more information on productivity with workers on the assembly lines. Small groups of workers on the factory floor, reacting to that information, were able to think up countless little changes that increased speed, cut costs, improved quality, and enhanced productivity. Quite suddenly, Japanese autos became globally supercompetitive.)

Uncentralized systems – a checklist

It may also be helpful to sum up – and thus oversimplify – the rationale for the uncentralized systems that seem likely to be more and more characteristic of the post-post-modern era now ahead of us: for any complex activity to run in an uncentralized manner, there have to be some rules of the game (like standards).

- These rules need to be adopted through a participatory or representative process so that nearly all the "followers" will feel they have been part of the "leadership."
- Until the rules become shared doctrine, there needs to be some interim authority – the policeman at a new urban intersection, the foreman

in an industrial process, the guru in an ashram, a parent in a family – to remind everybody about the rules.

- In time, the rules become internalized standards of behavior – and the resulting community does not need anybody to be "in charge." Procedural reminders can be mostly automated.
- The rules are then learned in families and schools, by adult training and experience, and by informal (but effective) peer pressure.
- In every well-functioning market, most of those involved in the myriad transactions are able to buy when they want to buy and sell when they want to sell, precisely because no one is in charge, telling them what to do. The discipline is instead provided by wide and instant knowledge of the prevailing price of whatever is sought or offered. Modern information technologies have made this knowledge spread possible on a global scale.
- The uncentralized way of thinking and working naturally becomes more complicated as civilization moves from the small homogeneous village to large multicultural societies, and beyond that to the governance of communities in cyberspace. But there is evidently a path from the need for standards through the practice of consensus and the constituting of interim authorities (whose mandate is to work themselves out of their interim jobs), to patterns of naturally cooperative human behavior.

It is a path that may become universally valid for organized human effort, however complex. Once upon a time, it seems to have required centuries and even millennia for human societies to find their way along a path without precedent. But everything else is speeded up these days. Maybe, once we can trace the path, our capacity to build uncentralized organizations will also be greatly accelerated – *if* we keep learning.

In any event, the motivation of men and women in organizations to keep learning – and their willingness to try what has never been done before – will be the priceless ingredient of progress in the uncentralized systems of the twenty-first century.

2 | Our world as a learning system: a communities-of-practice approach

WILLIAM M. SNYDER AND
ETIENNE WENGER

E live in a small world, where a rural Chinese butcher who contracts a new type of deadly flu virus can infect a visiting international traveler, who later infects attendees at a conference in a Hong Kong hotel, who within weeks spread the disease to Vietnam, Singapore, Canada, and Ireland. Fortunately, the virulence of the Severe Acute Respiratory Syndrome (SARS) was matched by the passion and skill of a worldwide community of scientists, healthcare workers, and institutional leaders who stewarded a highly successful campaign to quarantine and treat those who were infected while identifying the causes of the disease and ways to prevent its spread. In such a world, we depend on expert practitioners to connect and collaborate on a global scale to solve problems like this one – and to prevent future ones.

Marshall McLuhan's assertion in 1968 that we live in a "global village" has come of age. During the past century, the world has become considerably smaller not only through the effects of the media – McLuhan's focus – but also through science, transportation, the Internet, migration, and the spread of global commerce. At the same time, there has been a proliferation of global problems: environmental degradation, the population explosion, increasing economic disparities between rich and poor nations, threats of biological and nuclear terrorism, disease pandemics, and breakdowns of financial systems. As the world becomes smaller, the problems we face are growing larger in scope and complexity.

We have survived these threats and, paradoxically, also caused or exacerbated them through dramatic innovations in science, technology, and organizational structures that increase our collective capacity to influence life on earth. Consider our ability to improve harvest yields and control diseases; to alter the genes in plants, animals, and humans; to create city- and world-spanning virtual communities; and to extend

35

corporations around the globe. Whether or not we take responsibility for designing our world, the evidence suggests that we are doing it already. For better or for worse, we are Prometheus unbound.

Yet we have just begun to discover the metaphors and mechanisms for participating in global stewardship and, even among cultural elites, incorporating an identity as global citizens. What does it mean to "think globally and act locally"? Does global stewardship primarily imply building international organizations that address social and environmental issues to compensate for the economic focus of global corporations? Is such a global perspective sufficient to address issues that are essentially local? How can we connect the power and accessibility of local civic engagement with active stewardship at national and international levels? What are the design criteria for such a system and what might it look like?

Design requirements for a world learning system

We believe there are three fundamental design criteria that help specify essential characteristics of a world learning system capable of addressing the scope and scale of the global challenges we face today. Problems such as overpopulation, world hunger, poverty, illiteracy, armed conflict, inequity, disease, and environmental degradation are inextricably interconnected. Moreover, they are complex, dynamic, and globally distributed. To address such challenges, we must increase our global intelligence along several dimensions: cognitive, behavioral, and moral. We must increase, by orders of magnitude, our societal capacity for inquiry; our ability to continuously create, adapt, and transfer solutions.[1] A world learning system that can match the challenges we face must meet three basic specifications:

- *Action-learning capacity* to address problems while continuously reflecting on what approaches are working and why – and then using these insights to guide future actions.
- *Cross-boundary representation* that includes participants from all sectors – private, public, and nonprofit – and from a sufficient range of demographic constituencies and professional disciplines to match the complexity of factors and stakeholders driving the problem.

[1] C. West Churchman, *The Design of Inquiring Systems* (New York: Basic Books, 1971).

- *Cross-level linkages* that connect learning-system activities at local, national, and global levels – wherever civic problems and opportunities arise.

Civic development is essentially a social process of action learning, in which practitioners from diverse sectors, disciplines, and organizations work together to share ideas and best practices, create new approaches, and build new capabilities. The full potential of this learning process is only realized when it connects all the players at various levels who can contribute to it.

There are a number of organizations – including the United Nations, the World Bank, and an array of nongovernmental organizations such as Doctors Without Borders, the World Council of Churches, Oxfam International, major foundations, and many others – whose mission is to address worldwide problems. But these organizations typically focus on solving the manifestations of problems – eliminating land mines from war-torn regions or reducing the incidence of AIDS, for instance. Given the urgency of these problems, it is understandable that these organizations do not focus on the underlying learning capacity of a city or country. While it is essential to address these and other urgent problems on their own terms, our society's long-term capacity to solve them at both local and global levels will nevertheless require step-change increases in our foundational capacity for intelligent social action.

What is the nature of large-scale learning systems that can operate at local and global levels? How can we take steps to create such learning systems? To what extent can they be designed and what does design even mean in such a context? These learning challenges are among our world's most urgent as we find ourselves today in a race between learning and self-destruction.

Cultivating learning systems

Fortunately, we have examples of transformative, inquiry-oriented learning systems in hundreds of private-sector organizations, with a growing number in public and nonprofit organizations as well – at both organizational and interorganizational levels. Strong, broad-based secular forces are driving this movement. Most organizations today, including domestic firms as well as multinationals, have been forced to confront large-scale learning issues to compete in the knowledge economy.

There is much we can learn from the experience of organizations about how to increase our society's collective intelligence. The most salient lesson is that managing strategic capabilities primarily entails supporting self-organizing groups of practitioners who *have* the required knowledge, *use* it, and *need* it. We call these groups "communities of practice" to reflect the principle that practitioners themselves – in active collaboration with stakeholders – are in the best position to steward knowledge assets related to their work. A well-known private-sector example of such practitioner stewardship is the network of "tech clubs" that Chrysler engineers formed in the early 1990s.[2] The company had just reorganized its product development unit into "car platforms" focused on vehicle types (small cars, large cars, minivans, etc.). Design engineers with specialties related to the various vehicle components – such as brakes, interior, and windshield wipers – organized communities of practice to foster knowledge-sharing across car platforms. The cross-boundary sharing of these communities was a critical success factor for the reorganization. We are now seeing a proliferation of organizations fostering the development of communities of practice across industry sectors, geographic locations, and various elements of the value chain.

Communities of practice are not new. They have existed since *Homo sapiens* evolved 50,000 years ago,[3] but organizations have now become increasingly explicit about cultivating these communities. Distinctive competencies in today's markets depend on knowledge-based structures that are not restricted by formal affiliation and accountability structures. The most distinctive, valuable knowledge in organizations is difficult or impossible to codify and is tightly associated with a professional's personal identity. Developing and disseminating such knowledge depends on informal learning much more than formal – on conversation, storytelling, mentorships, and lessons learned through

---

[2] See chapter 1 in E. Wenger, R. McDermott, and W. M. Snyder, *Cultivating Communities of Practice* (Boston: Harvard Business School Press, 2002).

[3] In 1902, in the preface to the second edition of his seminal book *The Division of Labor in Society* (New York: Free Press, 1964), Emile Durkheim traced the history of professional groups – communities of practice – from ancient times through the twentieth century. He argued that these groups would be essential in the twentieth century and beyond for reweaving the fabric of social capital that would be torn apart as industrialization took hold in countries worldwide.

experience. This informal learning, in turn, depends on collegial relationships with those you trust and who are willing to help when you
ask. Informal learning activities and personal relationships among colleagues are the hallmarks of communities of practice. Hence, we see
an increasing focus on informal community structures whose aggregate
purpose is to steward the learning of an organization and its invaluable
knowledge assets.

Communities of practice have three basic dimensions: domain, community, and practice. A community's effectiveness as a social learning
system depends on its strength in all three structural dimensions.

- *Domain*. A community of practice focuses on a specific "domain,"
  which defines its identity and what it cares about – whether it is
  designing brakes, reducing gun violence, or upgrading urban slums.
  Passion for the domain is crucial. Members' passion for a domain
  is not an abstract, disinterested experience. It is often a deep part of
  their personal identity and a means to express what their life's work
  is about.
- *Community*. The second element is the community itself and the
  quality of the relationships that bind members. Optimally, the membership mirrors the diversity of perspectives and approaches relevant
  to leading-edge innovation efforts in the domain. Leadership by an
  effective "community coordinator" and core group is a key success
  factor. The feeling of community is essential. It provides a strong
  foundation for learning and collaboration among diverse members.
- *Practice*. Each community develops its practice by sharing and developing the knowledge of practitioners in its domain. Elements of a
  practice include its repertoire of tools, frameworks, methods, and
  stories – as well as activities related to learning and innovation.

The activities of a community of practice differ along several dimensions – face-to-face to virtual; formal to informal; public to private.
Further, activities are orchestrated according to various rhythms – for
instance, in one community, listserv announcements come weekly, teleconferences monthly or bi-monthly, projects and visits occur when an
opportunity presents itself, back-channel e-mails and phone calls are
ongoing; and the whole group gathers once or twice a year face-to-
face. (See Figure 2.1.) These activities form an ecology of interactions
that provide value on multiple levels. Beyond their instrumental purpose of creating and sharing knowledge, they increase the community's
"presence" in members' lives and reinforce the sense of belonging and

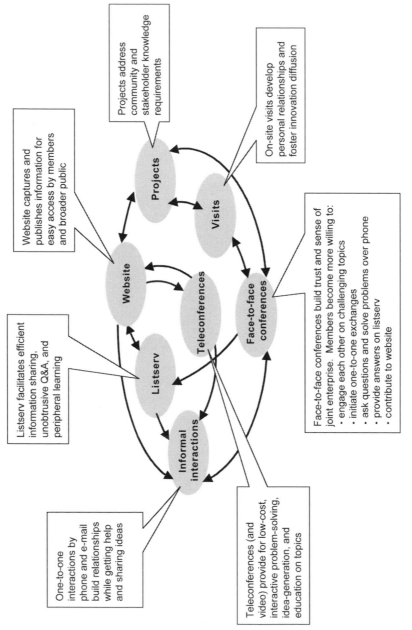

Projects address community and stakeholder knowledge requirements

On-site visits develop personal relationships and foster innovation diffusion

Website captures and publishes information for easy access by members and broader public

Face-to-face conferences build trust and sense of joint enterprise. Members become more willing to:
• engage each other on challenging topics
• initiate one-to-one exchanges
• ask questions and solve problems over phone
• provide answers on listserv
• contribute to website

Listserv facilitates efficient information sharing, unobtrusive Q&A, and peripheral learning

Projects

Visits

Website

Teleconferences

Face-to-face conferences

Listserv

Informal interactions

One-to-one interactions by phone and e-mail build relationships while getting help and sharing ideas

Teleconferences (and video) provide for low-cost, interactive problem-solving, idea-generation, and education on topics

Figure 2.1. A typical ecology of community learning activities.

identity that are the foundation for collective learning and collaborative activities.

Communities of practice do not replace more formal organizational structures such as teams and business units. On the one hand, the purpose of formal units, such as functional departments or cross-functional teams, is to deliver a product or service and to be accountable for quality, cost, and customer service. Communities, on the other hand, help ensure that learning and innovation activities occur across formal structural boundaries. Indeed, a salient benefit of communities is to bridge established organizational boundaries in order to increase the collective knowledge, skills, and professional trust of those who work in formal units. For instance, at DaimlerChrysler, brake engineers have their primary affiliation with the car platform where they design vehicles. Yet they also belong to a community of practice where they share ideas, lessons learned, and tricks of the trade. By belonging to both types of structure, they can bring the learning of their team to the community so that it is shared through the organization, and, conversely, they can apply the learning of their community to the work of their team.

Pioneering, knowledge-intensive organizations have recognized that beyond the formal structures designed to run the business lies a learning system whose building blocks are communities of practice that cannot be designed in the same manner as formal, hierarchical structures. Communities of practice function well when they are based on the voluntary engagement of members. They flourish when they build on the passions of their members and allow this passion to guide the community's development. In this sense, communities of practice are fundamentally self-governed.

Our experience suggests, however, that while communities do best with internal leadership and initiative, there is much that organizations can do to cultivate new communities and help current ones thrive. The intentional and systematic cultivation of communities cannot be defined simply in terms of conventional strategy development or organizational design. Rather, sponsors and community leaders must be ready to engage in an evolutionary design process whereby the organization fosters the development of communities among practitioners, creates structures that provide support and sponsorship for these communities, and finds ways to involve them in the conduct of the business. The design of knowledge organizations entails the active integration of these two systems – the formal system that is accountable for delivering products and services at specified levels of quality and cost, and the community-based learning system that focuses on building and diffusing the capabilities necessary for formal systems to meet performance objectives. It is crucial for organizational sponsors as well as community leaders to recognize the distinct roles of these two systems while ensuring that they function in tandem to promote sustained performance.

The fundamental learning challenges and nature of responses in business and civic contexts are very similar. The size, scope, and assets of many businesses create management challenges that rival those of large cities, or even small countries. In both cases, one needs to connect practitioners across distance, boundaries, and interests in order to solve large-scale problems. Organizations have found that communities of practice are extremely versatile in complementing formal structures. They are known for their ability to divide and subdivide to address hundreds of domains within and across organizations; they lend themselves to applications where scalability, broad scope, and the need for extensive, complex linkages are relevant. Hence there is much we can learn from the early, highly developed business examples. The approaches for building large-scale learning systems in organizations – by combining both formal and informal structures – provide a blueprint for thinking about how to build such systems in the messy world of civil society.

Civic communities of practice: local, national, and international

Communities of practice already exist in the civic domain, where they complement place-based communities as well as the ecology of formal organizations, including businesses, schools, churches, and nonprofits. In the civic arena as well as in organizations, our challenge is not to create communities of practice so much as to foster them more systematically.

Our analysis of societal learning systems – whether at local, national, or international levels – focuses on cities (which we define as an entire metropolitan region) as high-leverage points of entry for a number of reasons. For one, as of the year 2000, there are more humans on the planet living in cities than outside them. In 2002, there were twenty megalopolises in the world with more than 10 million people, and by 2015 there will be nearly forty. Cities have always been the font of new ideas, new applications of technologies, new cultural movements, and social change. They constitute natural nodes in a network for disseminating innovations. In the problems they face and the opportunities they offer, they also provide a microcosm of the world. Finally, cities possess an organizational infrastructure and established leadership groups with the potential to see the value and to sponsor the design of a local learning system.

In many cities, multisector coalitions or alliances are formed to take on a pressing issue such as improving urban schools, increasing access to low-income housing, cleaning up a business district, or building a stadium, park, or cultural facility.[4] These coalitions, however, generally do not take sustained responsibility for stewarding a civic domain or for bringing together the full array of stakeholder constituencies to identify and address short- and long-term priorities. One way to assess the level of civic stewardship in any city or region is to map the prevalence, inclusiveness, and effectiveness of civic communities of practice (also known as coalitions, associations, partnerships, and alliances, among other terms) who take responsibility for clusters of issues related to particular civic domains, such as education, economic development, health, housing, public safety, infrastructure, culture, recreation, and the environment. The reality is that in many cities these domains have no explicit stewardship, or they are left to public agencies or to a menagerie of disparate, often competitive and conflicting organizations that carve out small pieces of the puzzle – regarding housing availability, for example – but do not coordinate efforts or leverage a common base of expertise and resources.

The city, reimagined as a learning system, consists of a constellation of cross-sector groups that provide stewardship for the whole round of civic domains. (See Figure 2.2.) Cultivating a learning system at the city level means taking stock of the current stewardship capacity in the city and accounting for the array of civic disciplines and the quality of active communities of practice stewarding them. This city-level

[4] P. S. Grogan and T. Proscio, *Comeback Cities* (Boulder, Colo.: Westview Press, 2000).

Figure 2.2. The city as a learning system: stewarding the "whole round" of civic domains.

assessment provides a template for what a nation can do. At the nation level, leaders might evaluate a representative sample of major cities and regions as a baseline assessment of its civic stewardship capacity. By extension, an evaluation of the top 500 strategic cities in the world could provide a benchmark for our civic learning capacity at a global level. At the national and global levels, the analysis also considers the strength and quality of linkages across cities both within and across nations. Of course, even at the city level, there are subsectors and neighborhoods that are fractal elements of the city, each with its own whole round of civic practices, and among which neighborhood-to-neighborhood linkages are as instrumental as ones that connect cities and nations.

A *city-based community: economic development in Chicago*

A city-based initiative to promote economic development in Chicago provides an example of an effort designed to leverage communities as agents of civic development.[5] In 1999, the City of Chicago established a cross-sector coalition, the Mayor's Council of Technology Advisors, to create 40,000 new high-tech jobs in the Chicagoland region. The coalition leaders began by pulling together a group of forty-five civic leaders to brainstorm ways to achieve this goal. According to a study commissioned before the group met, the greatest challenge they faced was encouraging business development in high-tech industries such as telecommunications and biotech. A related challenge was cultivating local sources of seed capital for start-ups in these industries.

The result of the group's first meeting was a slate of long and short-term initiatives – including the introduction of technology in schools; encouraging young women and minorities to explore technology careers; and building a stronger digital infrastructure in the city, especially in underserved areas. Several of the groups focused on initiatives specific to the industry sectors identified in the initial study: telecommunications, software development, biotech, venture capital, and emerging areas such as nanotechnology. The industry groups were particularly successful in this initiative, largely because they were able to coalesce communities specific to development challenges in each industry sector.

The civic leaders in Chicago understood that coalescing communities of practice – in this case, along industry lines – was the foundation for building relationships, generating ideas, and catalyzing business initiatives. As one leader put it, "Our first objective was to create communities, period. The technology industries were fragmented without a sense of commonality. For example, we have more software developers than in Silicon Valley, but here it's only 9 percent of the workforce. So we started getting people connected and networked and building a sense of community in our high-tech sectors."

The Chicago Biotech Network (CBN) is one of the more mature high-tech communities in Chicago and provides an illustration of the

[5] For a more extensive review of this initiative, see W. M. Snyder, *Organizing for Economic Development in Chicago: A Case Study of Strategy, Structure, and Leadership Practices* (2002) available at http://www.socialcapital.com.

influence and stewardship such a community can have over time. CBN started as a grassroots group that held about five seminars a year for diverse constituents interested in biotech developments. At first, it was more for individuals interested in life sciences. Then companies (such as Abbott Laboratories and Baxter, two *Fortune* 500 pharmaceuticals located in the Chicago area), started to attend the meetings as well, and they brought different perspectives. Over time, the community came to include scientists, university deans, lawyers, venture capitalists, angel investors, city and state business development staff, and others. Anywhere from twenty-five to two hundred people showed up at the meetings, which were held at various places and sponsored by members. These gatherings provided an opportunity for members to discuss science and industry trends and build relationships. One of the leaders summarized the community's evolution: "Early on, people mostly came for the personal value of networking and discussing ideas. Now the domain of the community is to promote science and business development in the biotech sector in the Chicago area. We focus on science ideas, business development know-how, and knowledge transfer processes." Offshoots of community activities include targeted events that link scientists, angel investors, and large pharmaceuticals to fund biotech start-ups that can commercialize promising innovations coming out of university labs. On a broader level, the community has helped increase biotech lab space in the city, lobbied at state and federal levels for increased research funding, and recruited biotech companies to locate in Chicagoland.

The leader of the Chicago-based biotech community estimated the value of the community's activities for generating start-ups and, by extension, job creation in the region: "I can't point to anything specific, but our events have brought structure to the interface between R&D scientists and the venture community; and we've gone from very little venture funding to the point where we now have $50 million coming to various biotech companies this year."

The Chicago Biotech Network illustrates how an industry-based community of practice can serve as a powerful force for civic development. In this case, the focus was on economic development, but the key point is that strong stewardship of civic issues, even in the hard-nosed area of industry development, depends on vital communities of practice. The purpose of the communities was not only to provide professional development and networking opportunities but also to cultivate thriving high-tech industries in Chicagoland. These communities advocated for their domain as a strategic focus for the city, built relationships among community members from various backgrounds, and shared know-how among practitioners. Finally, as one community leader stated, they worked to serve the city they loved and ultimately their children, who would inherit their civic legacy.

A *national community: SafeCities to reduce gun violence*

Communities of practice can also provide powerful stewardship for civic issues at the national level by connecting innovative civic groups across cities. The SafeCities community, for example, was organized in March 1999 by Vice-President Al Gore's Reinventing Government initiative to reduce gun violence in the United States. The announcement of the SafeCities community coincided with publication of the FBI's crime-rate statistics, which showed significant variation across cities in injuries and fatalities caused by gun violence. Senior executives in the National Partnership for Reinventing Government (NPR) office began by convening officials from relevant agencies and developing a shared vision for what the network would be about and how they would work together. They sent out an invitation to cities and regions nationwide and selected ten coalitions to participate in the SafeCities community, basing the selection on criteria that included multisector collaboration, a track record of innovation, and commitment to improved results. These local coalitions provided stewardship for public safety issues in their cities, as did the industry-focused communities in Chicago. A striking characteristic of the initiative was that it offered participants no funding – the value of participation was to get connected, to learn, and to enhance the capacity to reduce gun violence. The scale of the initiative was also distinctive – connecting civic coalitions from across the nation for the purpose of sharing ideas, collaborating on innovation initiatives, and helping to shape policy at local, state, and federal levels.[6]

[6] For a more extensive review of the SafeCities initiative and others sponsored by the NPR office and other federal agencies, see W. M. Snyder and X. de Sousa Briggs, *Communities of Practice: A New Tool for Managers,* IBM Endowment for the Business of Government (2003), available at http://www.businessofgovernment.org.

The SafeCities community can be described in terms of the three structural dimensions of communities of practice. Each of the coalition members was focused, broadly speaking, on issues related to the domain of public safety. Their specific domain targeted a subdomain within this area – defined as reducing injuries and fatalities due to gun violence. The specificity of this domain was crucial for coalescing a community with overlapping interests, focusing its learning activities, and attracting sponsors. The community was composed of members at local and national levels and from various disciplines and constituencies, such as officials from the FBI, the Bureau of Alcohol, Tobacco, Firearms and Explosives, and an assortment of divisions within the Justice Department at the national level; and mayors, police chiefs, faith leaders, hospital and social workers, school principals, neighborhood activists, and district attorneys at the local level. Finally, the practice of SafeCities members included community policing strategies, after-school programs, crime-mapping methods, prosecutorial strategies, the design of local gun-possession laws, and ways to improve the interaction between at-risk youth and law-enforcement professionals.

After a couple of preliminary teleconferences, SafeCities was launched at a face-to-face meeting in Washington, D.C., explicitly billed as a community-of-practice launch. The sponsors and community coordinating team (based in the NPR office) posed three basic questions for the group to address during the two-day conference: What is SafeCities about (domain)? Who is part of SafeCities (community)? What does SafeCities do (practice)? The conference included opportunities for members to meet informally, including an evening reception and knowledge-sharing "fair." A nationally renowned police chief from Highpoint, North Carolina, gave a talk about his city's success in reducing gun violence through both rehabilitation and enforcement efforts that focused on the city's most violent individuals. (He was so impressed with the gathering that he asked NPR officials if his coalition could join, and they agreed to make his group an honorary member.) During the conference, members outlined a design for how they would learn together – including teleconferences, visits, a website, and other activities. The issues they identified became topics for their biweekly teleconferences. The conference was instrumental in coalescing members around a shared agenda and in building trust and reciprocity. The SafeCities teleconferences subsequently became more active and members were more forthcoming about selecting topics and offering to speak to the group about their experiences. Fostering "community" – a sense of mutual trust, shared identity, and belonging – took on more prominence as an important structural element that made SafeCities successful.

One of the outcomes of the initial conference illustrates the value of network participation for members. After hearing the Highpoint police chief talk about his success, groups from Ft. Wayne, Indiana, and Inkster, Michigan – including police chiefs, mayors, and faith leaders from both cities – visited Highpoint and observed programs in action. Both coalitions then adapted the Highpoint model for their own locales with coaching from Highpoint.

SafeCities operated successfully from March 1999 until June 2002, spanning the transition from a Democratic to a Republican administration. Political appointees from both parties, as well as senior civil servants in the justice and treasury departments (where the sponsorship was primarily based) believed in the cross-level, cross-sector approach that SafeCities embodied. Sponsors were impressed to see such active participation on the part of senior civic leaders, even though they received no government funding for participating. These local leaders felt strongly about the value SafeCities provided – in terms of ideas, access to expertise, and opportunities for national visibility and influence based on local success.

Agency sponsors ultimately decided to close the SafeCities community in favor of a more conventional federal program. The decision confused many of the participants, given the minimal federal costs associated with the initiative, principally the cost of funding the community's full-time coordinator (a junior staff person, albeit a talented leader) and intermittent attention by agency champions. The coordinator's role was particularly important – arranging speakers for teleconferences, documenting insights on the website, arranging peer-to-peer visits, and coordinating with state and federal officials. The loss of the coordinator and agency attention was a fatal blow to the community. In its place, the US Justice Department enacted a new program, called SafeNeighborhoods, which provided funding for local initiatives such as after-school programs. The program managers intended to build on the SafeCities foundation, but they did not appreciate the distinctive characteristics of the community – opportunities for peer-to-peer learning and collaboration across cities, sectors, and levels of government. While SafeCities members were glad that the government was providing new funds to support local initiatives, they passionately argued that such funding could never substitute or compensate for the value of the SafeCities community.

The SafeCities story thus validates the power of cross-city communities of practice while highlighting a key challenge: how to educate senior leaders with the power to sponsor such initiatives – from public, private, or nonprofit sectors (including foundations). These and other questions about starting, sustaining, and scaling such initiatives must be addressed for communities to succeed at local, national, and international levels.

An international community: Ayuda Urbana on city management

At the international level there is a myriad of professional groups and organizations that focus on global civic issues. In recent years a number of these have developed a stronger emphasis on peer-to-peer learning and innovation among members from diverse disciplines. The Ayuda Urbana initiative was started in conversations about developing municipal capabilities between World Bank urban specialists and several mayors of capital cities in the Central American and Caribbean region. They recognized the value of connecting with peers across borders to address problems and challenges that all cities in the region face. A group of ten cities decided to participate in the initiative: Guatemala City, Havana, Managua, Mexico City, Panama City, San José, San Juan, San Salvador, Santo Domingo, and Tegucigalpa. The people involved in the project include the mayors and their staff in each of the ten cities. Additional partners include the World Bank, which provides overall coordination, some regional organizations to provide local legitimacy, and the British and Dutch governments to provide funding.[7]

The project was to create a constellation of communities of practice that would take advantage of the knowledge available in the participating cities. The domains would focus on a challenge of urban development and management the cities shared, including e-government,

---

[7] For a more extensive review of this initiative, see E. Wenger, *Ayuda Urbana: A Constellation of Communities of Practice Focused on Urban Issues and Challenges in Central America, Mexico, and the Caribbean Region* (2003), case 333, available at http://www.beep-eu.org.

urban upgrading, environmental sanitation, municipal finances, urban transportation, renovation of historical city centers and poverty alleviation, and disaster prevention and management. The communities would consist of urban specialists in each domain from the participating cities and from local organizations. Together they would build their practice by comparing experiences and sharing resources across cities, with input from World Bank experts about what had been learned elsewhere.

The communities of practice were officially launched through a series of two-day workshops, each focused on one of the topics. Each workshop brought together specialists from the participating cities as well as a few World Bank experts. The purpose of the workshops was to

- create an initial forum to develop relationships and trust through face-to-face interactions among participants
- provide an opportunity for each participating city to share its experience
- engage participants in a discussion of lessons learned based on presentations by World Bank experts
- establish a prioritized list of the most pressing issues and most frequently asked questions
- introduce Web-based tools for use in facilitating an ongoing learning process and train participants to use the system
- choose a person to coordinate the collection of resources to be shared via e-mail and the website.

The project has created an interactive website, available to the public, which serves as a repository for the various communities of practice. The site includes a library of resources, downloadable manuals, bibliographic references, and proceedings of meetings. In addition, the site hosts an online forum to give participants the opportunity to discuss issues, ask questions, share relevant information, and stay in touch. For example, a community member asked how to price waste management services. Another member, from San Salvador, responded with a posting that explained how his city determined the price of such services.

The Ayuda Urbana initiative illustrates the value of collaboration across borders to address urgent issues in urban development, and it raises salient issues common to international communities. Creating communities of practice among cities from different countries is not all that different from similar efforts within a country, but there is additional complexity. The regional focus of Ayuda Urbana meant that participants spoke the same language and shared a cultural context. The situation would have been more complex if the project had expanded beyond the region. Another issue is the role of the convener when members do not share the same national government. Sponsorship has to come from an organization like the World Bank, which can appreciate the vision of cross-border communities and the subtleties involved in cultivating such communities. Indeed, Ayuda Urbana represents the latest development of a broader initiative at the World Bank to focus on knowledge as a key lever in the fight against poverty. The Bank started an initiative in 1998 to support the development of communities internally, and since then the number of communities has grown from twenty-five to more than a hundred – and the influence of several has been considerable. An external study of the communities found that they were the "heart and soul" of the Bank's new strategy to serve its clients as a "knowledge bank."

The Ayuda Urbana initiative highlights the importance of a skilled convener who is committed to a community-based approach as a way to address societal challenges. In this case, the World Bank is applying the same knowledge strategy with client countries that it has been applying internally. Indeed, the Bank's experience in cultivating communities of practice was critical to the success of the Ayuda Urbana project. The result is a new model for facilitating knowledge development among countries. Experts at the Bank consider it their task not just to provide their knowledge to clients but to build communities of practice among them as a way to develop their capabilities. The Bank experts still have a role to play, but not in a one-way transfer. Instead, their contribution takes place in the context of a community of practice that emphasizes peer-to-peer learning. This approach models a shift in the traditional relationship between sources and recipients of knowledge.

The fractal structure of large-scale learning systems

Cultivating civic learning systems involves many of the challenges that organizations face in cultivating internal learning systems, but many of these become amplified in the civic context. The domains are especially complex; the communities tend to be very diverse; and the practices involve different disciplines, varied local conditions, and less well-defined opportunities to work together on projects. But perhaps the greatest challenge is the scale required for civic learning systems to leverage their full potential and match the scale of the problems they address.

How do you significantly increase the scale of a community-based learning system without losing core elements of its success – identification with a well-defined domain, close personal relationships, and direct access to practitioners for mutual learning? The principle to apply is that of a fractal structure.[8] In such a structure, each level of substructure shares the characteristics of the other levels. Applying such a design principle, it is possible to preserve a small-community feeling while extending a system from the local to the international level. Local coalitions such as the Chicago Biotech Network and each of the SafeCities partners created a local focus of engagement that made it possible for members to participate in broader networks at national and international levels. The idea is to grow a "community of communities" in which each level of subcommunities shares basic characteristics: focal issues, values, and a practice repertoire. Each dimension of a community of practice provides opportunities for the constitution of a fractal learning system.

Fractal domain. In many cases, domains may start more broadly and eventually subdivide as members discover nuances and opportunities to focus on different subtopics or to apply a topic to different localities. Ayuda Urbana, for example, is spawning subdomains related to particular civic practices and engaging members with particular expertise and interest in those areas. The city-based coalitions of SafeCities focused on the same issues but within the context of their situations. All these subdivisions retain a global coherence that gives the entire system a recognizable identity and allows members to see themselves as belonging to an overall community even as they focus on local issues.

Fractal community. Topical and geographic subgroups help create local intimacy, but they must be connected in ways that strengthen the overall fabric of the network. A key to this process is multimembership. Members such as those in the SafeCities network join at the local level but end up participating in multiple communities in ways that help

---

[8] See J. Gleich, *Chaos: Making a New Science* (New York: Penguin Books, 1987), pp. 81–118; and M. J. Wheatley, *Leadership and the New Science* (San Francisco: Berrett-Koehler, 1994), pp. 80–86.

interweave relationships in the broader community. As a result, they become brokers of relationships between levels in equivalent types of communities. This works because trust relationships have a transitive character: I trust people trusted by those I trust. The police chief in Highpoint, for example, had developed strong relationships with FBI officials, which in turn encouraged his peers to work more closely with federal agents.

Fractal practice. Useful knowledge is not of the cookie-cutter variety. Local conditions require adaptability and intelligent application. A fractal community is useful in this regard because it allows people to explore the principles that underlie a successful local practice and discuss ideas and methods in ways that make them relevant to circumstances elsewhere. A fractal community can create a shared repertoire and develop global principles while remaining true to local knowledge and idiosyncrasies. Moreover, if one locality has a problem or an idea, the broader community provides an extraordinary learning laboratory to test proposals in practice with motivated sites. In the SafeCities community, local coalition members were ready and willing to share results quickly and convincingly with peers and then translate these into action. A SafeCities member from Michigan reported, for example, that a meeting with innovating colleagues in Highpoint "added ideas and motivation to an initiative that we had been planning for a year. Once our mayor visited, he wanted to do it." Highpoint members then helped the Michigan coalition adapt their model successfully.

Each locality constitutes a local learning experiment that benefits from and contributes to the overall learning system. The key insight of a fractal structure is that crucial features of communities of practice can be maintained no matter how many participants join – as long as the basic configuration, organizing principles, and opportunities for local engagement are the same. At scale, in fact, the learning potential of the overall network and the influence at local levels can increase significantly. The key challenge of a large-scale learning system is not whether people can learn from each other without direct contact but whether they can trust a broader community of communities to serve their local goals as well as a global purpose. This depends on the communities at all levels – local, state, national, and international – to establish a culture of trust, reciprocity, and shared values. Developing this social capital across all levels is the critical success factor for going to scale. The evolution of a learning system must therefore be paced at the time-scale of social relationships, not according to an externally imposed objective to achieve short-term results. Organizers must be careful not to scale up too fast. They need to establish trust and shared values at different levels of aggregation through various mechanisms, including a network of trusted brokers across localities.

Challenges for supporting civic learning systems

In the civic domain, the institutional context can be fragmented and the issues politically charged. This presents particular challenges for finding sponsorship, organizing support, and managing potentially conflicting constituencies.

Sponsorship. All three communities depended on sponsorship from executives such as the Mayor of Chicago, the Vice-President of the United States, or representatives of the World Bank and funding governments. Sponsorship is especially important for large-scale learning systems that will require additional activities to connect localities. It can be difficult, however, to identify the "client" who benefits when a learning system is so dispersed. When you try to engage a city to sponsor a constellation of cross-sector communities of practice to address an array of civic domains, where do you start? A civic community of practice is such an innovative approach that leaders typically do not have enough context to see its value. Sustained sponsorship, furthermore, requires community members to make the value visible enough to demonstrate the payoff of sponsor and stakeholder investments. Finally, the legitimacy of sponsorship can be contested in a politically fractious context, where the role of institutions such as the World Bank or the federal government in orchestrating local affairs is not universally welcome.

Support. Process support was key to the communities we have described. They needed help with local event planning, finding resources, coordinating projects across levels, finding others to connect with, and designing ways to connect. All three communities needed facilitation at meetings, and SafeCities and Ayuda Urbana both required moderation for their online interactions. A challenge for civic learning systems is that there may be no clearly defined institutional context or financing model for process support. The Ayuda Urbana experience also suggests that one must be ready to provide a lot of support at the start to help develop members' local capabilities and prepare the group to operate more independently. Civic communities of practice also need help to build a technology infrastructure for communicating across geographies and time zones, and for building accessible knowledge repositories. This can be particularly difficult when communities span multiple organizational contexts.

Conflict management and collaborative inquiry. Civic communities of practice organized around contentious issues such as housing, education, and health will face considerable obstacles from formal and informal groups with entrenched and opposing views and interests. There are good reasons these basic conflicts have been so intractable: views and values are divergent and trust among players is often low. Moreover, businesses, nonprofits, governments, and universities have reasons to resist the development of communities of practice. These formal organizations and their leaders have developed established, privileged positions in society, and changes initiated by community members may not be welcomed. Inevitable mistakes early on could further diminish low trust levels and reduce the low-to-medium public readiness to invest time in these unfamiliar social commitments. Communities that face such tensions will have to develop expertise in collaborative inquiry and conflict management and learn to build trust over time through activities that enable members to find common ground.

Where do we go from here?

There is an emerging, global zeitgeist about community and learning. These issues have become commonplace in multinational organizations – private, public, and nonprofit. Still, when one looks at the learning requirements of the world, the complexity of the required learning system may seem so overwhelming as to discourage action. But the advantage of a community-of-practice approach is that it can be evolutionary – starting small and building up progressively, one community at a time. It is not necessary to have broad alignment of the kind required for designing or changing formal structures. We can start wherever there is opportunity, energy, and existing connections. We can build on what already exists. Indeed, we have found successful examples of initiatives to cultivate learning systems: within cities, across cities at a national level, and across cities internationally. Taken together, these early examples paint a picture of what a mature world learning system may look like, and they give some indication of what it will take to cultivate such a system.

We now need to develop frameworks for describing the organizational nature of civil society as a community-based action-learning system – and tools and methods for cultivating such systems. This chapter is thus not only a call to action and a proposal for what is possible. It also calls for a new discipline. A discipline that expands the field of organization design and applies analogous principles at the world level. A discipline that promotes the development of strategic social learning systems to steward civic practices at local, national, and global levels. A discipline whose scope is the world and whose focus is our ability to design the world as a learning system – a discipline of *world design*.

This chapter is only a beginning. There are many established and emerging disciplines – political science, economic sociology, social network analysis – that can inform the work in this domain. A community-based approach to world design is not a silver bullet for solving the problems of the world. While the emphasis here has been on community, a complete discipline of world design would address how the power of communities can be most fully realized by aligning community activities within a broader ecology of formal and informal structures – institutions, cultural groups, laws, and social networks.

To steward such a discipline, we need a community of practice ourselves – or indeed a constellation of communities on the topic of world design, at local, national, and global levels. For instance, a small group of people passionate about civic development may gather to outline an approach to cultivating the city as a learning system. They might connect with various civic leaders and extant initiatives, and organize a gathering for the purpose of assessing the implicit structure of the city today as a practice-based learning system. Which practices have active stewardship? What groups are providing it with what sorts of initiatives and results? Who is represented? Where is the focus of sponsors – such as local government, corporations, universities, the media, and foundations? To what degree is there a shared language and understanding across constituencies of the nature of cross-sector civic governance and of how to participate effectively? These questions become the concerns of "meta-communities" at various levels, which can link together – as a community of meta-communities – and build their own practice to support the development, effectiveness, and influence of civic communities at all levels.

The complexity and intelligence of such a social learning system must match the complexity of world-design challenges and the knowledge requirements associated with them. The messy problems of civil society require a commensurate capacity for learning, innovation, and collaboration across diverse constituencies and levels. The challenge to intentionally and systematically design and develop the world as a learning system must be a global, diverse, interwoven social movement. This social movement is not simply about advocacy; nor is it a political revolution. Rather, it is about the transformation of civic consciousness – a way of thinking about governance as an action-learning process, as a role for civic actors across sectors, as a process that links the local and global in clear and concrete ways. And it depends, fundamentally, on individuals finding a way to participate locally – whether that means a community of place or practice, or both – a way that gives them access to the entire learning system. Let us begin.

3 | *Developing talent in a highly regulated industry*

KAREN KOCHER

THE insurance industry is not known for risk-taking – and with good reason. Our job is to help our customers *avoid* risk; this is the cornerstone of our business and everything we do. For us, taking a conservative approach is not a choice so much as a calling.

I understand this style of doing business because I come from a long line of insurance people. My grandmother was an Aetna employee in the 1970s. My father, my uncle, and my aunt worked in insurance. We were an insurance family. So, after college, I worked in various aspects of the business myself, from medical cost containment to workers' compensation.

When I was hired to manage the CIGNA Technology Institute (CTI), an education-focused organization that helps CIGNA implement technology and ensures that all employees use technology productively, I knew I would be facing a big challenge. CIGNA, a leading provider of employee benefits in the United States, with a workforce of 40,000, established CTI in 2001. As I took over the leadership of CTI, I realized that not only would I need to find ways to encourage innovation within the confines of the tradition on which our company thrives, but I would have to do this while meeting the demands of a highly regulated environment.

In this chapter I describe how we at CIGNA have tried to achieve a balance between innovation and conservatism, between helping employees do their best work and helping them and the organization observe important guidelines. Training plays a crucial role in this balancing act, so first I set out the essentials for training in a regulated industry. Then I discuss the challenges and risks involved in implementing innovative approaches and some strategies that have led to significant success in our approach at CIGNA.

Three essential training areas: compliance, certification, and business development

As in the manufacturing and banking industries, compliance is crucial to the industries in which CIGNA operates: insurance, healthcare,
and financial services. These industries must adhere to standards of
practice that are carefully measured and mandated by federal and state
guidelines. Training our employees to meet these standards is of utmost
importance. Likewise, we must help them maintain their professional
certification in fields like nursing and underwriting so that they will be
able to continue to do the work they were hired to do.

In manufacturing, the line employee is most affected by government
regulations. In banking, upper management takes responsibility for
any regulatory discrepancies. But in health-related fields, regulatory
pressures typically apply to *all* employees and affect basic as well as
advanced work activities. Consider, for instance, the Health Insurance
Portability and Accountability Act of 1996 (HIPAA), which requires
adherence to specific privacy, portability, and accountability guidelines. Complying with the act meant having to educate our employees
on specific regulations, processes, procedures, and performance standards. Some employees, such as clinicians, nurses, and claim payors,
need the full dose of HIPAA-related education. Others, whose roles
are peripheral to the healthcare business – accountants, financial managers, education employees – need a minimal amount of education. But
all CIGNA employees are touched in some way by this act.

In addition to mandated learning requirements in compliance and
certification, we also find it necessary to devote part of our training
budget to developing employees' business skills. Like any competitive business, regulated or not, we want continually to improve our
customer service, build management skills, and teach employees how
to use new software and other technologies that could improve our
offerings.

Many companies in the service and retail sectors have wonderful
training programs that address many aspects of doing business. These
employee development programs are vital to a company's ability to
grow and succeed in the marketplace. However, there is a major distinction between what we do and what they do: in most cases, their training
programs do not determine whether or not the company is *allowed* to
stay in business. Each of these three areas of training (compliance,

professional certification, and business development) can be thought of as legs of a stool. If one is given short shrift, the stool will not be stable, and our goals for employee development overall will be jeopardized. Tempting as it may be to focus entirely on the "must-have" areas of training (compliance and certification), we cannot realize success unless all three legs are intact and balanced.

Challenges and risks

One of the primary challenges of managing learning in a regulated industry is simply determining how to allocate resources. And I do not just mean money. I am also talking about time – both employees' and trainers'. And I am talking about developing people and the criteria we use for making investment decisions.

Requirements from professional and state insurance departments affect areas such as nursing, clinical practice, underwriting, actuarial, and claims. Juggling all these requirements – and all these people – adds significant complexity to the overall talent-management landscape. For too many years, our culture focused inordinately on the needs of high-potential managers. Mid-level employees, a group which constituted approximately 70 percent of our workforce, had minimal access to training. We basically did only what was necessary to maintain expertise and provide the bare minimum of instruction required for regulatory compliance. Fortunately, this trend is changing.

A large number of our training needs are required by law and therefore fall into the must-have category. These include things like teaching agents the intricacies of HIPAA and meeting our fiduciary responsibilities with regard to customers' investments. Recently, though, we have made a conscious effort to find ways to offer training beyond what is mandatory. Just like companies in the service and retail sectors, CIGNA has many training needs that are not required by law but are none the less important, such as improving customer service and developing management skills. Our desire to offer not only must-have training but also nice-to-have training represents a culture shift for us.

Must-have training needs do not tend to require the same level of creativity or innovation as nice-to-have ones. In many cases, regulations include a number of clearly prescribed education requirements: you are told which topics need to be addressed, you are notified of deadlines by which the training must be completed, and you are given metrics to prove your success.

And, as I have said, the must-have programs, which are just a smattering of the overall education initiatives in play at a given time, in many cases affect CIGNA's entire employee base. Targeting education to 40,000 employees on a frequent and ongoing basis is difficult, especially when learning technologies are still in their infancy.

Challenging as it is, our must-have training also presents a number of wonderful opportunities. For one, when you are working in a heavily regulated world, you follow a clearly marked path. If you obey all the rules, you will most assuredly get a thumbs-up from the state and federal governments. Not only that, but you know that you have been given the same rulebook as your competitors.

There are two sides to this issue. On the one hand, as a regulated industry you are freed from the responsibilities of setting guidelines and benchmarking your success. On the other hand, you may feel that you have fewer opportunities to differentiate your company from competitors. Here are some of the challenges we face at CIGNA as we try to balance the three-legged stool and find ways to innovate.

Example 1: Microsoft XP

Not all the training I have been calling must-have training is regulatory. Like any other organization in any other industry, we at CIGNA need to keep up with technological advances, and introducing new technology to our workforce is a tremendous challenge, especially in an organization unused to taking risks. Consider what we experienced in 2002, when we decided to roll out a new e-learning component to support the company's upgrade of its operating system software to Microsoft XP. Upgrades like this can have a significant impact not only on a company's hardware and software infrastructure but also on employees' behavior and the corporate culture. We anticipated that our workforce would need help learning the new software, so we developed an e-learning sequence as our primary method of educating everyone about the features of Microsoft XP.

Because 3,600 CIGNA employees in our systems community had been using e-learning successfully for the past year and a half, it seemed a natural decision that we should also use e-learning to educate those in the greater CIGNA population about Microsoft XP. The rollout of the new system and of the training to support it was to take place over the course of thirty months and would affect all employees.

Shortly before we were to unveil the e-learning component to the first set of people migrating to the XP environment, we discovered a problem caused by an unfortunate and unforeseen hardware change – a big problem that stopped us in our tracks. (As you read this, remember that most companies run into problems from time to time. How a company solves its problems reveals a lot about its culture.)

When we first developed the specifications for our e-learning module, we based them on the use of a particular type of IBM hardware that we already had. Midway through our software development, that model was discontinued. So the company purchased 8,000 desktops of a different model to finish the rollout of the new operating system – models that required service packs provided by Microsoft in order for our e-learning to work.

It was clear to us that installing the service packs would involve some degree of risk. The upgrade might result in software incompatibilities. Our e-learning modules might not even run properly on the models that had the service packs installed. We did not know how such changes might affect productivity. Could we afford a thorough period of analysis, which might last six months or longer? We knew that the service packs, after all, were created by Microsoft to fix any known problems with the current version of their software, not with the XP version we would soon be using.

Other companies might have decided to continue with the rollout and work out any difficulties after the fact. And, in fact, the team that selected our e-learning modules felt certain that any problems could be overcome. But when business managers were faced with the decision to go ahead, they pushed back. Eventually, they chose not to install the service packs, which made our e-learning module unusable to this group. Why did they decide this? Because a possible disruption of service was more of a risk than the company wanted to accept.

In truth, this affected only 8,000 of CIGNA's employees. But it was a lesson for us – we learned just how deeply our company was committed to risk avoidance!

CIGNA does, however, take on new challenges. Actually, the fact that we embraced an e-learning program, accessible to all, is proof positive that our corporate culture is changing in some very exciting ways. At one point in the company's history, learning opportunities were not so democratic. Nice-to-have learning was limited to management training for high performers in the company's upper tier. Now, through e-learning and a number of other initiatives, we're changing the culture around CIGNA so that a continuous learning environment will encourage and enable more of our employees to take charge of their own career development. This is a success in its own right.

Example 2: HIPAA – general training

Failure to comply with regulations outlined in the HIPAA carries with it tremendous consequences that can include huge fines and jail time for the chief learning officer and anyone else closely involved. Even if a company is not formally reprimanded, the mere hint of noncompliance or a serious investigation is enough to hurt the value of a company's stock.

When you look at the learning needs of a service-oriented company or a retailer in a non-regulated industry – say a chain of ice cream parlors or a large network of hardware stores – the requirements are relatively simple. At the most basic level, companies in the service and retail sector want to make sure their employees develop the skills they need to serve customers well. If a company's training program is successful, its customers will presumably value that company over its competitors and will keep doing business with it.

It is a different story in a regulated industry such as ours. CIGNA is required by law to demonstrate competency and compliance in a number of areas. To show compliance in most regulatory matters, a company must be able to demonstrate, first of all, that employees have been educated on the regulation in question. Then, the company must demonstrate knowledge by periodically auditing documents pertaining to compliance. This includes a scan of transmissions and transactions for errors. Finally, companies must also document what training has occurred and maintain that documentation for six years.

The HIPAA Privacy Rule, one part of the larger HIPAA, requires that a workforce be trained on policies and procedures pertaining to protecting consumers' health information. When CIGNA set out to create its training program regarding this rule, our objectives were straightforward. We wanted a program that would focus on basic privacy concepts and explain CIGNA's privacy policy as well as the HIPAA

Privacy Rule. With 40,000 people to train, we needed a large-scale, efficient solution, which meant e-learning was our best option.

Example 3: More HIPAA – legal compliance

Sometimes, buy-in from one department is essential to success. In the case of the HIPAA program, which was required by law, getting feedback and approval from our legal department was central to the program's success. We worked closely with members of the legal team, who have in-depth understanding of the HIPAA laws and regulations, to ensure that our training programs were teaching employees to comply. We also worked hand in hand with the legal department to identify which people required which specific training, and to confirm that our ongoing HIPAA training plans and actual learning content would enable CIGNA to remain compliant. Developing and delivering the training for HIPAA compliance was truly a joint effort.

In addition to legal input, we also needed approval from each division of the company at each stage of development because everyone wanted an opportunity to provide input on the content and reporting functions for training. For instance, the Healthcare Division wanted specific reports to demonstrate that the compliance-education initiative was on track. CIGNA Retirement and Investment Services as well as the Systems Division were not all that concerned with reports, since their employees were minimally affected by HIPAA, but they were very interested in making sure that the training would not be a drain on employees' productivity.

So, to ensure a smooth implementation across the company, we obtained buy-in from all stakeholders at each development milestone through structured review sessions and a multifaceted communication plan.

Example 4: Patriot Act

Even companies that have, until now, escaped the grip of regulations are facing a new set of circumstances with the passage of the Patriot Act. This federal law, passed by Congress in the fall of 2001, was designed to help the United States defend itself against the threat of terrorism from any factions identified as hostile to the government. One of its provisions requires that any and all institutions involved in transacting funds, which is to say, any company *doing business*, must be able to demonstrate that it has educated employees on how to spot a potential terrorist transaction.

At a minimum, this act targets employees working in finance and accounting, because anyone handling money would need to understand what sorts of banking transaction might be suspect. So, even if your company has not previously considered itself to be "regulated," you will soon find yourself having to demonstrate compliance with Patriot Act regulations in much the same way we in insurance and healthcare have had to demonstrate compliance with any number of other federal and state regulations.

CIGNA's strategies and triumphs

The challenges of surviving in a regulated environment – let alone growing our business and nurturing employees – have led us to think hard about our strategies. We have had to figure out how to maintain a focus on balancing the must-haves of compliance and certification with the development of business knowledge. I hope that as you read about our approaches, you will see how we have maintained a spirit of innovation, and that these strategies might add practical value as you develop and implement your training programs.

Strategy 1: Putting people first

CIGNA's People Strategy is an initiative designed to help us do a better job of attracting, developing, motivating, and retaining good employees. This strategy, which includes a number of employee retention and satisfaction programs, has helped us articulate our core beliefs and communicate that we value people and want to enable their optimal performance. To make it work at every level, managers are held accountable for implementing the program, and their success is measured by a set of performance metrics.

This initiative has been truly innovative for CIGNA and motivating for our entire workforce because it makes it clear to employees at all levels that they are critical to CIGNA's success. Demonstrating to employees that they are valued, and that CIGNA is investing in activities that will help them take initiative, represents a huge cultural shift for CIGNA. This new corporate strategy is visibly promoting what many executives and managers have long felt but had not institutionalized.

Strategy 2: Developing a learning organization

A lot has been written about the benefits of developing a learning organization. We targeted an area to do just that, and the learning extended all the way to our clients.

At CIGNA, service representatives routinely took calls from clients about their retirement plans. The reps prided themselves on how fast they could answer the phone, how many calls they could handle in a day, and how quickly they could help clients take loans and withdrawals from their retirement plans, not addressing the fact that it is really not in anyone's best interest – the client's or CIGNA's – to take money from a 401(k) account.

A pilot group of service representatives was charged with determining how to provide 401(k) plan participants with more information and education. Because representatives do not have the required SEC and NASD licenses to act as financial advisers, they cannot give advice *per se* on which funds investors might choose. But they can be expected to help customers better understand the value of their portfolio at retirement. They can also be expected to advise customers on the outcomes if they increased their contributions to their 401(k) account and kept their money in it, instead of taking money out through loans. The ultimate goal was to help clients save appropriately for retirement.

The group first looked for a vendor who would "teach" them how to do this; but group members quickly found that no one was able to play that role. So they looked to themselves for the answers. They had the experience, the management support, and the knowledge to assess the situation and information and educate participants.

They started with a very clear objective and began to determine which practices they used to educate clients and influence them to build their retirement nest eggs. As a team, they spoke about their successes, shared experiences, and tested and refined their theories about what worked and what did not. They learned how to help clients think through the ramifications of taking a loan and to offer options that could address clients' needs without jeopardizing the value of their 401(k) accounts.

Today, when service representatives get calls from clients who want to take withdrawals or borrow against their 401(k) accounts, they talk to clients about the potential impact to the 401(k) and they walk customers through various options. Ultimately, the clients must make their own decisions, but those decisions may be dramatically different from what they had originally intended. And their decisions are not only in their best interest, but are actually better outcomes for CIGNA as well. This new approach to learning has succeeded in just over three months and is credited with a $4 million increase in assets under management.

Strategy 3: E-learning

E-learning is just one of many tools available to help us educate our workforce. We have also begun to use strategic learning, a method that educates people through on-the-job situations, simulations, experiences, and expertise. The approach is about learning while doing. We first used this approach with one of our business divisions, CIGNA Retirement and Investment Services. By using the expertise within the organization, having clear objectives, and providing an environment that encourages learning, this group has significantly improved both customer and representative satisfaction.

On the basis of CIGNA's specific content – for instance, teaching individuals how to perform customer service functions and use proprietary techniques and processes – and considering in-house subject matter expertise, the complexity of CIGNA's computing environment, and our concerns about cost, we decided to develop the content to support our unique issues and our specific technology applications internally rather than purchase software already on the market.

For the HIPAA e-learning component, we chose a staggered rollout over seven months to accommodate each division's business cycle. Our healthcare division was the single largest constituent, with more than 70 percent of CIGNA's employees. The most challenging aspect of the project was creating the tracking and reporting component. We needed to track multiple education requirements, over an extended period, for a large number of roles performed by an overall population of 40,000 individuals. In addition, because of the staggered HIPAA requirements, we needed to be able to prove compliance at different points for people who perform a variety of roles. To succeed, we leveraged our existing systems area work teams and processes – adapting them to meet the needs of this endeavor. Instead of buying or building something new, we re-used a reporting and tracking system originally created for an internal process-change initiative. After some modifications, we found ourselves with a cost-efficient way to track and report on HIPAA education.

Strategy 4: Blended initiatives

Blended initiatives are also working well for CIGNA. Such approaches are usually not appropriate for mandated training, which must be accomplished within a specific time-frame for large numbers of employees. They are generally most effective when the knowledge and skills can be transferred over an extended period.

For example, CTI has recently completed a blended learning solution for technical training with a pilot program on Cisco systems. This solution included e-learning, instructor-led classroom instruction, hands-on Internet labs, e-learning mentors, subject matter experts, and CIGNA mentors. Fifteen students, five mentors, and eight managers from three locations participated in this program, meeting simultaneously in a virtual classroom and participating in weekly learning labs online. Students also had "anytime, anywhere" access to e-learning modules through their home or business computers.

This blended learning solution enabled CIGNA to save $1,675 per student over its previous approach, which relied exclusively on classroom training. Several participants earned Cisco Certified Network Associate certification as a result of this endeavor. CTI plans to extend this new method of training to other programs on the basis of the compelling results from this pilot.

Blended solutions were also incorporated into CTI's Java Re-Skilling Boot Camp. This four-month program, developed in a partnership between CIGNA and Hartford's Capital Community College, uses a combination of classroom, online, laboratory, and workshop training to give mainframe developers at CIGNA an opportunity to learn new skills and be retrained for web developer roles. Using a blended approach to learning, participants get all their training without taking time away from their current jobs.

Succeeding and innovating in a regulated industry

Some people are naysayers. Unfortunately, a good many people in regulated industries use the fact that they are working within the confines of a very narrow space to say they cannot be expected to innovate. Luckily, I get a kick out of trying to find the angle that enables me to do what I need to do despite any barriers I may encounter.

To succeed in developing and maintaining talent in a heavily regulated industry, you have to be able to strike a balance between your priorities, your resources, and the corporate culture for which you are aiming. It is back to the three-legged stool. Just as we must balance many variables when determining which education initiatives to focus on, we must strike a similar balance when determining what education approaches to use. We must balance the time we have, the money and other resources that are available, the population that needs to be served, the business priorities in action, and the learning technologies available.

At CIGNA, it is our job to help others minimize risk. It has been a tremendous source of challenge and opportunity that when we approach the task of creating learning opportunities within the company, we find ourselves taking chances. This may mean taking a personal risk, as is the case when an employee agrees to learn something new. It may mean taking a risk with our infrastructure, as is the case when we roll out new software. Or it may mean taking a risk with our corporate culture.

We are developing a learning culture not because it is easy but because it is the right thing to do. CIGNA is slowly but surely shifting from a mindset of conformance to a mindset of creativity and innovation in which we exceed expectations and chart our own path. Incidentally, in the process, we are becoming the premier provider of employee benefits.

4 | *The invisible dogma*

MITCH RATCLIFFE

WHEN the World Wide Web was young, really just embryonic, I worked for a company that ran successful technology trade shows. This company wanted to be on the cutting edge, so I found myself on a team charged with building a three-dimensional virtual trade show on the Web. Our team met in person constantly, ignoring what our own experience was telling us about the limits and possibilities of virtual work and the potential for online events. We spent hundreds of thousands of dollars to build elaborate virtual booth space to sell to our exhibitor customers. "Attendees" could stroll the virtual aisles, collecting virtual brochures and tchotchkes (promotional knick-knacks) as though there were no difference between the Javits Convention Center in New York City and a computer screen.

We failed to see that our assumptions about how people would adapt to networked meetings were leading us down a blind alley. Even though technology was changing trade shows, we assumed that people would still be looking for all the flourishes of the physical events. In retrospect, I would say we were praying that the Internet did not mean the end of meeting in physical venues with tens of thousands of other people to collect brochures and listen to sales pitches. And our tools, which let us create all sorts of nifty virtual realities, encouraged errors every step of the way, precisely because we were not thinking critically about how those tools were reshaping the services our company offered. Things were changing in the trade show industry, but we clung to the artifacts of the physical events and tried to build them in cyberspace.

Those who attended the first virtual trade show were not enthusiastic about the experience, and no exhibitors wanted to buy booth space in the second. Eventually, the expense of the project was chalked up as a lesson learned. But that company and many others still have not learned the larger lesson that there are all sorts of assumptions – about how people should act, what needs to be done to be "effective" and "efficient" and "profitable" – wrapped up in the tools we select to support our businesses. Some of those assumptions are embedded in the tools themselves, while others rise out of our purchasing decisions, because we often select tools that reinforce what we think should be or, worse, hope can be the future of an industry.

The evidence that this lesson has not been learned? That trade show company, and nearly all the other companies in that industry, are struggling to stay afloat as communication between customer and vendor migrates online into environments that look nothing like conferences or trade shows.

Every company relies on tools to reach its goals. Those tools, which include systems for accomplishing our work ranging from the written articles of incorporation to information systems, are selected in the hope of achieving optimal results. Many of the tools we use have become so commonplace that we never think about them or their impact on our day-to-day work. Computer technology, in particular, is generally thought to be inherently neutral, a shapeless, omnifunctional thing to which we have given form by installing instructions in the form of code and, hence, not likely to shape our behavior as much as we shape it. Yet, most companies strive to repair broken human processes with technology, blindly redefining them as they do so.

Smart companies and accomplished learning organizations can stop reading here.

You are still reading. This is a good sign. Either you recognize that even the best organizations can never stop seeking new insights or you know that technology cannot repair broken human systems. The catch is, even when information technology (IT) is the right answer, it must be monitored – not just for performance and efficiency but also for its *continuing* influence on the processes an organization is addressing through automation. Prevention of built-in errors and institutional stupidity, as with forest fires and sexually transmitted diseases, begins with you.

Active engagement with our tools is the key to successfully applying technology to the problems of operating a company. It is management's responsibility to engage in this way rather than apply IT like an all-purpose salve for broken human processes. This chapter will tell you what to engage with and the mistakes to watch out for every day, not just on the day you make a buying decision in order to help create a culture in which people can learn.

Operating on autopilot

Anyone who has made a technology buying decision knows the process. An organizational issue is raised, such as, "We're not sharing enough information to learn from our customers and design a better product," which is followed by the debate about *what is wrong*. The problem is reduced to a missing step in the information collection, analysis, and presentation process, because that is what companies do today, right? Granted, companies do manage knowledge, often forgetting in large or small ways what they actually deliver to a customer, be it a product or service. So, having decided that a step is being missed somewhere, someone draws up a Gantt chart or a process analysis and then the diagnosis is handed over to the IT department, which is expected to fix the problem. Simple as that. How many of these scripted exercises, which ideally fit into one or two meetings, have you been involved in over the years? How many have failed?

Here is the secret about software: it is a simulation of reality, especially the reality between our ears and the reality of what passes between us when we meet and talk. Effective software draws users into a shared irreality field in which differences in perceptions of data are bridged just enough to make everyone believe they are actually collaborating, a kind of suspension of disbelief that a movie audience experiences. Most software designed for groups, however, never achieves this goal; most of it is a simulation of a solitary tool, like a typewriter or a spreadsheet, which is worked on serially rather than collaboratively. For all the talk about "friction-free" value chains, new tools are a hassle because they require a change in behavior. This is why IT is a management issue in the first place, because we managers have to coach people through the process of adapting to new inconveniences in order to reach a corporate goal. It is all about people, even if we are told that IT is transparent and easy to use.

Coming face-to-face with such a discontinuity between reality and the models used for planning reveals what I call "invisible dogmas," assumptions that mislead our efforts and analysis or that shape the channel of communication to reinforce preordained conclusions. Most companies suffer from "repetitive mistake syndrome," because they refuse to learn when they live in a shared irreality field maintained by poorly designed tools for knowledge-sharing.

Dogma: remnants of priestly practices

In everyday business and organizational life, invisible dogmas are subtle and difficult to identify because technology decisions are still treated
as mysterious despite the fact that the priestly caste of programmers
supposedly passed with the decline of the mainframe computer. We
have to keep firmly in mind that the vision and skill of the people who
apply technology can expand or constrain the conduits for ideas. The
evidence of the Internet bubble is that high inspiration does not often
yield practical results, because doing something cool with a computer
is not always a path to doing something useful.

When confronted with the reality of supporting complex human
interactions, technology can be a Typhoid Mary of poor thinking. IT,
because it is a conduit that shapes our communication, can impose
simplistic assumptions about how people should interact or ideological
interpretations about the meaning of information and how it should
be distributed. Technology is rife with invisible dogmas that can foul
management's best-laid plans, leaving learning organizations in ruins
as people and networks route around the rigid stupidity they perceive
in misapplied technology.

For managers reading this chapter, I want to make one point that
you should never forget: what technology does is basic; it stands in for
human services, so any tool for managing knowledge is something that
you should be able to understand easily. If a programmer or a software
sales rep shows up at your door and spouts a bunch of buzzwords that
you do not understand or that do not map to the realities of your business, their tools are not ready for you. Tell them to come back when they
know something about what you do. It is exactly like being in a meeting
in which someone, put on the spot, falls back on management fads or
prevarication to explain away mistakes, instead of taking responsibility
and sharing the lesson with everyone at the table. In such situations,
you ask the person to learn something or find another job.

I cannot count how many times I have been subjected to demon-
strations of new products, especially products designed to "enhance
productivity," that consist of the guy who built the tool sitting down
and with astonishing flourish and speed setting up and managing a
complex project document while he talks over his shoulder about all
the great features of the software. His hands seem to know instinctively
where to go on the keyboard or how the mouse saves three steps. It

is really impressive. Here is why: people like this have reduced their brains to computer code and they can operate their code-filled brains really well. They do not run up against the mistakes in thinking and the realities of your business that come into conflict with their tools, because the software carries every assumption they made and, so, supports all those assumption with nifty features.

Then, they give you the software – or, worse, they sell it to you – and two weeks later you cannot figure out what it does or even how it is supposed to help you achieve your goals. Of course, there are consulting services available to customize (fix) the software or to beat your team into the patterns of work and information flow that the software demands. It all comes down to the fact that you cannot think using another person's brain, which is what you have on your hands.

Not all software is like this. Well-made applications accommodate many different ways of working, which is why, for instance, Microsoft Word is a vast application of which you and your team regularly use only one-fiftieth. Eventually, the effort of supporting a mass market makes the application so unwieldy that it becomes impractical – this is what is happening with Word and other productivity applications today.

Flexible type; immovable blobjects

IT is not a bad investment for a company. Refusing to use computers and networks would be a grave mistake. However, we also need to recognize that the knowledge tools introduced over the last fifty years will have negative consequences, just as type and broadcast media and the interstate highway system have given us propaganda and air pollution, to name just a couple of the downsides of other paradigmatic technologies.

Granted, a computer connected to a network is a remarkably versatile tool for managing information and can carry almost anything, from simple facts to complex theories. At every layer of its design, however – the computer, its operating system, application software, network connections, network protocols, interfaces between computers, and databases on the networks – this tool shapes information. The people who define and build each of those layers often have unchallenged control over the implementation of ideas. And we customers often ignore how such tools sculpt what we know into what we want it to be. Assumptions, presumptions, biases, and ideologies are injected into software and data services by programmers, designers, even the customer who will use the tools. Simple decisions made early in the life of an IT project become embedded in the hardware and software, whether those decisions were right or wrong. Early errors are compounded by upgrades that ossify the original features. Managers, programmers, and support personnel who build careers around a particular technology platform do not just maintain that system; they defend it from change – just as monks fought the Renaissance – and can narrow channels of communication within an organization so that they shut out or reshape much of what the systems were intended to let flow freely.

E-mail, though it creates many problems related to information overload, is an example of a successful tool for communicating over a network. As e-mail has matured, generations of software that was supposed to facilitate workgroup productivity have fallen by the wayside. When "groupware" first came into vogue along with the first practical and affordable commercial networking technologies in the early 1990s, I tried repeatedly to introduce shared word processing and message boards into a technology trade publisher's offices. Invariably, the staff would try out my latest discovery and then go back to e-mail, which was the simplest way to send a message. But e-mail was the least efficient way, from a purely statistical perspective, to update a document that a group was writing together. The most recent version of the document was seldom available to everyone, because it had not been sent to the entire group or someone would forget to attach it to e-mail. Rectifying all those changes in the final document was, and still is, painfully time-consuming, but the short-term convenience of sending an e-mail that said "Here's my latest draft of the proposal" outweighed the value of the time saved by the person charged with compiling changes. I have compensated for reality by adopting e-mail as my primary tool for communicating with and managing teams, but I make sure, whenever possible, I am not the one who has to clean up the final draft.

Now, if my solution to the inefficiency of e-mail is to make sure someone else does the extra work required to concatenate the results of an e-mail exchange, there is something wrong. While many companies have adopted e-mail as their primary tool for communicating textual and graphical information, we are reaching the limits of returns from this particular mode of shared irreality. Yet companies charge on into the breach, using the mail metaphor to address more processes within organizations.

The technology itself is so enticing that it is often difficult to see beyond the tantalizing features to the shortcomings embodied in the product. For example, I am typing this chapter on an Apple PowerBook G4 Titanium, which is so cool that Apple CEO Steve Jobs pronounced, "Titanium is sex" when it was introduced. It is the epitome, from a technologist's perspective, of what industrial designer Karim Rashid calls "blobjects," about which science fiction writer and futurist Bruce Sterling says this: "Though they are merely made things, blobjects tend to be fleshy, pseudo-alive, and seductive." This laptop cost more than other computers with similar, though not identical, functionality, even though it runs software that is cranky when it deals with 90 percent of the rest of the computers in the world. I bought it because it is cool, because it seduced me. Just like every information tool you see this year, it promises to deliver improved efficiency, better analysis of corporate data, or the implementation of Six Sigma processes with nary a bump in your quarterly goals. Blobjects entice, but each one carries an agenda that spreads like a virus, unevenly, in bursts of rapid adoption, reinforcing dogmas along the way.

Invisible dogmas can take many forms, from the decision to filter out certain words deemed unsuitable for a community to presumptions about the way people should use hardware or software. Take the example of public libraries that want to provide informational resources to the entire community, including children, so they filter out access to websites with the word "breast," inadvertently blocking women from learning about breast cancer. If they filter the word "ass," Jesus does not ride into Jerusalem on Palm Sunday.

Invisible dogmas can wipe out reality and replace it with wishful thinking. At a minimum, they sanitize reality, leaving people charged with responding to rapidly changing situations with very little authentic information on which to base their next decision. Dogmas, however, are the results of remarkably practical decisions that are easily justified by management, employees, and contractors or the companies that build knowledge tools.

If there is a general sense that information management systems must sacrifice complexity to come in under budget, the resulting tools will not deal well with increasingly complicated data. Budget and beliefs result in shortcuts based on cost-benefit analyses that can have profound effects on what the organization can achieve. These are the realities we must keep in mind when erecting the foundation for a company, a learning organization, or a government bureaucracy built on IT. Nevertheless, we often make these decisions in response to messages that appeal to our fears of failure or our desire for success and not with a clear view of how each new tool changes our company in small or large ways.

The DNA of dogma

Simple enough to say, but what exactly are we to look for when trying to cobble together a foundation from which teams can collaborate and learn? And cobble we must, because there is no end-to-end solution that allows groups to collaborate and learn with equal facility in all settings.

The answer is to look for biases, opinions, or beliefs that have been arbitrarily laid down as rules about what people should do with technology, as well as when they should do it and how they should behave. Here is where inflexibility will interfere with the flow of ideas. When I was attempting to introduce workgroup software into organizations in the early 1990s, my bias was that being able to open and share a document from any workstation was more efficient than e-mailing a document around a workgroup. While that may or may not be true, I was making an assumption that e-mail was inherently less efficient, and I tried to *block* people from using it in conjunction with the workgroup tools.

Dogmas can be correct, which makes them all the more diabolically difficult to eliminate. There is no doubt in my mind or any manager's that an organization should pick tools that enforce its priorities to some degree. It would be impossible to cook a meal in a kitchen where knives were forbidden, and every company, because companies do largely deal with the manipulation of information, needs to define the range of data it will try to process. So, some dogma is a very good thing. The very act of defining an organization requires managers to invent a bit of dogma, a dollop of determinism in an otherwise chaotic environment. A deterministic system is purposeful and supports goal-setting. However, if that system eliminates the organization's ability to make choices, it writes failure into the DNA of the organization.

Participation and modality biases

Rules that define how and when users should contribute to the group's dialog are participation and modality biases. These biases may take the form of forcing people to use a particular application or learn some esoteric mark-up language. Fact is, some of your team is most comfortable using e-mail, while others thrive on the phone or in a shared workspace or teleconference; there may be a guy who loves entering data in forms on his computer, but the IT system does not allow that mode of entry in some situations. Now, for the purposes of argument, why can he not use his preferred mode of communication to contribute to the group's success? Because a programmer said so? Not a good enough reason when he earns $80,000 a year already and does just fine working as he always has.

Even transient events, such as a decision by a manager just passing through, can redefine how a software application is used in an organization. Imagine how a poor choice by a sales manager hoping to streamline her prospecting process across a large sales force could shut down some of her staff and give others who happen to thrive in the application unprecedented and unearned influence.

Herein lies the importance of invisible dogma: if a bias changes the performance of a tool and the tool changes the performance of a group of people, then we managers need to be very conscientious about the choices we make with technology. Simple example: how do your people react to being interrupted? Say, interrupted right in the middle of a meeting? The walkie-talkie-like press-to-talk feature of the Nextel wireless service, which lets someone butt right into your day via cell phone, is about to become a major service feature across most wireless networks. It will be played up in advertisements, and the notion that one would ignore a "call" of this type will be judged rude by some, unproductive by others, and all the while half the world will think it the worst sort of interruption. What we have here is a participation and a modal bias – first, there is a presumption that the press-to-talk service is useful and necessary (why else would your company have paid for it on the phones issued to employees?), a participation bias, and then there is the related assumption that being available at the push of a button is a good thing, even if the person on the receiving end of walkie-talkie chatter cannot stand using the phone in the first place, which is a modality bias.

The crux of a participation or modality bias, then, is a requirement that an individual user act or contribute in a particular way or through a particular channel. A system with this kind of bias will invariably draw complaints that it does not let people express themselves in a way they think is effective or that it "interrupts" their work or is "annoying."

Technology, because it is usually deployed *en masse*, is a blunt instrument that often hits everyone the same way. This is especially apparent within the confines of a small group, where individual differences are starkly evident and can be exaggerated by the introduction of a tool that favors one form of participation or mode of dealing with knowledge over others.

Once a new tool is installed in your organization, have you noticed that some people who had been middling contributors suddenly take on leading roles? Is there a cadre of stars who seem to have had their energy reduced recently? Does any of this have to do with a change in management practices or is it due to the tools changing around these people? In the film *The Matrix*, Morpheus introduces the hero Neo to life inside a computer simulation as they engage in a Kung Fu match. "Do you think I beat you because I am stronger or faster than you? Do you think that is air you are breathing? Are you aware of the game?" Participation and modality biases are elusive and difficult to understand until you accept the practice of questioning processes anew each day. Then they become apparent and pop up everywhere. Do you want to know what the Matrix is? Look around.

Speed and skill biases

Speed and skill biases are based on the presumption that everyone has the same amount of time each day to participate in a group project and that it takes everyone the same time to perform similar chores. This is a particularly difficult bias to identify when dealing with software because "ease of use" is assumed to be a uniform characteristic, yet not all people have the same skill level or aptitude for learning new commands and shortcuts with each new application. Consistency between different applications is often a remedy for speed and skill biases – the simple fact that people do not need new habits and commands with each new tool they use is a significant benefit. The reason the original Macintosh operating system was so popular was that Apple strictly enforced its Human Interface User Guidelines across all applications that ran on the computer – the same commands worked the same way regardless of what you were doing with a Macintosh. Likewise, Microsoft's Office suite provides widely but not completely consistent commands across a core set of productivity tools – it is just easier to get used to than a collection of tools with different commands. "If one has to spend precious brain energy learning the peculiarities of the [application] interface, there is less energy left to learn the topic at hand," says Cliff Figallo, a veteran of building online communities.

For example, I serve on the board of advisers of a company that builds software for workgroups. Among the founders and advisers there is a real passion for a type of collaborative editing tool, called a "wiki" (Hawaiian for "quick"), that allows a group to make changes to a shared web page. I do not like wikis because I have to use a set of formatting commands that are similar to those of other tools but dissimilar enough that I often get confused. It just takes me more time to get information into a wiki than I want to spend. Only one other adviser does not "get wikis," in the words of the rest of the team. Compounding my distaste is the fact that each time someone edits a wiki page on the company's site, a percentile ranking of his or her input to the company's efforts is displayed at the top of the page. "You are in the 25th percentile of contributors," I am informed when I do take the time to work on a wiki page.

Am I just whining about my poor performance rating? No, wikis are an example of both participation and modality bias (some folks like their wikis and others like e-mail as a primary channel for textual communication) and speed and skill bias (because wiki pages require learning a special mark-up language and doing the editing is more time-consuming that tapping out an e-mail). I prefer e-mail. But, because the company's founders like wikis, those pages display my contribution percentile while not a single e-mail comes with a ranking of input, even though I send a lot more e-mail. The system is tilted in favor of what the team wants to sell rather than how its customers may want to behave.

The important question for the company I am advising is whether the wiki serves its needs. I may not be the right adviser for the company if wiki collaboration is the primary mode of exchange it seeks to encourage (in fact, wikis are just one part of a larger whole the company is building, but because wikis are the flavor of the month and the subject of intense development, the group is fixating on the *wikification* of everything these days). Maybe they ought to jettison me and find someone who will contribute more? Or, perhaps, the preference for wikis is shutting out input that would be given if other forms of communication were more highly valued.

Speed and skill biases are most closely related to the lack of time people have to keep learning. Do you really want your team focused on picking up new computer skills when they need to be learning about the market and the world so that they can spot new challenges before the competition does? If you have asked yourself that question about a communications tool, you are facing a speed or skill bias.

Most executives I know would prefer to use the phone. Almost no CEO I know makes day-to-day decisions that would be served by ranking their input percentile on a wiki. If one were to put a wiki in place as the sole mode of communication within an organization, it would be a disaster. At the same time, the largest freely accessible and collaboratively produced encyclopedia on the planet, Wikipedia, was created using a wiki less than six years after the technology was introduced. In its proper place, any technology can be a powerful tool. The hoe comes to mind when I head out to the garden, but I would not want to paint a house with one.

Semantic biases

Language is a messy business, because of both its constant evolution and the differences in the way people use it. Semantic biases are evident in the range of options available for categorizing information, such as labeling every new topic as a problem instead of an opportunity (in software, this evolved from quality-assurance practices among programmers) and in the limited ranges of choice in a knowledge tool that prevent the group from straying outside well-defined lines.

Semantic biases are most prominent in networked environments where different cultures and standards come into conflict. Let me remind the reader, again, that we are only at the earliest stage of the information age. From a historical perspective, we are just learning to grunt and gesture with computationally enhanced communications. Only the most basic forms of networked transactions have been possible during the greater part of the history of computing, and differences between systems were wiped out in the interest of "compatibility" so that information such as product specifications could be provided across an industry. For example, there is a Performance Review Institute that administers the standardized product specifications for the aerospace industry. Achieving this kind of compatibility required that the basic structure of data be standardized, and once companies were able to communicate about their products or services and the needs they had, customers have defined how sellers describe their offerings by buying more, less, or none of a particular product or service. Albeit, sellers have ladled a heavy dose of marketing on the facts. Nevertheless, when it came to decision-making, product specifications have been the gold standard – if the product did not do what the customer needed, it was returned.

When computing evolved past managing data to collecting and distributing knowledge, meaning became infinitely shaded. Information technology decisions are now made for convenience or budget's sake that can fundamentally alter the substance of what is communicated. The value of information depends on the system analyzing it, just as no two people see the same event in precisely the same way. During a bullfight, one spectator may watch carefully the cape work of the toreador while another is watching the *señoritas* in the stands and wondering how much tequila is in his Margarita. Both will be able to recall the event, but they will not remember the same elements. Knowledge management is similarly complex, and, as I have written elsewhere, computers let you make more mistakes faster than any invention in human history, with the possible exceptions of handguns and tequila.

Within a group or organization, shades of meaning can be managed by strictly enforcing a schema, such as, "A four on a scale of one to ten means the company should not pursue this opportunity at this time, but the idea should be reviewed again later." This may work internally, but open the discussion to the outside world and it becomes a useless metric, because one person's "four" is another's "six."

Semantic bias is perhaps the most dangerous type of invisible dogma, because it can convince an entire team that its interpretation of reality *is* reality.

Historical biases

"That's the way we've always done it," is the signature of the historical bias, the preservation of outmoded knowledge because of the rigidity of technology. Imposing a practice in technology is like setting it in cement.

The self-organizing qualities of a learning organization are anathema to the way centralized IT departments have dealt with change. Self-organization grows from "a different mindset from the prevailing approach to software development and managing vast amounts of information," says Greg Elin, a developer of "social software." "In the new organization, there is no central control, errors are good, flexibility and self-repair are highly valued." History does matter.

Historical bias is often well founded in the stories of the past. In other words, some ideas are good or were good. Enduring ideas, however, can interfere with necessary evolutionary activity, preventing the organization from considering new information and the changing context of the marketplace until it is too late to react effectively. What if your company has moved from making buggy whips to airplanes, and the software you use is designed for a buggy whip company? Often, it is the failure of software to evolve with the organization that makes it utterly useless – this has happened in many media companies, for example, where digital technology was designed for outputting paper or television signals according to day-part pricing schedules and has locked companies that could be exploiting the Internet and on-demand multimedia networks into increasingly outmoded business models.

When they fade into the background and go unexamined, dogmas do the most damage. Necessity dictates decisions that emphasize certain priorities or subtract options from future consideration, because they are deemed unnecessary elements, at every phase of organizational and application development. This is the reality of developing tools on a limited budget. In advance of a truly universal computational environment that can accommodate any information or mode of input with total flexibility to manipulate data for accurate re-representation to many users, compromise over what can be programmed into a knowledge platform is a dirty fact of life. An organization can face these realities by assessing how it will shape the resulting knowledge for good or bad, increased or decreased accuracy and clarity, and for the potential to re-use information as technology continues to develop.

Most dangerous of all is the tendency to settle on a set of technologies, with their attendant biases, and treat this initial state as the foundation for future decisions, without returning to examine the compromises reflected in the original technology selection. Everyone knows we make compromises in the process of choosing knowledge tools, but no one records these compromises with the same kind of eye as, for instance, a literary critic or historian reviewing a book. There is a real urgency to *get on with business*, which forces compromises into the past and out of sight almost reflexively. It enforces a kind of institutional amnesia that can and should be prevented.

If we were to engage in a practice of reviewing our tools critically, recording the compromises made along the way, it would be much easier to tune both the tools and our organizations over the long run. We may all be dead in the long run, but the people who follow us are going to be even more ignorant of the compromises than we are if they cannot access these critical records of corporate and software development. I find this especially ironic in an age when many business books published each year attempt to explain the longevity of successful companies. Recording the history of your own company and its decision-making, including how the tools you use shape those decisions and how the decisions shape the tools, needs to be far more important to you than finding out how Lou Gerstner made the elephants at IBM dance. Gerstner succeeded because he accessed his own experience and internalized the experiences of the company he took over at its darkest hour. He thought hard about IBM and his own decisions, about the compromises he would have to make at that time and the reparations he would pay later to correct earlier shortcuts.

The scientific method, which demands that scientists examine with rigor their data, their analytical choices, and their results, is the model for abolishing – or, at least, substantially reducing – built-in biases and limitations. It takes practice and is a practice that cannot be carried out by a corporate librarian or even a chief technology officer working on her own. From the beginning of a company's life, records need to be prepared that exceed the requirements for simple reporting to shareholders or the US Securities and Exchange Commission. Internal accountability, in the form of frank discussion and writing down what has been left undone, is the foundation for successful growth. But metrics alone, which have dominated business schools in recent years, are not sufficient. Management is part science and a lot art. I would suggest that a practical and profitable investment among business leaders would be the development of a discipline of business historiography. This is the study of how histories are influenced by the historians' times – a history of the New Deal era written during the McCarthy era will read very differently from one written in the 1970s. Why? Because each decade is flavored with a different set of hopes and fears. In business, each epoch in the life of a company is defined by distinct priorities and, below those priorities, more hopes and fears.

Would a company investing today in technology to support organizational learning be treated with skepticism by an investor who, having lost more than a third of his portfolio value when the Internet bubble burst, prefers a company that "focuses on core competencies"? The resulting limits on available capital might require the company to assume that only e-mail and database access are necessary. Nevertheless, the addition of a wiki and other collaborative tools, as well as the staff to support them – not to mention the entire consultative services division that could evolve from the environment of learning facilitated by these tools – could accelerate the company's growth. If, after making the case for funding to build these tools, the company opts for a stripped-down information infrastructure, should the analysis of the opportunity not be retained and taught to future managers? Successful companies, notably Royal Dutch Shell, have made a religion of these practices through the use of scenario development that incorporates past lessons.

Every company needs to embrace such practices, not necessarily in the guise of scenario development but in terms of recording and talking about the tools they use, the compromises they have accepted, the blind alleys they have gone down. A business historiography will take all that data and the perspectives gained over time to provide management with an evolving analysis of opportunities missed and those that are re-emerging.

Where we have been and do not want to visit again

We are flirting with a dark age in business and organizational thought, precisely because a great many people are interested in imposing what they think is the right approach to group dynamics through the unenlightened use of technology. Invisible dogmas – unstudied and facile management fads or simple faith in a particular way of doing business imposed at some stage in an organization's life – are akin to the religious fervor that laid civilization low in the early fifth century. Rigorous thinking was replaced by faith reinforced by dogma, which became unquestioned truth, very much like the company that, when asked why it does something one way and not another, cannot respond with a well-considered reason. Alas, it is not as easy to detect as religious dogma, because you are not asked to kiss as many rings as you are during a visit to the Vatican. But we all know from personal experience what it is like to be ushered into the mahogany offices of an executive who operates like the Pope.

One of the reasons invisible dogmas crop up so frequently is that the decisions that shape the collecting and processing of knowledge are highly political. It is often uncomfortable to ask acknowledged experts if they might be installing unfounded biases in a system of knowledge. Yet we must ask such questions. Knowing how and why design decisions are made, recording those decisions for future use by programmers as well as managers, and recognizing when a decision is based on a controversial position or promoted by an influential individual, together constitute a tightrope act of competing agendas and personalities.

Unfortunately, most experts concentrate in one area and cannot conceive of the complexities or concessions required to build, for example, a simple application for communicating information (as distinct from knowledge). Even the dedicated polymath, who learned a programming language in graduate school but has not kept up with the latest software advances, is likely to be many technological generations behind the leading edge by the time he or she turns forty. So we must encourage the development of questioning skills that allow the parties to a technology-supported learning culture to identify and eliminate the invisible dogmas that they *must* create in order to get any working software into workers' hands.

If there is nothing simple in city government or academic bureaucracy (and there seldom is), then how do you codify the current state of a discipline, like accounting or quantum mechanics, in which the scope of the known is changing constantly and debates are reshaped with a single finding?

This may seem trivial today, but for the future user of information or for knowledge architects, the products of invisible dogmas will appear as incongruous as the discovery of an American colonial musket in the midst of an Egyptian archeological dig. If a decision today does not make complete sense today, the results will become mysterious after a couple of generations. When making our initial decisions about a technology, we need to ensure that the rationales are recorded so they can be resurrected and reconsidered in context during future upgrades and at new junctures in the life of a company. Doing so will substantially reduce the cost and complexity of significant changes in a business process or a wholesale transformation of a company.

Simply put, the source of dogmas is our own laziness. We opt, for instance, to make people collaborate by using "collaboration" software instead of teaching them to work together respectfully and constructively. We fail to appreciate how these tools change the requirements when hiring new employees and often blame the employees when they fail to thrive in the stunted learning environments we have created. The institutionalization of critical thinking about our choices of information tools is absolutely essential to the manager's role in the information age.

The introduction of the printing press and the vernacularization of the Bible broke the back of the priest caste that dominated intellectual life in the Middle Ages by allowing the layman to think about and question the dogmas of the church. Today's information-rich workplace is the institutional equivalent of the Gothic cathedral, and the mysteries of our tools need to be stripped away and made plain and comprehensible. This means that managers have to lead the task of disseminating and thinking about the invisible dogmas that reside quietly in our tools but have profound effects on the success of organizations. From the way we organize our companies to the tools we use to share information, the assumptions of the past must be questioned every day if we hope to build on the shoulders of the giants that have gone before.

5 | Looking back on technology to look forward on collaboration and learning

DAVID GREBOW

I once accepted a job with an international company that focuses on learning and collaboration. My new CEO wanted me to get a sense of the corporate culture by meeting the heads of the various divisions face-to-face. So I took a trip around the world on a one-way ticket east that started and ended – sixteen days later – in the little town of Carmel, California. When my journey was over, one of the things I had collected was a huge stack of business cards from London, Paris, Johannesburg, Sydney, Brisbane, Auckland, and points in between. I had spoken with, and could reconnect to, more than a hundred people around the world. A new community of learners, which crossed national and organizational boundaries and cultures, was spread out in my hands. All I needed to do was enter their e-mail addresses into my address book and I could reach out to almost anyone, anywhere and anytime.

As I flipped through the business cards, I had one of those moments of insight that had me scrambling for paper and pen. It was not just this small community that was reflected in these cards but the whole world. What I wrote down was something like this:

We have reached a milestone in human evolution, a point where we as individuals can connect with countless other individuals, mind to mind, regardless of time, distance, space, culture, borders, and nationality. We are still evolving, but in a relatively short time we have come a long way. Think about the earliest human beings: minds isolated inside themselves, unable to connect except in the most rudimentary fashion. From a lonely, speechless perch somewhere on the African continent, the human mind has evolved into an interconnected, worldwide community of learners.

Communication, connection, learning, sharing, and community: the human mind has achieved all this through invention, through technology.

As one looks back over the last 30,000 years of human evolution and invention, it seems as if there has been an innate drive – an almost mindful evolution. Many of our most important inventions have been designed to help the mind break free of various constraints; first the body, then other physical limitations: borders, boundaries, even time and space. We have been driven to connect with other minds, to create a worldwide community of learners. Now this evolutionary scheme has been fulfilled in many ways. My stack of business cards is the proof.

How did we evolve toward this vast community? What were the signposts along the way? What inventions and technology enabled it to happen? And how could the journey we have taken over the past 30,000 years inform us about the inventions and technology that will continue to shape this community?

In recent years, I have sought insight into the development of the worldwide community of learners – specifically, the technology that learners have found useful and enabling. I have studied the crucial moments of invention and technological discovery that brought us to this point: learning to speak, writing, the gathering of knowledge, printing, and the transmitting of information without wires. I imagine these points as five peaks in a vast range of inventions, the key inventions and technologies that have made it possible for the mind to overcome various barriers and connect with other minds. After they appeared on the scene, we lived our lives differently. We evolved in a very real sense into something greater than we were before. We evolved into an ever-larger community.

In order of appearance upon the historical stage, this is a snapshot of those five moments:

(1) *The invention of language (approximately 30,000 years ago)*: Learning to speak to one another and create communities of learners that could extend beyond pointing and miming. Our minds evolved beyond being alone, unable to communicate with one another, and we began developing the first communities of learners.

(2) *The invention of writing (4,000 years ago)*: The origin of communities that could finally be free from the limitations of time and space. We evolved beyond our immediate physical boundaries and created the first virtual learning communities. This invention meant that communities of learners could develop and communicate anywhere and anytime.

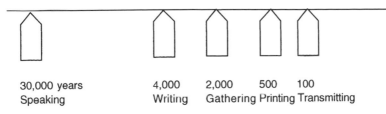

Figure 5.1. Timeline of key inventions and technologies.

(3) *The building (and destruction) of the library at Alexandria (2,000 years ago)*: The first international learning community in history, which gave rise to numerous others after it was destroyed. Our minds spread out into the known corners of the world then and forever. We evolved into many communities around the world focused on learning and sharing what was learned. And through that sharing, from that point, our evolution accelerated.

(4) *The invention of the printing press (500 years ago)*: The first great portable learning technology, which enabled the spread of learning communities throughout the world. This invention gave us a way to disseminate learning much faster and farther than speech or writing or collections of pre-printing books ever could. Our minds could reach out to one another with ideas and dreams, fact and fiction. The first technology to enable communities of learners spread rapidly all over the "civilized" world in less than a hundred years.

(5) *The invention of the radio (100 years ago)*: The first virtual learning communities, set free of physical boundaries. With radio technology, almost anyone could talk to anyone else almost anywhere about anything. A first true worldwide virtual community evolved. This development gave rise to the idea and invention of television, and ultimately the Internet.

Graphically, the timeline is as shown in Figure 5.1.

Let us start at the beginning.

The invention of speech

It is a shame that talking to one another is taken for granted, because speech is truly an amazing invention. Jared Diamond describes speech as one of "the Great Leaps Forward" and claims that it evolved simultaneously in several regions of the world. He believes we invented speech because of "the perfection of the voice box" and that this was the anatomical basis of modern language. Others suggest that there was a basic change in the organization of the brain at the same time as what we now call the language centers developed, and those changes together led to the invention of speech. Whatever the cause, one thing is certain: we began naming things and talking to one another. We broke out of the cage that held our minds captive and alone. The "we" in this case were our Cro-Magnon ancestors, who, before they could talk, had already invented art: ancient, forgotten music and paintings on cave walls. At some point around 30,000 years ago, according to various anthropologists, we invented speech.

The invention of speech was the great technological advance that helped create the first communities of learning. Anthropologists, archeologists, linguistic scientists, and others have all located "gatherings" where various tribal groups came together to trade. One of the things they traded was words, the name of a thing. We do it to this day: words for technology and culture are constantly finding their way across boundaries and languages.

Perhaps most important, speech overcame the limits of concrete thought. It opened the world, literally and figuratively, to abstract conversation in the form of storytelling, the development of mythology, the enabling of complex creation tales and religious rites. Speech helped us look up and outward together and tell one another what we saw. It was the first great step in becoming a human community – the ability to share the secret and perhaps frightening thoughts and ideas that had been locked away for so many years.

When I was in Johannesburg, South Africa, during my world tour, I was not too far from where most archeologists, anthropologists, and others believe speech was invented. I can imagine some Neanderthal genius looking at something and making a sound, then realizing that he could associate the sound and the thing and, in a sense, make them one. What is even more astounding to imagine is this person then realizing that another Neanderthal could learn to do the same thing: point, make the sound, and have that sound mean "that thing." It would not be too far a leap to realize that the thing itself is no longer actually needed, that the sound would magically conjure up what "it" was. Add to the word the sign for eat or danger or want or need, and you had speech. According to most people who study the invention of speech, a hybrid of signing came first and then sounds were associated. For all we know, the first sounds might have been music. It took almost 30,000 years of hard inventing before language moved beyond the concrete to the abstract and speech began to sound like it does today.

I can imagine Cro-Magnons and their Neanderthal predecessors using their bodies and hands to communicate. If you have ever watched people sign to the hearing impaired, you realize something very quickly: you need a line of sight – you need to be able to see the body language and the hands signing. It is very limiting. So inventing this technology called language, speaking to one another, naming things, and expressing them, is all about overcoming the constraints of the body. Without language, communities of learning are limited to very small groups of people who are in the same place at the same time. People need to be from your tribe or group to understand your signs. And the signs can communicate only relatively simple concrete thoughts. You can learn how to do only basic things like grind corn into meal, skin a carcass, or make fire. Learning is coupled with surviving, not with evolution, enrichment, or enlightenment. It took a long time before we named enough things and ideas to have a true language. This was perhaps the most time-consuming and difficult piece of evolution the mind has performed. Language needs no thing to point to or accompanying sign. It exists unto itself. In a very real sense, it is the universe abstracted and encapsulated into sounds. I am surprised that Descartes did not say, "I speak therefore I am."

And because the invention of speech enabled a one-to-many relationship between speaker and listener, teacher and learner, it helped us form the first communities of learners. Instead of a teacher slowly and carefully passing information to a student, a teacher could now pass on the knowledge to many students. If we look at tribes and groups whose language is still relatively concrete, we can see that their learning happens individually, not communally. Mothers show daughters, fathers show sons, and peers use language sparingly because there is not much language to use. There are no indigenous classes or instructor-led groups because there is no language to support that kind of knowledge transfer.

That would come thousands of years later, after we had named enough things to enrich language and cover abstract ideas as well as concrete things. I imagine that the first abstract ideas revolved around birth and death. Where did we come from and why are we here are more good abstractions that need words. The word "we" often enters into abstract discussions since the idea of a world that is more than just "I" is an abstraction. The ideas of family, group, tribe, nation, state, and country are all abstractions, as is the idea of a community of learners. So before we could evolve into such a community, we needed to invent the language that would help us create one.

There are not only many words but also many different words for the same thing. And in many cases, there are many words in one culture for a thing that another culture has not yet named. But words are about much more than naming things and imagining we have control over them.

Words are about sharing. I believe they were invented to extend our mind's ability to think and to be part of a human community, to share what we know and wonder together about the universe and the things it contains.[1]

The invention of writing

If speech gave us the words to create a community and to share things and ideas among the members of the community, then writing gave us a way to move those words from the speaker to anyone who could read or listen. The result was the ability to make the community larger, perhaps spanning time and space. Writing could be read to or by a community of people that spanned both those boundaries.

The Bible was among the first writings that were used to pass knowledge to a large and widely separated community of learners. The writing was captured on what we call the Dead Sea Scrolls, and it helped

---

[1] For more information on the origins of speech, see J. Diamond, *Guns, Germs, and Steel: The Fates of Human Societies* (New York: W. W. Norton & Co., 1999) and *The Third Chimpanzee: The Evolution and Future of the Human Animal* (New York: HarperCollins, 1992); M. Ruhlen, *The Origin of Language: Tracing the Evolution of the Mother Tongue* (New York: John Wiley & Sons, 1996); L. L. Cavalli-Sforza, *Genes, Peoples, and Languages* (Berkeley: University of California Press, 2001); L. L. Cavalli-Sforza and F. Cavalli-Sforza, *The Great Human Diasporas: The History of Diversity and Evolution* (Reading, Mass.: Addison-Wesley, 1995); and B. Grimes, *Ethnologue: Languages of the World*, 13th edn. (Dallas: Summer Institute of Linguistics, 1996).

enlarge the community that the spoken word had created. You no longer had to hear the sound of my voice to know what I said. It is true that writing was probably first invented to keep a record of grain and cattle and other things given as taxes or stored away in the case of a bad harvest. Yet to help the mind in its quest to reach out to other minds, writing was soon taken over and used by learning communities. Just like speech, the invention of writing became yet another enabling tool. Small, isolated communities of learners had slowly begun to evolve. With the invention of writing – and later the printing press – they could grow and connect more quickly.[2]

The invention of knowledge gathering

A library by definition is a place where written materials are managed and stored. While it is not a technology, it is, like speech and writing, a very human invention. Libraries around the world tend to be quiet places, where fingers cross lips in the universal sign to stop talking. Today, one of a library's primary roles is to provide a place for focus, for reading and research, writing and thinking. The library at Alexandria was like the Grand Central Station or the Piccadilly Circus of learners by comparison.

According to the most recent scholars, the library was built by Demetrius, under the patronage of Ptolemy I, Ptolemy Soter, around 200 BC, and was composed of several small libraries. Prior to that time, libraries were modeled after Greek private collections and were built by individuals, such as writers and philosophers, for their pleasure. Aristotle's library, for example, in which he collected his own and other's works, is famous enough to have been written about.

Ptolemy I's great ambition was to possess all known written works, to amass written knowledge from all cultures and schools of thought, and to have the greatest minds read and discuss them. He wanted to include all domains of study, from religious texts to the sciences, arts, and literature. The library housed hundreds of scholars, librarians, translators, scribes, teachers, visitors, and students in a beehive of activity and conversation, research and exploration. Scrolls, tablets, codex,

---

2 For more information on the invention of writing, see J. DeFrancis, *Visible Speech* (Honolulu: University of Hawaii Press, 1989); R. Logan *The Alphabet Effect* (New York: Morrow, 1986); and D. Diringer, *Writing* (London: Thames and Hudson, 1982).

parchment, linen, even early versions of paper all captured in writing the knowledge of the known world. It was the first time a place was dedicated to the writings of people from different cultures, countries, backgrounds, and beliefs. Entire new disciplines emerged, such as grammar, manuscript preservation, and trigonometry.

In an odd way, it was the destruction of the library by fire around 48 BC, when Julius Caesar occupied the city, that saved it. Even though many of the irreplaceable texts were lost, the energy of the first learning community, composed of people from all over the region, streamed into their countries and inspired people to form other communities whose sole purpose was learning – gathering and sharing the knowledge of their time and place, and adding whatever they could from other cultures. So the idea of a community of learners was born in Alexandria and took root in all the countries to which learners returned after the library was gone.

And the influence reached beyond libraries. Alexandria helped create learning communities that eventually became the prototype for monasteries, private schools, universities, and colleges. Libraries themselves expanded to incorporate the written records from other countries and cultures. For the first time, they were opened to the public. The library at Alexandria was one of those experimental human peaks from which the human mind made a quantum evolutionary leap. It instilled in many countries a culture of learning that was to become part of everyone's life, a life in which reading and writing were skills that almost all were expected to have.[3]

The invention of printing

Just as the Bible represented some of the first words written to be shared among a community, it was also an early player in the development of print technology. It was literally among the first books off the printing press.

[3] For more on the library at Alexandria and other early libraries, see R. Macleod, *The Library at Alexandria: Centre of Learning in the Ancient World* (London: I. B. Taurius & Co., 2002); L. Canfora and M. Ryle, *The Vanished Library* (Berkeley: University of California Press, 1990); D. A. Flower, *The Shores of Wisdom: The Story of the Ancient Library at Alexandria* (Philadelphia: Xlibris, 1999); and D. H. Tolzmann, A. Hessel, and R. Peiss, *The Memory of Mankind: The Story of Libraries Since the Dawn of Mankind* (New York: Oak Knoll Books, 2001).

In 1450, the church in Europe controlled the minds and hearts (and souls) of the people. It told them what to think and read. So some of the first printed books were not really books at all but forms. They were pages of the Bible that, thanks to moveable type, contained the Scripture. Those pages and words were then shipped off to monks in scriptoriums to illuminate with their amazing floral borders and drawings of death and life, the sacred and the profane. The "books" that were produced during the first fifty years of the printing press are called incunabula. The learners they were reaching were the true believers, and you could get many more bibles out to that community with this new invention than monks could working in their scriptoriums.

It took until the late fifteenth century for the printing press and the printed word to take their place in history. Books from Greek classics to English editions of *How to Play Chess* were being produced for everyone throughout Europe and eventually the rest of the world to claim as their own. The church had unwittingly shown the power and the glory of the printed word in the creation and maintenance of geographically dispersed communities.

It is important to remember that most people could neither read nor write at the time. Communities of learners were very focused – church, guilds, governance, and business – and relied on those who could read to keep them abreast of the newest ideas, methods, approaches, and innovations. Yet, as different types of printed materials appeared, new communities emerged, and even if you could not read, you could go to the town meeting, where a reader informed you of the latest happenings. As with speech and writing, printing once again served the evolutionary aims of the mind and spread knowledge more widely than ever before. Learning communities were now given the condensation of almost 30,000 years of evolution – speech and writing – between the artfully created covers of a book, which could be read, shared, discussed, and valued as part of the heritage of the human mind.[4]

---

[4] For more information on the development of printing, see R. Tames, *The Printing Press: A Breakthrough in Communications* (Oxford: Heinemann Library, 2001); B. Steffens, *Printing Press: Ideas into Type* (London: Lucent Books, 1990); E. Eisenstein, *The Printing Press as an Agent of Change* (Cambridge: Cambridge University Press, 1979); and W. J. Ong, *Orality and Literacy: The Technologizing of the Word* (London: Routledge, 1988).

The invention of transmitting

By the end of the twentieth century, communities of learners were speaking to each other, writing to each other, and gathering in groups. They read the printed thoughts of minds long dead, from faraway places, and saw the world through a multitude of apertures. And these communities were growing all over the world, separated mainly by distance. Still, they could reach out and contact one another through letters and other forms of writing. The world was smaller in the late 1900s than it was 30,000 years before, when tribes met to swap stories and share new words.

Guglielmo Marconi was partly responsible for making the world smaller. The telegraph was already in existence when in 1895 Marconi produced the wireless telegraph that was soon to be called the radio. Following his initial experiments between his house and garden, he eventually sent a signal clear across the Atlantic Ocean from Cornwall to Newfoundland on December 12, 1901, a distance of more than 3,500 kilometers. It was a signal heard well beyond the sending and receiving stations in Britain and America. Without the constraints of time or space, speech could now be transmitted around the world. Information could be given and received, entertainment and amusement shared, dramatic broadcasts and rescues enabled. The human mind was in one sense returning to its first invention – speech – but now it was free of expensive and cumbersome infrastructure, such as wires, poles, and transoceanic cables. Anyone with electricity could have a radio and with that radio talk with anyone else in the world who also had one. An entire subculture – a learning community with radios called ham operators – evolved and spread news among themselves and other communities. Even today, ham radio operators form a thriving worldwide community. And they were not the only ones who took to this invention. Radio broadcasts began from experimental stations in the United States and abroad in the 1920s, and by 1930 the radio was a part of most people's daily lives. With 608 stations broadcasting in 1930, you could receive everything from news to entertainment programs of all kinds, from Private Eye weekly series to sporting events, as well as a new type of program called science fiction. Radio drew the whole world together with real-time reporting of events that were shaping our lives – from the *Hindenburg* disaster to the Cuban missile crisis.

Many of those reading this are not old enough to remember the world when radio was the way people connected. I am old enough, and I remember many summer nights sitting on what we called the sun porch listening to baseball games or Buck Rogers, walking around with the newest transistor radio glued to my ear, sometimes thinking about all the other people I could not name or see who were listening at that very moment. The human mind had created yet another amazing invention that brought the voices of strangers into my home, my living room, even my bedroom. From that would follow the television, and then the ultimate invention of the 30,000-year evolution, which brought the world together into a global community of learners.'

Inventing the future: from atoms to digits

On a recent trip back to California from Boston, I was sitting next to a senior executive of an investment bank. Looking for a good stock tip, I asked him what he thought the next "big thing" would be. He smiled and said, "The Internet."

"The Internet?" I replied. And as I thought about it, I realized why he was right.

We have gone through the first stage of the Internet and are rapidly heading for the next generation. And it is the Internet that unites every invention and technology of the past and the present together, creating the first worldwide community that will be able to use all the inventions and technologies our mind has invented. Today we are in the incunabula stage of the Internet. Just as the first half-century of printing did not foreshadow how that technology would be used and improved, what we have seen so far in the digital age can in no way tell us what is to come.

The Internet is the most recent invention of the human mind. It allows all the previous inventions to come together into a single realm. And it changes the rules in a way that expands the power of the human mind, allowing it to move faster, reach further, grow and learn more quickly,

---

[5] For more on the invention of the radio, see B. Birch, *Guglielmo Marconi: Radio Pioneer* (New York: Blackbirch Marketing, 2001); T. Lewis and D. Ossman, *Empire of the Air*, audiocassette (Bloomington, Ind.: LodesTone Media, 1996); and S. J. Douglas, *Inventing American Broadcasting* (Baltimore: Johns Hopkins University Press, 1997) and *Listening In: Radio and the American Imagination* (New York: Times Books, 2000).

and find communities more easily. And with it, we are gradually shifting from an analog world composed of atoms to a digital universe of electronic digits. And that means that we no longer depend on voice boxes for speech, trees for paper, or bricks and mortar for libraries and classrooms. The power of digital technology and the Internet was most clear to me when I was talking to a Hebrew scholar one day about the Dead Sea Scrolls. He was telling me that until they had been digitized and spread around the world over the Internet, scholars had been on waiting lists that were many years long. After the Scrolls had been digitized, they could be reviewed, discussed, published, and finally shared with learners throughout the world.

What will follow the Internet's incunabula period? How will the technology develop? I know it will connect us more closely and more easily, and it will overcome some of the remaining barriers to minds meeting minds in a community of learning. Typing ability will not matter because we will have speech recognition. On-the-fly translators will break down any remaining language boundaries. Conversation over the Internet will improve and be used more widely. Collaborative tools such as instant messaging, shared Web meetings, and more realistic classrooms-in-a-box will become widespread and commonly used. We will unhook our technology from phone lines and go wireless and global. The world will be digital and take advantage of all things digital – hypertext will become the norm, as will faster, always-on connections and communities that form, disperse, and reform as quickly and fluidly as the Northern Lights. Speech, writing, libraries, schools, and universities – and everything from radio to television to movies – have already been changed by this new digital world. Computers – desktops, laptops, and palmtops – may be relegated someday soon to a museum along with the abacus, quill pen, and analog radio and television. What we think of today as computers will become embedded devices, part of a utility of computing enabling numerous and, by today's standards, strange new communities of learners. Who is to say that the smart refrigerator of tomorrow, which scans your food's bar codes, tells you what you have got on hand, goes on the Internet for recipes, and then communicates with the supermarket for another delivery, is not part of a community in which information has been learned and shared?

If I extend my imagination into the more distant future, I see us melding computer and communications technology directly with the mind. I think that after all these years, that would be the mind's greatest evolutionary desire: biotechnology. Eyes will see what today we call heads-up displays. Ears will hear conversations that now require cell phones. Fingers will point and televisions will turn on, garage doors will open, computers will light up, and pointers will follow your hand to menus that will engage at the command of your thoughts. If you think I am stretching too far, many of the first experiments in these areas have already been conducted. Communities of learners in the distant future may be able to connect minds in ways that we can only imagine in our science fiction of today.

And there will be cultural and social changes to support the new technology. I believe that more organizations will recognize that knowledge shared – not knowledge held or hoarded – creates real power. Democratizing countries will continue to free minds to join the community. The human mind does not like to be shut away or fettered or silenced. It is all part of the evolutionary scheme of the mind trying to connect with other minds, share what it knows, and learn what it needs to know. To wonder together. To connect with one another.

Participating in various communities of learners will become a daily activity. We will include the idea of community into the act of learning, so that the separate, isolated learner, struggling along in what we today call "self-paced mode," will become a relic. Instructors will morph into facilitators or coaches. Mentors and experts will be available in a variety of ways, outside the course or class, to guide learners through their education. A course will be considered the beginning, not the end. And classes in schools and universities will take on a different appearance. Small groups will be connected over the Internet to other small groups to form a larger community. Learners will be able to participate in events and experiences, from space flight to archeological digs, and form interactive real-time communities with the scientists and others whom they once could only read about or watch. Problems at home and at work, professional and more personal, will be solved as a community. Access to information will be shared more easily and quickly among the community than ever before. Digital spaces for various communities to come together virtually will become more real and usable. As these communities of learners become ubiquitous, they will shape the entertainment I choose, the things I buy and use, the way I think about the world and myself. These communities of learners will drive and direct, consciously and unconsciously, the way I dress, the language I speak, the very culture in which I live.

Perhaps someday we will start to develop a collective wisdom about what it means to live here on Earth and share that wisdom as today we trade knowledge. Perhaps that was the endgame that the mind envisioned when this evolution toward a worldwide community of learners began more than 30,000 years ago.

I thought about this as I happily entered the names and e-mail addresses I had collected on my trip into my address book, from people whose only ticket into my new community was a business card. I was looking forward to all the interesting and wonderful things I would soon begin to learn.

6 | Using measurement to foster culture and sustainable growth

LAURIE BASSI, KAREN L. MCGRAW,
AND DAN MCMURRER

D O organizations invest enough in helping their employees
learn? Do they invest too much? What specific learning initiatives would be the most worthwhile investments? Where
are the answers to these questions? As knowledge becomes the foundation of our economy, these questions are increasingly important to
the financial health of businesses around the world. Yet even though
many managers believe they must invest in employees through formal
and informal training, knowledge management systems, and human
capital development programs, the accounting systems embedded in
their organizations are inadequate for measuring, reporting, and evaluating these key investments. As a result, many managers find themselves unable to make well-informed decisions in an area that may be
vitally important for their organizations' survival and success.

The accounting and reporting systems that executives, managers,
and stock-market analysts rely on are a relic of the industrial age. They
focus undue attention on quarterly earnings and essentially ignore the
capabilities and culture necessary for creating lasting value. Using the
information these systems provide, most businesses cannot answer
the fundamental question: Do training investments create value for an
organization? Leaders are not certain whether additional investments
improve profitability or whether the stock market will recognize and
reward them for these investments. And investors have no idea how
much companies focus on learning or knowledge creation, or how these
investments improve long-term earnings prospects.

Not surprisingly, rational managers respond to this information
problem by shying away from human-capital development, and rational investors respond by ignoring learning culture altogether when
picking potential winners in the market. Those of us who believe in
the importance of creating organizational cultures that value learning struggle to overcome these strong inclinations. Of course, learning
cultures will thrive only if they help organizations produce business

results. In order to promote learning cultures, measurement systems must provide the understanding and insight an organization needs to optimize its investment in learning *and* appease the finance department. Without a compelling measurement framework that can identify the actual effects of a learning culture on organizational performance, those concerned only with the bottom line will prevail far more often than not.

The time has come to develop measurement systems that look beyond current earnings – systems that can assess an organization's capacity to be productive and profitable, and measure how investments in learning create that capacity. Such metrics can allow organizations to be driven with the steering wheel rather than the rear-view mirror. They can provide sound, analytically responsible guidance for improving, rather than merely justifying, human-capital investments.

Human capital and organizational performance

Despite the mantra that "people are our most important asset," current accounting and reporting systems usually reinforce the treatment of people not as assets but as costs. During downturns, the incentive to boost quarterly earnings by cutting "people costs" is too overwhelming for many organizations to resist – despite compelling evidence that layoffs have a high probability of destroying not only corporate culture but also shareholder value.[1] Even in the absence of layoffs, accounting for people – and especially for investments in their learning – as costs perpetuates a chronic underinvestment in employees and hinders the growth of the culture required to support long-term performance and profitability.

The accounting and reporting systems that have developed over centuries reflect the evolution of economic history, albeit with a lag. Each era has been defined by the factor of production that has served as the foundation for wealth creation. In most developed nations, the currently accepted accounting principles and their related reporting requirements rest on the assumption that physical assets

---

[1] See, for example, W. F. Cascio, C. E. Young, and J. R. Morris, "Financial Consequences of Employment-Change Decisions in Major US Corporations," *Academy of Management Journal* 40 (1997), pp. 1175–1189; and R. G. Atkins and A. J. Slywotzky, "You Can Profit from a Recession," *Wall Street Journal*, February 5, 2001.

(land, machinery, buildings, natural resources, and inventory) generate wealth. Human capital does not even appear on the balance sheet. There is, of course, a reason for this that transcends history: unlike all other factors of production, human capital cannot be owned, so spending on the development of people does not meet the traditional accounting concept of an investment. But in the knowledge era, human capital – not land, machinery, or natural resources – is the primary foundation of wealth creation, and successful organizations must be able to invest in it and measure those investments.

It is a basic truth that organizations perpetually make choices among competing options in determining where to invest their resources. Budgets must be divided among all the factors of production necessary for an organization to be effective: buildings, equipment, technology infrastructure, R&D, and people (including their salaries, benefits, and development).

According to the logic of economics, in order to maximize profitability an organization must invest in each of these factors up to the point at which the marginal return on an additional dollar spent is equalized across all factors.[2] The widely used "law of diminishing marginal return" states that overinvestment in any factor will result in a lower return on that factor. Conversely, underinvestment in any factor will result in a *higher* return on that factor (indicating that an organization has failed to maximize its productivity and profitability by failing to invest sufficiently in that factor). This logic leads to the conclusion that in an organization that is investing effectively, the return on people should be identical to the returns on other factors of production.

This insight from economic theory seems helpful in interpreting the findings that emerge from a small but growing body of empirical research on the relationship between an organization's performance and its investments in creating a learning culture.[3] This research

[2] These marginal returns should all be equal to the opportunity cost of capital (sometimes referred to as the "internal rate of return").

[3] In addition to the works cited below, there is a relatively large body of case study analysis that we have not considered here. We have excluded these works because case study analysis is a notoriously poor methodology for identifying cause-and-effect relationships. The studies cited here are based on large-scale, empirical analysis of hundreds of organizations. Even with this level of rigor, identifying causal relationships according to the strictest of academic standards is not fail-safe. None the less, these studies represent the best available evidence.

consistently finds that organizations that make an extraordinary investment in people enjoy extraordinary returns.[4] As noted above, higher than normal returns are indicative of underinvestment in a factor. The inescapable conclusion from the research evidence is that most organizations generally underinvest in people. Organizations that make larger than average investments will therefore consistently outperform those that do not.

One notable study in this area was conducted by Bruce Pfau and Ira Kay of Watson Wyatt.[5] On the basis of an analysis of 750 large publicly traded companies, both inside and outside the United States, Pfau and Kay draw three major conclusions:

(1) Superior human-capital investment practices are a leading indicator of financial performance.

(2) Organizations with the best human-capital practices provide returns to shareholders that are three times greater than those of companies with weak human-capital practices.

(3) Specific practices drive shareholder value, while others actually diminish it.

Pfau and Kay find that shareholder value is increased through such human-capital practices as rewards and accountability; collegial, flexible workplaces; recruiting and retention programs; communications integrity; and focused human-resources technologies.[6]

Another study that focuses on predicting shareholder value was conducted by two of the authors of this chapter – Laurie Bassi and Dan

---

[4] Most of the studies cited herein are based on analysis of publicly traded companies, since these are the only companies for which reliable financial data are available in a consistent format. It is reasonable to assume, however, that the findings from these studies are also applicable to privately held firms, as well as not-for-profit and public sector organizations (with, of course, the exception of shareholder value).

[5] A summary of their findings can be found at http://www.watsonwyatt.com/research/resrender.asp?id=w_488&pages=1. Their research is also discussed in the appendix of B. N. Pfau and I. T. Kay, *The Human Capital Edge* (New York: McGraw-Hill, 2001).

[6] Somewhat perplexingly, they conclude that there is a negative relationship between employee training and development and future shareholder value. We believe that this finding, however, is driven by the unusual manner in which they have defined "training." They define firms that make unusually large investments in training by two dichotomous variables: whether the company reports that employees have access to training needed for career advancement and whether the company maintains its training programs even in difficult economic circumstances. Because neither of these variables

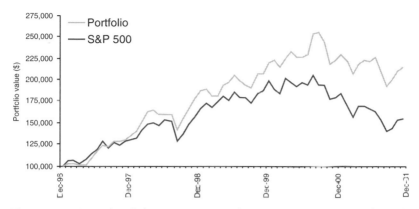

Figure 6.1. Growth of $100,000 invested on January 1, 1997 through December 31, 2001: hypothetical portfolio of companies with high training investments vs. S&P 500 index. Portfolio of companies selected using knowledge asset management formula; return reported net of hypothetical fees/expenses.

McMurrer.[7] The study focuses on the effect of investments in employee education and training in 600 publicly traded US companies. It found that from 1997 to 2001, a hypothetical portfolio of companies that made large investments in employee development outperformed the S&P 500 index by a factor of two the year following the investment (Figure 6.1).

Other researchers have conducted large-scale empirical studies that point to the centrality of learning cultures, as evidenced by human-capital development and management, as drivers of financial performance:

- Jonathan Low and Pam Cohen Kalafut (Cap Gemini Ernst & Young) identify human capital as one of the four most important determinants of a company's future financial performance (along with networks and alliances, brand equity, and technology and processes).[8]

appears to be a particularly authentic way of capturing the intensity of a firm's investments in human capital, we conclude that this particular finding should be given little weight.

[7] L. Bassi and D. McMurrer, *Investing in Companies that Invest in People*, published on HR.com, February 2002. A copy of the paper can be downloaded at http://www.knowledgcam.com/downloads/Article_hr.com.pdf.

[8] J. Low and P. Cohen Kalafut, *Invisible Advantage: How Intangibles Are Driving Business Performance* (Cambridge, Mass.: Perseus, 2002).

- Marcus Buckingham and Curt Coffman (Gallup Organization) point to the importance of the quality of management in driving employee retention, customer satisfaction, and productivity.[9]
- Brian Becker, Mark Huselid, and Dave Ulrich point to the importance of high-performance work practices in creating superior financial results.[10]
- Laurie Bassi and Mark Van Buren find linkages among investments in employee development, employee satisfaction and retention, and customer satisfaction.[11]

Taken together, these studies offer two major conclusions:

(1) There is a financial payoff to organizations that invest in cultures (including both policies and practices) focused on exceptional human-capital development and management.

(2) Given the economic logic outlined above, it follows that these organizations enjoy this payoff in large part because there are relatively few that do a good job of developing and managing people.

But even business leaders who embrace the idea that long-term organizational success is inextricably tied to human-capital investment practices find themselves stuck with antiquated measurement systems. It is a fact of corporate life that what gets measured gets managed; businesses can approach learning as a strategic investment only if it is measured as such.

Forces that perpetuate shortsightedness

The treatment of all people-related expenditures (including those associated with employee development) as expenses creates an external force from financial markets that promotes underinvestment in human capability. This is particularly true in publicly traded companies.

---

[9] See especially the appendices of M. Buckingham and C. Coffman, *First, Break All the Rules: What the World's Greatest Managers Do Differently* (New York: Simon & Schuster, 1999).

[10] See especially the appendix of B. E. Becker, M. A. Huselid, and D. Ulrich, *The HR Scorecard: Linking People, Strategy, and Performance* (Boston: Harvard Business School Press, 2001).

[11] L. Bassi and M. Van Buren, *Measuring What Matters: Core Measures of Intellectual Capital* (Alexandria, Va.: American Society for Training and Development, 2000).

Imagine two organizations that are comparable in all but one respect – company A makes substantial investments in individual and organizational learning and company B does not. What will be evident to analysts is that A has higher expenses and therefore lower earnings than B. Consequently, A's stock price will be lower – at least in the short run – than B's. What will not be evident is that some of A's higher "expenses" can be expected to generate productivity gains and financial benefits. In short, A invests in learning despite pressures from financial markets. That such pressures exist is a direct result of the fact that learning investments are treated as a cost rather than an investment, making expenses seem artificially high for companies that invest in learning.

In addition, there are internal forces that can result in underinvestment in people. In at least some organizations, there is the perception (and perhaps the reality) that employees are apt to leave after large investments have been made to develop them. Certainly, this happens in individual cases. And there are probably organizations in which this is a chronic problem. But the existing research suggests that employee-retention problems are more likely to occur in organizations that lack a learning culture and human-capital infrastructure than in those that make significant investments in learning.

Another internal force that causes underinvestment in human capability is the difficulty of demonstrating the return on such investments. Unlike investments in R&D that lead to revenue streams associated with new products, advertising campaigns that can result directly in increased sales, or customer relations management that can point to increased customer retention rates, the effects of investments in people are much more difficult to isolate. Paradoxically, it is precisely because the potential benefit associated with the development and management of employees is ubiquitous that it is so difficult to identify. The skills and knowledge of employees touch virtually every element of an organization's operations.

To make matters worse, the measurements used by human-resources practitioners and chief learning officers in many organizations provide little defense against budgetary axes. All too often, these measures focus only on inputs or activity levels, such as the number of people who attended a course or the number of hits received by the self-service HR website. At best, they may report on efficiencies within the HR function, such as reductions in the cost per hire. The focus of HR scorecards and benchmarks produced by organizations such as the Saratoga Institute is on the HR function itself instead of on the impact of HR practices.

Even when an attempt is made to identify the return on a specific HR or learning intervention (usually classroom training), the attempt often backfires because return on investment (ROI) is calculated incorrectly or is used for the wrong reasons (for self-justification instead of for optimizing and improving business results). Some of the mistakes made most frequently in calculating ROI include the following:

- Attempting to measure the value of education and training not tied to business results. If the learning intervention has not been linked, either directly or indirectly, to a business goal, then its value will be virtually impossible to determine.
- Focusing on the wrong metric; that is, measuring "outcomes" that have little relevance to business objectives.
- Underestimating costs, including direct costs associated with the intervention; indirect costs, such as the wages and benefits of employees participating in a learning intervention; and opportunity costs from lost productivity and the cost of capital.
- Overstating benefits. When done well, learning is typically one component of an integrated bundle of interventions designed to improve performance.
- Failing to discount the flow of future benefits; that is, to calculate the present discounted value of the benefit stream.
- Failing to gain agreement up front on what metrics will be used to measure success and what standard of evidence will be used to determine whether success has been achieved.
- Insisting on the achievement of precision. The metrics and standards of evidence that are appropriate when benefits are quite specific and can easily be quantified (such as sales training) will not be appropriate when benefits are extremely diffuse or inherently difficult to quantify (such as leadership development).

In our view, an important step in improving measurement is to shift the language away from ROI analysis because even when done correctly it does not yield insights that can improve outcomes. It is fundamentally backward-looking and is not measurement as a means for generating value. What is needed is a measurement system that is forward-looking, predictive, and diagnostic.

Guiding principles for transforming measurement systems

Overturning our outmoded measurement systems and creating new ones to take their place seems like an overwhelming challenge. You may have a vision of where you want to end up: in an organization that understands the profound influence of learning on performance, that helps employees learn through strategic investments. But how do you craft a measurement system that can move an organization toward that vision? It might help to start with some principles that we have articulated after many years of research.

(1) Some measures are more important than others

Organizations should focus on the measures that matter. But how do you figure out what matters, when what matters is so highly intangible? An emerging body of research suggests that key metrics to track include:

- Employees' satisfaction with the quality of their learning and development opportunities
- Employees' satisfaction with the management skills and abilities of their immediate supervisors
- Employees' satisfaction with the extent to which they are treated fairly and feel appreciated and acknowledged for their work
- Employees' sense that the work they do makes a difference
- Retention rate of key employees.

These factors can and should be linked to more concrete measures of performance such as customer satisfaction, customer retention, sales per employee, and unit labor costs. And they should be combined with measures that assess the effectiveness of the interventions an organization uses to improve its human-capital advantage.

(2) Measurement should be used to generate accountability through improvements in performance, not to justify a budget

Measurement systems need to be simple but powerful, and they should yield meaningful measurements and actionable recommendations. Measurement that is designed solely for the purpose of budget justification lacks credibility with senior management. CEOs and CFOs are more likely to be convinced by measurement systems that are designed to promote accountability by specifically identifying and tracking the strategic outcomes that are targeted for improvement. Budget justification should be the byproduct of such a measurement system instead of the primary motivation for it.

(3) Money is necessary but not sufficient to improve performance, so measurement systems must examine more than just spending

Optimizing the impact of investments in a learning culture requires systematic thinking – not just implementation of the latest e-learning initiative or knowledge management system. It requires full support for the human-capital enablers (culture, governance, time) that are necessary if a learning initiative is to be institutionalized and well integrated. It also requires that staff and other human-capital resources are available to support new learning initiatives. In addition, it requires examining operations that tie the initiative to development and performance management practices. Without each of these – human-capital enablers, supporting resources, and operations – major learning initiatives will almost certainly fail to produce the desired benefits. Consequently, measurement systems must have the capacity to identify in advance the areas that must be strengthened so that these initiatives can deliver on their promise. For example, many companies have spent enormous amounts on e-learning or knowledge management technologies only to find that their corporate culture treats these initiatives as a virus and attempts to reject them.

(4) Only multiple tiers of measurement can demonstrate the returns on investments in learning

Organizations need to be able to link their investments in learning to financial performance and business results. However, the relationship is most often not a direct one. The impact of such investments on financial performance is mediated through a variety of outcomes or performance measures, such as employee satisfaction, customer satisfaction, competency levels, and innovation. Demonstrating the link between investments in learning and business results requires multiple tiers of measurement: traditional financial measures, followed by human-capital outcomes, and, finally, granular measures of the organization's human-capital infrastructure (enablers, resources, and operations).

(5) A systematic, benchmarkable measurement system promotes continual improvement

Organizations should use measurement systems that help them identify their relative strengths and weaknesses across an array of factors that are known to drive performance. A systematic, forward-looking, benchmarkable measurement system ensures the rigorous measurement of investments in learning. It also lets the organization compare itself with others and use measurement to continually improve organizational performance.

The measurement agenda outlined above represents a huge stretch for most organizations. But if human capital is to be managed as the strategic asset it has become, then this is a challenge that forward-looking organizations must tackle in earnest.

The Human Capital Capability Scorecard

After years of working with economic and leadership challenges, and coming to understand the guiding principles of measurement, we realized that if we wanted to use the type of knowledge-age measurement system we had been searching for, we would have to create it ourselves. No existing model focuses directly on the relationship between financial measures and human capacity measures. Furthermore, many of those models that do exist are idiosyncratic and therefore cannot be benchmarked across organizations or business units. After extensive research, we developed the Human Capital Capability Scorecard (HCCS), a measurement framework and set of data collection instruments. The three measurement tiers and the components within each tier are tightly linked to a knowledge base of best practices in organizational learning, culture, and human performance (Figure 6.2).

Even though this might look complicated at first, it is fairly straightforward. It can be read from the bottom up. The lowest level of the HCCS measures the organization's human-capital infrastructure: the enablers, resources, and operations that allow people to do their jobs. This includes twelve areas that, when examined together, provide a means of measuring the strengths and weaknesses of the organization's

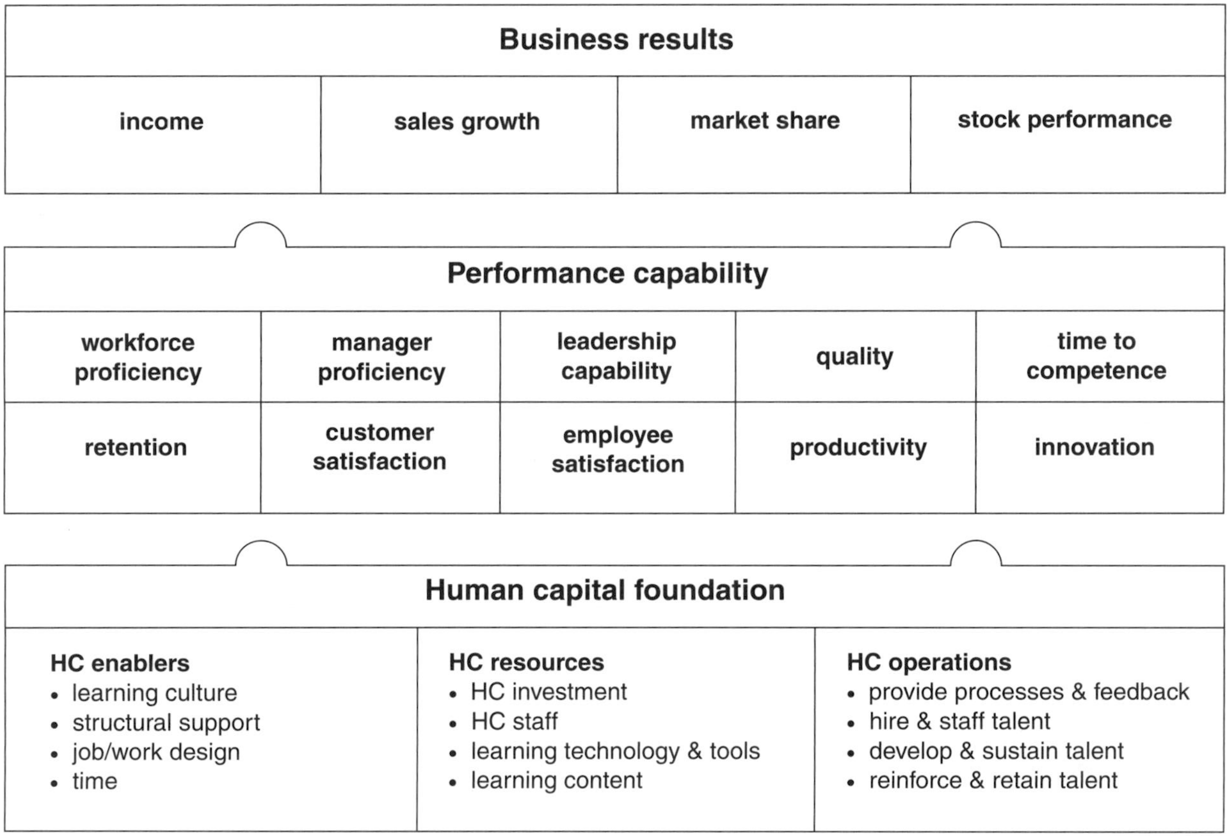

Business results

income	sales growth	market share	stock performance

Performance capability

workforce proficiency	manager proficiency	leadership capability	quality	time to competence
retention	customer satisfaction	employee satisfaction	productivity	innovation

Human capital foundation

HC enablers
- learning culture
- structural support
- job/work design
- time

HC resources
- HC investment
- HC staff
- learning technology & tools
- learning content

HC operations
- provide processes & feedback
- hire & staff talent
- develop & sustain talent
- reinforce & retain talent

Figure 6.2. HCC Scorecard framework.

learning culture. These factors, individually and collectively, have been demonstrated in the research literature to be the consistent drivers of performance outcomes and business results.

The middle tier includes nonfinancial organizational-performance outcomes that drive business results more directly. These are a core set of ten measures that have universal applicability across industries, such as customer satisfaction, quality, innovation, productivity, and workforce proficiency. (It should be noted that this list is not necessarily exhaustive. For example, industry-specific measures can certainly be added, such as safety for manufacturing firms or regulatory compliance for pharmaceutical companies.) This middle tier of measures is the domain in which most "balanced scorecard" efforts operate – measuring key, nonfinancial outcomes such as quality and customer satisfaction. Collecting such information is an important step in developing predictive measurement systems.

Although this middle tier focuses on leading (rather than lagging) indicators, this type of information still does not generate diagnostic information about what must be done to improve organizational results. Such information is available through the twelve categories of third-tier measures. When examined together, they provide a means of measuring how an organization develops and manages people within the context of a performance-based measurement framework. Researchers have found that these factors, individually and collectively, are the consistent drivers of organizations' nonfinancial performance (middle tier), which, in turn, drive top-tier results.

The top tier – organizational results – consists of traditional financial measures (such as income per employee) as well as measures of strategic goals and other key outcomes. These measures will, of course, vary from organization to organization. For example:

• Publicly traded companies might include total stockholder return among the financial variables they track in the top tier, whereas not-for-profit and public-sector organizations obviously would not.
• Strategic goals include those that are the focus of an organization's governing board. These could range from improving free cash flow in a *Fortune* 500 company to reducing the dropout rate in a school system.

Other key results are particularly important for not-for-profit and public-sector organizations. These could include event attendance (for an arts organization) or compliance with congressional mandates (for a federal agency).

The measures in the first tier are the easy ones; virtually every organization already knows how to measure those that are relevant to its success. They are, however, "lagging" indicators in that they capture the outcomes of what has been produced in the past. To begin to understand the "leading" indicators of performance, it is necessary to dig down to the middle tier – nonfinancial performance measures that have consistently been identified in the research and best practice literature as the key drivers of future organizational performance.

We have included a specific, benchmarkable set of "human factors" – the nonfinancial performance measures in the middle tier. These include leadership capability, managerial capability, time to competence, workforce proficiency, employee engagement, and retention of key employees. These are the factors that consistently emerge from the research and best practice literature as the human predictors of organizational results.

The data at the top tier (organizational results) and much of the middle tier (performance measures) are collected through various online questionnaires from finance executives or other selected organizational leaders. Much of the lowest tier (human-capital infrastructure) data is collected from frontline employees through a fifty-item online survey that takes ten to fifteen minutes to complete. Survey questions address such issues as the time that is available for learning and thoughtful decision-making, the extent to which learning and training support departmental operations, and whether managers encourage teamwork and collaboration.

To identify an organization's current standing in each of the HCCS categories, scoring algorithms are applied across all tiers of data. These algorithms have been designed to generate inherently meaningful metrics, based on a capability and maturity model, with a low score indicating an absence of capability and maturity on a given factor and a high score indicating the extensive presence of those qualities. The result is a scorecard that shows in numeric, benchmarkable, and graphic terms (color-coded scores) an organization's strengths and weaknesses with regard to promoting the development and management of people within a performance-driven framework. This scorecard represents an analytically responsible, fact-based foundation that is used to make recommendations to improve organizational performance and to document the effectiveness of the organization's environment for developing and managing people.

Organizations have used the HCCS for many different purposes. American Standard, a 122-year-old manufacturer of brand-name products in air conditioning systems, bathroom fixtures, vehicle control systems, and more, employed the scorecard as a critical component of its efforts to transform the company into a world-class organization in which operational excellence is the norm, customer service is superior, and financial objectives are consistently met.

In the view of the CEO and the senior vice-president for human resources, American Standard's success hinges on the people it employs and the systems for developing and managing them. World-class systems in these areas are necessary to achieve the organization's world-class goals. In order to establish baseline measures of its strengths and weaknesses in people management and development, American Standard implemented the HCCS in 2002.

The scorecard revealed wide disparities in maturity and quality across business units and plant locations, and in the methods used for managing and developing people. In many cases, these findings confirmed management's understanding of its strengths and weaknesses. In a number of other cases, however, the scorecard's findings identified areas where problems were more serious than had been previously understood and pointed to potential production and union problems that were likely to emerge.

The human resources vice-president used the information from the scorecard to intervene within business units and specific plants in an effort to begin systematically addressing deficiencies and neutralizing problems before they reached boiling point. The leadership of American Standard views the system and its insights as essential components of its transformation into a world-class organization, and has made plans to employ the scorecard regularly as a compass in mapping its path.

We have also seen operating executives use the HCCS in the following ways:

- To identify the root cause of underperforming divisions
- To determine the initiatives that must be undertaken to retain high-potential employees in an arts organization that offers low pay

- To understand the support that is necessary to ensure that teachers are able to use state-mandated content standards
- To provide a CEO with tools for managing conversations with Wall Street analysts.

When the HCCS is deployed across an organization, it is possible to assess human-capital foundation and performance measures together with the business results of different units or divisions. As expected, higher "capability" scores in human-capital areas correlate positively with higher performance measures and with business results.

We have also seen executives discover, as a result of the HCCS process, what is actually going on in their organizations. Many business units "talk the talk" regarding their support for learning; they say that learning is critical for strategy. But when their statements are compared to scores in such areas as resources (money, staff to support learning, time to allow for learning on the job), it becomes clear that less successful business units do not "walk the talk" very well. Organizations need this type of hard, empirical evidence to align the "walk" and the "talk" on the importance of employee development and organizational learning.

In addition to the HCCS, there are some excellent free or inexpensive research-based resources. Two of the most notable are the following. The American Society for Training & Development (ASTD) has developed a free benchmarking service for measuring investments in learning outcomes of education and training along with diagnostic measures of barriers to, and enablers of, learning transfer, and core measures of human and intellectual capital, and employee satisfaction. Again, the Gallup Organization has done extraordinary research on the fundamental determinants of employee retention. The distilled and practical implications of this research are available in Marcus Buckingham and Curt Coffman's *First, Break All the Rules*.

Taken together, these resources can go a long way toward providing organizations with practical tools for measuring and managing investments in human capital.

It is fashionable for CEOs to say their organization has a strong learning culture. Measurement can determine the extent to which that is true and identify the impact of learning on performance. It can help organizations move beyond HR scorecards, which measure just the HR function, and balanced scorecards, which are notorious for their lack of insight into the people side of business. Whatever tool you use, it must accurately measure the results of the learning culture. Only when an organization can demonstrate that learning is having a positive effect on its people and its profits will the culture of learning have an unshakeable foothold.

HCCS and Human Capital Capability Scorecard are registered trademarks of McBassi & Company, Inc.

Illustration © Eileen Clegg

7 Innovative cultures and adaptive organizations

EDGAR H. SCHEIN

M ANAGERS and students of organizations are increasingly concerned about the capacity of organizations to adapt to rapidly changing environments. The rate of technological, economic, political, and sociocultural change is increasing, and organizations are, therefore, finding it more and more important to figure out how to adapt.

Adaptation in turbulent environments involves more than minor adjustments. It often requires genuinely *innovative* thrusts: new missions, new goals, new products and services, new ways of getting things done, and even new values and assumptions. Most important, adaptation involves managing perpetual change. Organizations will have to learn how to learn and to become self-designing.[1]

The difficulty is that organizations are by nature, and often by design, oriented toward stabilizing and routinizing work. They develop

The ideas expressed in this chapter are the result of extended conversations with Tom Malone, Diane Wilson, and various other colleagues. Our goal was to identify the main characteristics of innovative, adaptive, creative systems and cultures. Special thanks also to Lotte Bailyn, Randy Davis, Marc Gerstein, Bob McKersie, Michael Scott-Morton, and John Van Maanen for their insightful comments on an early draft, and to the Management in the 1990s project for the financial support that made possible the research on which this chapter is based.

This chapter is updated and adapted with permission from an article written for the *Sri Lanka Journal of Development* 7 (1990), pp. 9–39. Citations given in the article have been included as footnotes here. Contact the editors for a copy of the article with the original citations.

[1] See, for example, E. H. Schein, *Organizational Psychology*, 3rd edn. (Englewood Cliffs, N.J.: Prentice-Hall, 1980); C. Argyris and D. A. Schön, *Organizational Learning* (Englewood Cliffs, N.J.: Prentice-Hall, 1978); and K. E. Weick, "Organization Design: Organizations as Self-Designing Systems," *Organizational Dynamics* (Autumn 1977), pp. 31–46.

cultures expressed in structures and processes that permit large numbers of people to coordinate their efforts and that permit new generations of members to continue to perform effectively without having to reinvent the organization each time.[2] How then, can one conceptualize an organization that can function effectively yet be capable of learning so that it can adapt and innovate in response to changing environmental circumstances? How can one conceive of an organization that can surmount its own central dynamic, that can manage the paradox of institutionalizing and stabilizing the process of change and innovation?

In this chapter, I want to address some aspects of these questions and to present a point of view based on my research into the dynamics of organizational culture. In particular, I want to focus on *innovation* as itself a property of culture. In other words, what kind of organizational culture consistently favors innovation?

This question is especially interesting because of the rapid advances in information technology (IT). Ample evidence suggests that the introduction of IT into organizations forces cultural assumptions out into the open and that the strategic potential of IT is not fulfilled unless organizations develop (or already possess) what I will define as an "innovative culture."

The definition of "innovation" is itself a major problem. For the purposes of this chapter, I will adopt a broad and imprecise definition – new ideas, behavior patterns, beliefs, values, and assumptions covering any aspect of the organization's functioning. I want to consider both "content innovation" – new products, services, and ideas – and "role innovation" – new ways of doing things, new definitions of roles, and new approaches to performing in roles.[3]

Defining what is "new," of course, is also problematic. In analyzing a case of culture change in a large corporation, I found that some of the major changes that the organization felt it had made actually

[2] See E. H. Schein, *Organizational Culture and Leadership* (San Francisco: Jossey-Bass, 1985).

[3] See E. H. Schein, "The Role Innovator and His Education," *Technology Review* 72 (1970), pp. 33–37; and J. Van Maanen and E. H. Schein, "Toward a Theory of Organizational Socialization," in B. M. Staw and L. L. Cummings (eds.), *Research in Organizational Behaviour*, vol. I (Greenwich, Conn.: JAI Press, 1979).

affirmed some of its most basic assumptions. What, then, had changed? Was there any innovation? My sense is that we must define innovation ultimately by the perceptions of both members of the organization and outsiders who interact with the organization and thus are in a position to perceive changes. If both insiders and informed outsiders agree that something is "new," then we are dealing with an innovation.

This definition will not satisfy the positivistic empiricist. Measuring consensus in perceptions is difficult and messy. However, if we are to understand what really goes on in this organizational domain, and if we are to develop better concepts and theoretical insights, we are at this stage better off with the rich and messy insight of the ethnographer and the clinician.[4]

There is a vast literature on organizational design and innovation. My goal is not to summarize what we know but to push into an area of cultural analysis that has not yet, to my knowledge, been well explored. In this chapter, I will provide my own view of the central variables needed to analyze organizations, make some hypotheses about the necessary assumptions of an innovative culture, and explore some of the key characteristics of IT and its relationship to an organization's capacity for innovation.

A sociotechnical paradigm for analyzing organizations

I will start with some of my underlying assumptions about the nature of organizations. There are many models for analyzing organizational systems. Many of them are flawed, however, because they separate the *task* and *technical* elements from the *human* and *organizational* elements. For example, most models of strategy and organizational design advocate that one should start with a mission or goal, and then design the organization to fulfill that mission or goal. The human elements are typically thought of as something that must be adapted to the mission and the technical and structural elements.

In contrast, a sociotechnical model integrates the human considerations with the technical ones in the initial design process. The initial

[4] See E. H. Schein, *Process Consultation*, vol. II (Reading, Mass.: Addison-Wesley, 1987).

formulation of the mission and goals of the organization is, after all, a product of human beings in entrepreneurial, technical, and managerial roles. The assumptions, beliefs, values, and biases of these human actors will limit and bias the technical and structural options, and will certainly affect the organizational design.

Furthermore, if the people who will be using a given system (however it may have been invented) are not involved in its design, all kinds of problems may arise that make the system less effective than its technical designers had forecast. We see this especially in IT, where the difficulties of implementation far outstrip the difficulties of invention.

For example, when an information system is initially designed, the human consequences are often either misunderstood or ignored. In a small example, Lotte Bailyn observed that the introduction of personal computers to an executive group was slowed down by the fact that executives do not type and do not like to go into a learner mode. The enthusiastic implementers created a typing program to deal with this issue and arranged for a bell to ring every time a mistake was made (on the theory that an aural signal would get better attention than a visual one). But the signal was public, and the executives did not want others to know when they were making errors, so the system had to be redesigned with the less vivid but more private feedback signal.

A larger example occurred in a division of an aerospace company. The general manager needed detailed performance and schedule information for each project and program in the company, so he designed a system that allowed him to identify schedule or performance problems as soon as they arose. He thought he needed that information to deal with outside stakeholders.

What this manager did not anticipate was that the project managers and engineers felt threatened knowing that their day-to-day behavior was being monitored. If the manager asked questions about problem areas, they found it difficult to respond because they had not had a chance to look at the reasons for the observed deviations from plan. The system designers should have anticipated this problem, inasmuch as it is a well-known phenomenon in the psychology of control. What typically happens is that subordinates who feel threatened or embarrassed by revealed information attempt to subvert the system by refusing to enter data or by falsifying information to protect themselves. Such behavior usually leads the system designers to invent more elaborate information devices, and thus resentment and tension escalate.

An even more dangerous outcome is that subordinates become dependent on the boss to be the control system and cease to exercise any self-control.[5] The sociotechnical solution is to involve all people concerned in the initial system design. In the above case, the manager eventually realized that he was creating resentment among his subordinates. So, the whole organization launched into a redesign of the system. It was concluded that the manager needed the information but not at the same time as all the employees. So the project members suggested a delay: they would get the information as soon as it was available so that they could work on any problems. The manager would get the same information a couple of days later so that by the time he inquired about problems, or even before he inquired, the project teams could tell him what was wrong and how they were dealing with it. The delay solved everyone's problem and led to a much more motivated and effective organization. The essential control stayed where the information was – in the project teams.

Enough is known today about the human problems of information and control systems, equipment design, and automation to make sociotechnical design entirely feasible. But cultural assumptions about the role of management and the role of technical designers in the initial creation of innovations often stand in the way. It is for these reasons that organizational culture must be analyzed first in defining the conditions for adaptation and innovation. (See Figure 7.1.)

The sociotechnical model emphasizes that one can study adaptation and innovation from the point of view of the organizational processes that must be present, the organizational structure that must be in place, and the information technology that must be available. However, inasmuch as the culture will determine how the technology is used and will influence organizational structure and processes, the cultural assumptions underlying innovation will influence each of the other elements. Adopting a sociotechnical model reminds us that we cannot bypass the analysis of the cultural and human forces at work in organizations.

[5] See D. McGregor, *The Human Side of Enterprise* (New York: McGraw-Hill, 1960) and *The Professional Manager* (New York: McGraw-Hill, 1967).

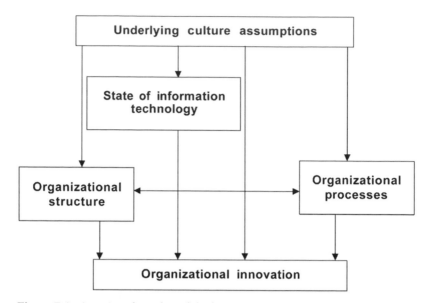

Figure 7.1. A sociotechnical model of organizational innovation.

Culture

The overarching determinant of how organizations work is the culture that evolves as members cope with the external problems of survival in the environment and their internal problems of integration. Culture can be defined as the pattern of learned assumptions that has worked well enough to be considered valid and, therefore, to be taught to new members as the correct way to perceive, think, and feel in relation to the problems of survival and integration.

Culture manifests itself in overt behaviors, norms, and espoused values – what can be thought of as cultural artifacts. Culture is also expressed in some of the less conscious and operational values that members share. But unless one deciphers the often implicit and unconscious pattern of assumptions, one has not really analyzed the culture *per se*.

Culture and its overt manifestations stabilize the daily life of members and provide meaning to what they do. Stability and hence predictability are essential. Without predictability, members of an organization cannot function and cannot avoid the anxiety that attends loss of meaning. Culture, once in place, is, therefore, an inherently conservative force.

The "strength" of a culture will be a function of several variables: the strengths of the initial convictions of the organizational founders; the stability of the group; the intensity of the learning experience in terms of number of crises survived and the emotional intensity of those crises; and the degree to which the learning process has been one of anxiety avoidance rather than positive reinforcement. The more the culture serves to reduce anxiety, the more it will resist change.

Cultural assumptions tend toward a consistent paradigm to the extent that the culture creators have a consistent set of assumptions in the first place and to the extent that the organization's learning experiences provide consistency. If the members of an organization learn inconsistent things in order to survive and remain integrated, they will have inconsistent and possibly ambiguous assumptions with which they can nevertheless feel comfortable.[6]

To the extent that culture is a learned product of group experience, there will be a culture wherever there is a group of people who share experiences over a period of time. Inasmuch as most organizations differentiate themselves over time into subgroups, one will have subgroup cultures in each of them, their strength varying as a function of the factors identified above. A total organization, then, can have a total culture as well as a set of subcultures, and any member of the organization will simultaneously "possess" elements of all the cultures of which he or she is a member.[7] And some of these will, of course, be family, community, occupational, and other groups that the person belongs to and identifies with outside of the organization.

Given that members of organizations have multiple group memberships and that they identify to different degrees with these various groups, a strong overall culture may have deviant elements within it, and entire subcultures may be deviant or countercultural because of

[6] J. Martin, personal communication, 1987.
[7] See J. Van Maanen and S. R. Barley, "Occupational Communities: Culture and Control in Organizations," in B. M. Staw and L. L. Cummings (eds.), *Research in Organizational Behaviour*, vol. VI (Greenwich, Conn.: JAI Press, 1984).

their connections to, for example, a professional group or international union.[8]

We know that culture evolves and can be changed, but we have not analyzed carefully enough what the characteristics are that would more or less facilitate change and innovation. Or, to put the question more directly, is it possible to conceive of a type of culture that would be innovative, that would have as its learning dynamic the invention of environmentally responsive solutions rather than conservative self-preservation? And is it possible to conceive of a type of culture that would favor sociotechnical design innovations instead of the traditional technology-driven ones?

Before answering these questions, some attention must be given to the other elements in the model.

Information technology

Cultures are built around and respond to the core technologies that caused the organization to be created in the first place. One may expect organizational cultures to vary, therefore, as a function of the technology involved. Chemical, high-tech, heavy manufacturing, financial, and other service industries will each evolve somewhat different "industry" cultures that will influence organizational cultures.

But all organizations have in common the need to communicate, to get information to the right place at the right time, to divide labor appropriately and coordinate members' efforts. The flow of information can be likened to the lifeblood of the system, and the information channels can be likened to the circulatory system. The state of IT in use at any given time is, therefore, likely to be an important determinant of the organization's capacity to learn. What then are the characteristics of an information system that maximizes the capacity of the organization to learn, adapt, and innovate?

IT is central to this analysis because its own evolution has made possible innovative leaps of extraordinary magnitude. Today some organizations are being designed on totally different premises by taking advantage of the capabilities of IT. We can conceptualize this best

[8] See J. Martin and C. Siehi, "Organizational Culture and Counter-culture: An Uneasy Symbiosis," *Organizational Dynamics* (Autumn 1983), pp. 52–64.

by distinguishing three kinds of utopian visions that have grown up around technology:

(1) *The vision to automate.* Most of the critical functions in the organization are taken over by robots or computerized systems run by highly skilled and trained operators.

(2) *The vision to informate.* By building accurate models of critical processes in the organization, it is possible not only to automate such processes but to make the processes themselves visible and understandable to everyone in the organization. This is what Shoshana Zuboff calls "informating" the organization, and it obviously has tremendous implications not only for workers but for managers at all levels.[9]

    (2a) *Informating up.* In this vision, IT is used to aggregate and centralize as much information about all the parts of the organization as possible to facilitate planning and control by top management. The organization becomes transparent to top management.

    (2b) *Informating down.* In this vision, the design of systems forces an analysis of the core production and other processes of the organization and makes those transparent to workers. Instead of understanding only a small piece of the total process, workers become familiar with the whole process and can, therefore, make decisions that previously were made by various layers of management.

(3) *The vision to transform.* A few organizations think of even more radical innovations by asking how one might organize the basic work, the communication patterns, and authority relations, to take advantage of the possibilities inherent in IT. Sociotechnical design considerations become primary to integrating the technical and human capabilities. Such organizations may be more like complex networks in which communication and authority chains shift according to the requirements of the task and the motivation and skills of the people.

Adaptation and innovation are involved to varying degrees in each of these visions, but in the vision to automate and the vision to informate up, we are talking only of making existing processes more efficient.

[9] S. Zuboff, *In the Age of the Smart Machine* (New York: Basic Books, 1988).

Thus robots and various other kinds of machine-controlled work are important innovations in the production process, and sophisticated information systems that permit high levels of centralized control are innovations in the degree to which information can be rapidly collected and centralized, but it is only with informating down and transforming that we get more radical innovation in the nature of the organization itself. In these instances, IT creates a new concept of how work is to be done and how the management process itself is to be defined. What this means is that the cultural assumptions about the nature and use of IT will themselves be a crucial determinant of how IT will be used to create further innovation.

Organizational processes

Over time every organization develops a set of processes, recurrent events that ensure that the organization fulfills its primary task and that members coordinate effectively. Such processes concern how members communicate, how they solve problems and make decisions, how they implement decisions, how they organize work, and how they supervise, reward, punish, and, in general, deal with people.[10]

Such processes are a reflection of the culture as defined above, but the basic cultural assumptions are largely implicit and invisible, whereas the processes are visible and analyzable. To understand an organization, therefore, we need to specify both the underlying assumptions and the observable processes. For purposes of this analysis, the question is what kinds of cultural assumptions facilitate organizational processes that will increase the likelihood that the organization will be able to learn, adapt, and innovate?

Organizational structure

Some processes become stable and are articulated in rules, manuals, organization charts, and other more permanent documents reflecting how management feels things should be done. The ultimate division of labor as embodied in job descriptions and organizational units, the

---

[10] See E. H. Schein, *Process Consultation*, vol. I (revised) (Reading, Mass.: Addison-Wesley, 1988) and vol. II (Addison-Wesley, 1987).

basic organization design in terms of who reports to whom and who is accountable for what are typically thought of as the elements of "formal" structure. But as in the case of organizational processes, these structures reflect underlying cultural assumptions. One common misconception is that structure can be analyzed as a factor separate from culture. But if one starts with a sociotechnical model of organizations, one cannot separate the two. One can, however, ask whether some formal structures are more likely to facilitate or encourage learning, adaptation, and innovation, and, if so, what kinds of cultural assumptions favor the evolution of such structures.

In most organizations one also finds an "informal" structure, those processes that are observed to be relatively stable but are supported only by implicit norms and are often regarded to be unsanctioned or even to run counter to the formal structure. It is the existence of such counterstructures based on subcultures that may be "countercultures," and they may determine in important ways what kind of innovation is possible.

The informal structure also includes "compensatory" or "parallel" structures designed to offset or supplement weaknesses and dysfunctional elements in the formal structure. Such structures may be relatively permanent, such as standing committees, or they may be temporary processes such as task forces and project teams.

Most organization theories acknowledge that without the informal organization things simply would not get done effectively, and, therefore, that the informal structure must be explicitly analyzed and well understood if we are to understand the total system.

To sum up, I argue that to determine the necessary and sufficient conditions for an innovative organization, we must specify the characteristics of the culture that favor the kind of information technology, organizational processes, and formal and informal structure that increases the likelihood of innovation.

Characteristics of an innovative culture

Organizational cultures can be analyzed along many dimensions. I will specify a minimum set, as shown in Table 7.1, and state in hypothesis form the assumptions necessary for innovation. Table 7.1 can also be used as a diagnostic device for analyzing a culture.

Table 7.1. *Cultural dimensions that influence innovativeness*

Organization–environment relationship

Environment dominant	Symbiotic	Organization dominant
		×

The nature of human activity

Reactive, fatalistic	Harmonizing	Proactive
		×

The nature of reality and truth

Moralistic authority		Pragmatism
		×

The nature of time

Past-oriented	Present-oriented	Near-future-oriented
		×

Short time units	Medium time units	Long time units
	×	

The nature of human nature

Humans are basically evil		Humans are basically good
		×

The nature of human relationships

Groupist		Individualist
		×

Authoritarian/paternalistic		Collegial/participative
		×

Subculture diversity/connectedness

Low		High
		×

The × on each continuum indicates the ideal condition for high innovativeness.

Organization–environment relationships

Hypothesis. *An organization's capacity to innovate will increase to the extent that it assumes that its environment is controllable, changeable, and manageable.*

Organizations can be distinguished by their assumptions about the degree to which they dominate or are dominated by their environments. At one extreme we have organizations that assume that their existence and survival are out of their control. They are passive in the face of environmental turbulence. They accept whatever niche the environment provides.

At the other extreme we have organizations that assume that their behavior will influence their environments and that survival and growth depend on the extent to which they are able to dominate some aspects of their environments. Implied is the assumption that progress and improvement are possible, a basically optimistic orientation.

Innovative capacity will increase to the extent that members assume that innovation is possible and necessary, which derives from their optimistic assumption that the environment can be influenced. Organizations that pessimistically assume either that they are dominated by others or that their environments are fixed will find it difficult to conceive of new ideas and will find it even more difficult to marshal the energy to try them out.

The nature of human activity

Hypothesis. *An organization's capacity to innovate will increase to the extent that human activity is oriented toward problem-solving and improvement.*

All organizations make implicit assumptions about whether members should be reactive, fatalistic, and oriented to getting what pleasure one can out of life (Dionysian); or proactive, optimistic, and oriented toward improving things (Promethean); or whether they should take the middle ground of trying to compromise between one's own needs and environmental constraints and possibilities (Apollonian). As will be noted, these assumptions are the individual-level counterpart to the assumptions relating the organization to its environment.

An innovator in the midst of reactive or harmonizing people will find it virtually impossible to get even an audience, much less a commitment to new ways of doing things. In Dionysian or Apollonian organizations, innovators are likely to be called whistleblowers, boat-rockers, or troublemakers. And if the culture is too fatalistic, it will of course not attract or retain innovators in the first place.

But if the culture strongly encourages innovation, will life be too chaotic and unpredictable, thus undermining innovation? I believe not, because if too much innovation becomes a problem, the organization will invent and evolve processes and structures that reduce it to a tolerable level. In other words, if the organization is going out of control, its own innovativeness will enable it to invent mechanisms to achieve greater discipline and control.

The reverse is not true. An organization that is too passive or fatalistic cannot invent proactivity. It will stagnate until it fails or is taken over by others who will forcibly change the culture by massive replacement of people with a different activity orientation. I am hypothesizing, therefore, that one cannot have too much innovativeness but one can have too much conservatism and passivity.

The nature of reality and truth

Hypothesis. *An organization's capacity to innovate will increase to the extent that it assumes that truth is to be arrived at by pragmatic (not moralistic) means.*

Organizations can be distinguished by their assumptions about how one determines whether something is true. When a complex decision has to be made involving uncertain futures and information of uncertain validity, what criteria does the organization use to determine when it has enough and the right kind of information to make the decision?

At one extreme is a heavy reliance on tradition, dogma, the authority of moral principles, or the wisdom of elders. At the other extreme is pragmatism embodied either in a search for scientific verification or a trial-and-error attitude if formal verification is not possible or practical.[11] If the decision is in a domain where verification by physical

---

[11] See G. England, *The Manager and His Values* (Cambridge, Mass.: Ballinger, 1975).

means is not possible, pragmatism implies that the decision-makers debate the issues and subject each alternative to sufficient scrutiny so that the one that survives can be accepted with some measure of confidence.

In organizations dominated by dogma or various authorities, it is not only difficult to articulate new ideas but even more difficult to get the sanction to try them out. An exception is, of course, when the innovator is the person in authority, a situation that arises from time to time but is hard to specify as an organizational condition or to predict. To increase the innovative capacity generally, a positive value must be put on novelty, on breaking tradition, on trying out new things even if they are risky, and such a value must be supported by an underlying assumption that "the truth" is not already known.

The pragmatic end of the continuum also implies a more positive attitude toward trial and error, risk-taking, and the acceptance of unsuccessful efforts or even failures. The more the organization institutionalizes dogmas, rules, systems, and procedures, the harder it will be for members to take the risks that innovation requires. The message in such moralistic organizations is "try new things only if you are sure you will not break rules or fail," a prescription for conservatism and playing it safe.

The nature of time

Hypothesis. *An organization's capacity to innovate will increase to the extent that it is oriented to the near future (not the past, present, or far future) and to the extent that it uses medium-length time units (not short ones that do not allow innovation to develop, or long ones that make innovation difficult to evaluate).*

All organizations hold implicit assumptions about the relative importance of the past, the present, and the future, and about the appropriate length of time for different kinds of tasks. Some organizations measure themselves in short units such as weeks and months, some use intermediate units such as quarters and years, and some use longer units such as five- or ten-year spans. All organizations use all of these units for various purposes and, as Paul Lawrence and Jay Lorsch pointed out years ago, the different functional units of an organization such as sales and R&D will have different assumptions about what it means to be "on time" and how long units of work are.[12]

It is likely that in each organization's culture there will be assumptions about the really important time units. The size of the relevant time units will vary from company to company, so the determination of what is "past," "present," "near future," and "far future" must be determined by getting members' consensus on these units. The size of such time units is also influenced by the core technologies the organization is working with. The development of new products, for example, takes much longer in the pharmaceutical industry than in the consumer goods industry.

An organization that lives in the past or present will find it difficult to place a value on novelty because it is focused on what has worked or is working now. People with new ideas can be dismissed because their ideas do not fit with what the organization likes to think about. On the other hand, an organization focused on the far future may be unable to launch any innovation because it assumes there is always plenty of time to try things out. A near-future orientation should, therefore, be most favorable to innovation.

It is also clear that too short a time orientation will always make innovation difficult because one can always show that short-run costs are too high to justify continuation of the trial and error involved in innovation. On the other hand, if the time units are too long, some innovations that are failures will be allowed to continue, the organization will lose money, and the whole innovation process will be undermined. The organization's ability to develop a sense of an optimal length of time for an innovation thus becomes a very important determinant of its learning capacity.

This optimal length of time will be subjectively defined in most organizations, and it must be measured within each organization. The precise length of the units is not as important as the members' ability to recognize that giving an innovation too little or too much time is equally destructive to the overall innovation process.

Optimal time units also play a role in the selling of an innovative vision, whether that comes from leaders or from innovators in the organization. The vision of the future cannot exceed members' ability

[12] P. R. Lawrence and J. W. Lorsch, *Organization and Environment* (Boston: Harvard Graduate School of Business Administration, 1967).

to understand what is proposed, nor can it promise benefits that will be realized only by the next generation. To be motivated to implement something new, people must know what benefits they will witness.

As Elliott Jaques has argued, the length of time over which members have "discretion" appears to vary with rank.[13] On the shop floor, supervisors check on employees by the hour or the day. At lower managerial levels, one has discretion over weeks, and so on up the ladder until the most senior management is supposed to define its tasks in terms of years. In communicating the impact of proposed innovations, it becomes critical then to consider over what time units the audience is used to thinking. "Optimal" time units, in this context, are partly defined by the proposed innovative task.

The nature of human nature

Hypothesis. *An organization's capacity to innovate will increase to the extent that it assumes people are ultimately neutral or good, and, in any case, are capable of improvement.*

Organizations make implicit assumptions about human nature, both in terms of whether it is ultimately good, neutral, or evil, and in terms of how malleable or fixed it is. If organizations are cynical about human nature (what Douglas McGregor calls Theory X), they will not encourage innovation and may even believe that innovators have ulterior motives. In such organizations, innovative capacity often is devoted to defeating organizational goals. Workers invent elaborate processes and devices to make life easier for themselves at the expense of organizational efficiency.[14]

On the other hand, if the organization is optimistic about human nature (McGregor's Theory Y), it will expect people to be innovative, will encourage innovation, will listen to new ideas, and will be more likely to trust them. At the same time, for innovation to be encouraged, members must feel that one's personality and contribution are not fixed.

[13] E. A. Jaques, *General Theory of Bureaucracy* (London: Heinemann, 1976) and *The Forms of Time* (London: Heinemann, 1982).
[14] See C. Argyris, *Integrating the Individual and the Organization* (New York: Wiley, 1964); F. J. Roethlisberger and W. J. Dickson, *Management and the Worker* (Cambridge, Mass.: Harvard University Press, 1939).

If one knows one can grow and improve, this knowledge acts as a powerful stimulant to personal development and innovation.

The nature of human relationships

Hypothesis. *An organization's capacity to innovate will increase to the extent that it believes in the ideal of individualism and the pursuit of individual diversity. But if an organization has a few innovative individuals whose ideas are adopted, it can implement some types of innovation faster if it assumes the ideal of groupism.*

Hypothesis. *The capacity of an organization to innovate will increase to the extent that it favors collegial and participative methods of decision-making. But if innovative people are in senior leadership roles, the organization can implement some innovations faster if it takes an authoritarian approach to decision-making.*

This dimension of culture has to do with prevailing assumptions about the ideal human relationship. Two dimensions are involved here:
(1) The degree to which the organization assumes the ideal of individualism (that all good things ultimately come from individual effort) or groupism (that all good things ultimately come from the group, implying that ultimately all individuals must subordinate themselves to the group).
(2) The degree to which ideal relationships are seen as collegial and participative (implying that power and influence in decision-making are a function of who has relevant expertise) or as autocratic and paternalistic (implying that power and influence reside in positions, statuses, and roles or are a function of an individual's personality).
Under certain conditions, innovation could occur anywhere along these two dimensions. A culture that values individuals and individual diversity will have more ideas to draw from and create more incentives for ideas to be put forward. However, when it comes to acceptance and implementation of ideas, the strongly individualistic organization may be at a disadvantage. In other words, in a groupist organization it will be harder to get new ideas articulated, but if they are adopted, such an organization will be far more effective in implementing them because dissenting individuals will suppress their opinions for the sake of the group.

In groupist organizations, the burden of innovation probably falls on the leaders, who are the most likely to get an idea adopted in the first place. The determinants of innovativeness in the leaders of groupist organizations then become the secondary but critical question.

Collegial and participative decision-making is more likely to identify areas in which innovation is needed, to bring good ideas to the surface, to stimulate creativity, and to help everyone understand the idea so that it will be properly implemented. Such decision-making influences many phases of the total innovation process, from invention to implementation, particularly if the innovation is complex.

If, on the other hand, an autocratic or paternalistic leader has innovative ideas that are sound, if the ideas are not too complex to communicate, and if the sociotechnical implications have been correctly considered, it is possible for the organization to implement ideas more rapidly and thoroughly.

But the danger of an autocratic leader is threefold: that the leader will impose a bad idea under conditions in which subordinates are neither motivated to point out, nor rewarded for having pointed out, potential problems; that the idea will not be successfully communicated, which will lead to paralysis and frustration; and that the idea will be implemented incorrectly because the leader did not discover that subordinates did not fully understand or accept the consequences of the innovation.

If predictions about the ultimate impact of IT are correct, then leaner, flatter, more highly networked organizations are the likely consequence.[15] Such organizations cannot work effectively, however, if managers are still operating from hierarchical models buttressed by autocratic assumptions.[16] The basis of authority in such networks will more likely be the degree of skill or expertise that a member has at any moment relative to the task at hand. Positional authority will mean

---

[15] See P. F. Drucker, "The Coming of the New Organization," *Harvard Business Review* (January–February 1988); T. W. Malone, "Modeling Coordination in Organizations and Markets," *Management Science* 33 (1987), pp. 1317–1332; and T. W. Malone, J. Yates, and R. I. Benjamin, "Electronic Markets and Electronic Hierarchies," *Communications of ACM* 30 (1987), pp. 484–497.

[16] E. H. Schein, "Reassessing the 'Divine Rights' of Managers," *Sloan Management Review* 30 (1989), pp. 63–68.

very little. Obviously such systems will function better if they follow a collegial, participative model of decision-making in the first place.

Subcultural diversity

Hypothesis. *An organization's capacity to innovate will increase to the extent that it encourages diverse but connected subcultures.*

As organizations grow and mature, they develop subcultures as well as overarching cultures. The nature and diversity of such subcultures will influence the organization's innovative capacity. For any group, culture is a homogenizing force. However, if the organization contains enough subsystems with their own subcultures, it can innovate by empowering people and ideas from subcultures that are the most different from the "parent" yet best adapted to a changing environment. Drawing on diverse subcultures is, in fact, the most common way in which cultures evolve, and this process, if properly managed, is therefore one of the most important sources of innovation.

The subcultures must be connected and part of a parent culture or their elements will not be seen as relevant. For example, in a highly geographically decentralized organization, new ideas may well spring up in an overseas subsidiary, but those ideas can be imported into the parent organization only if the subsidiary is perceived to be genuinely part of the larger culture. If the ideas are brought in through a transfer of people from the subsidiary, those people will have credibility and influence only if they are perceived to be part of the larger culture and sympathetic to it.

It is this theme of diversity within unity that accounts for so many current management statements that the effective organization is one that can both centralize and decentralize, that can be loose and tight at the same time.

To summarize, in order to be innovative an organizational culture must assume the following:
(1) The world is changeable and can be managed.
(2) People are problem-solvers by nature.
(3) Truth is arrived at pragmatically.
(4) The appropriate time horizon is the near future.
(5) Time units should be geared to the kind of innovation being considered.

(6) Human nature is neutral or good and can be improved.
(7) Human relationships are based on individualism and the valuing of diversity.
(8) Decision-making is collegial and participative.
(9) Diverse subcultures are an asset, but they must be connected to the parent culture.

Having stated these conditions for what must be true in the overall culture, what further conditions must be present in the state of information technology?

Characteristics of an information technology that promotes innovation

I am making the assumption that any open system can function only if it can take in, move around, and appropriately process information. Information is the lifeblood of the organization, and information channels are the circulatory system. If the organization is to be capable of innovation, what must be true of the information system?

Parenthetically, I am assuming that if the above cultural conditions are not present, the organization is not likely to develop or implement an ideal information system, or if such a system should be present, it will be misused in ways that I will detail below. So having an ideal system from a technological point of view will not solve the problem of innovation. Technology alone will not cause things to happen. However, given the right cultural conditions for innovation, it is possible to specify how an information system will enhance the chances for innovation.

Networking capacity

Hypothesis. *An organization's capacity to innovate will increase to the extent that it has total networking capacity.*

My assumption here is that to generate new ideas and implement them, everyone must be able to connect to everyone else. Those connections do not need to be operational at all times, but the capacity for total connectedness will favor innovation. Especially important will be channels between subcultures so that new ideas that may arise in one can be seen by others and by the parent culture.

The network does not have to be electronic. It can exist in the form of frequent meetings that involve everybody, a travel schedule that gets everyone to all parts of the organization, an efficient mail system, or a good phone system. Sophisticated technologies become more relevant as the constraints of time and space become more costly.

Routing and filtering capacity

Hypothesis. *An organization's capacity to innovate will increase to the extent that it can open and close channels and filter information in the channels.*

My assumption here is that a fully connected network is not always desirable. For certain kinds of tasks and for certain stages of the innovation process, it may be more efficient to keep open only certain channels. The organization must be able to diagnose its information needs, and it must have the technical capacity to implement its diagnosis in the sense of opening and closing channels as needed.

In arguing for this capacity, I am not reverting to an authoritarian system – that is, some higher authority that determines which channels are opened and closed. I am suggesting that such capacity can be available in a collegial, participative system, in which members open and close channels themselves as they perceive this to be appropriate.

Just as the organization needs the technical capacity to open and close channels, so it needs the capacity to filter information flows along given channels to avoid information overloads, prevent inappropriate information from getting to some members, and to ensure that appropriate information gets to those who need it. Again, this implies a diagnostic and technical capacity, and, again, it implies that such filtering can be designed without reverting to an authoritarian system. A good example of such a system is the information lens and object lens technology developed by Tom Malone, which allows members of the network to specify rules for routing and filtering that are then automatically implemented.[17]

---

[17] K. Y. Lai and T. W. Malone, "Object Lens: A Spreadsheet for Cooperative Work," *Proceedings of the ACM Second Conference on Computer Supported Cooperative Work* (Portland, Oreg., September 1988); and T. W. Malone, K. R. Grant, K. Y. Lai, R. Rao, and D. A. Rosenblitt, "The Information Lens: An Intelligent System for Information Sharing and

Connectivity to environment; openness of the system

Hypothesis. *An organization's capacity to innovate will increase to the extent that it has multiple channels to and from its environments.*

Organizations are open sociotechnical systems embedded in multiple environments. If they cannot accurately track what is going on in those environments, they cannot identify areas in which innovation is more or less important, and they cannot assess the effects of their innovative and adaptive efforts.

Multiple channels to the environment are necessary, but they must be connected to the appropriate decision points within the organization so that the incoming information can be processed. Many organizations know a great deal, but the knowledge stays in departments that cannot effectively integrate and act on it.

Capacity to evolve own IT system technologically

Hypothesis. *An organization's capacity to innovate will increase to the extent that it understands and implements innovations in information technology itself.*

What is implied here is the organization's capacity to modify its use of IT as new possibilities become available and as new ideas arise on how to use existing technology. This means that somewhere in the system must reside good information on current capacities and on future possibilities. Such information may come from internal or external sources, but it must get to the right places to be acted on appropriately. Various aspects of IT, such as office automation and CAD/CAM, must not only be well understood but also be flexibly adopted to support the organization's mission.[18]

Interaction of culture and information technology

Implied in the above analysis is that cultural assumptions determine how or whether IT is used. The kind of information network described

Collaboration," in M. H. Olsen (ed.), *Technological Support for Work Group Collaboration* (Hillsdale, N.J.: Erlebaum, 1989).

[18] See R. J. Thomas, "The Politics of Technological Change: An Empirical Study," Sloan School Working Paper 2035–88, MIT, July 1988.

above will not be installed in organizations that do not believe in mastering their environment and in participative decision-making. But that is not the whole story. The technology itself will gradually affect organizational cultures, and in some cultures the interaction between culture and technology will, in the long run, destroy the organization's adaptive and innovative capacity. In order to examine these interactions we must first discuss some of the properties of IT.

If one thinks of the IT community as itself a subculture, one can identify certain of its assumptions that, if implemented, lead to the unfreezing of other cultural assumptions. Specifically, the IT community assumes that it is intrinsically good for organizations to have more information, more widely distributed, and more rapidly disseminated. The designers of IT are therefore likely to highlight the following properties of the technology.

(1) *Accessibility*. More people can more easily access information that is electronically available in a network.

(2) *Rapidity*. Information and feedback can be obtained much more rapidly by electronic means in computer-based networks.

(3) *Simultaneity*. Information can be presented to large numbers of people simultaneously even if they are in different time zones.

(4) *Presentational flexibility*. Information can simultaneously be presented in different ways to different people.

(5) *Complexity*. Complex relationships and contextual factors in information can be more easily represented with computer-aided systems (such as three-dimensional modeling).

(6) *System awareness*. Creating information systems requires accurate modeling of processes, and these models then become transparent to users (the essence of what Zuboff means by "informating").

(7) *System/network accountability*. Networks make it possible for all members to become aware of their interdependence, of the fact that there is no necessary higher authority in the network and hence that all members are accountable for network output.

(8) *Teamwork capacity*. The combination of simultaneity and network accountability makes it possible for real teamwork to occur where every member realizes his or her part, and where all contributions are transparent, thus forcing mutual trust.

(9) *Task-based authority*. In a functioning network it is possible to designate decision-making power to whoever has the most relevant information, and this authority can rotate among members as the task changes.

(10) *Self-designing capacity*. It is technologically and psychologically possible for the network to constantly redesign itself and to adapt to changing circumstances if power and flexibility have been built in initially.

As can be seen, these characteristics introduce a strong bias toward collaborative teamwork in that such work becomes not only much more feasible in an electronic environment but also more appropriate to the complex tasks that most organizations will face in the future.

What all this means is that the introduction of IT is a force that may stimulate culture change, first, by forcing cultural assumptions out into the open (such as assumptions about formal authority and managerial prerogatives) and, second, by making possible alternative methods of coordination. Thus if either the leadership of an organization or some subculture within the organization introduces sophisticated IT networks, this will force cultural re-examination and reveal which cultural assumptions will aid or hinder the use of technology. The further implication is that the introduction of IT may be one of the most powerful ways of unfreezing a culture and increasing an organization's innovative capacity.

Presence of an IT subculture

Hypothesis. *An organization's capacity to innovate will increase to the extent that it has a fully functioning, technologically sophisticated IT system that can be a demonstration of IT capacity and a source of diffusion to other parts of the organization.*

In other words, there must be among the subcultures of the organization at least one that is congruent with the assumptions of IT, or there will not be any place within the organization where IT can be appropriately used. However, such a subculture is only a necessary and not a sufficient condition for organizational innovation, because the larger culture may prevent diffusion of the innovation.

Destructive interactions between culture and IT

Hypothesis. *The provision of IT for purposes of automation to a management that operates according to McGregor's Theory X (a cynical view of human nature) will in the short run increase productivity but*

Table 7.2. *Positive and negative interactions between IT and culture*

IT vision	Theory X	Theory Y
Automate	Negative	Positive
Informate up	Very negative	Positive
Informate down	Very negative	Very positive
Transform	Not feasible	Very positive

in the long run will lead to employee dependence and anxiety, which reduce the probability of innovation.

Hypothesis. *The provision of IT for purposes of upward informating to a management that operates according to Theory X will give management a level of surveillance and control that will alienate employees and lead to resistance, rebellion, refusal to use the system, falsification of data, and, ultimately, total dependency and abdication of personal responsibility.*

Hypothesis. *The provision of IT for purposes of informating down to a management that operates according to Theory X will produce short-run productivity and involvement gains but will, in the long run, be subverted by management's need to control and assert what it considers its prerogatives.*

Hypothesis. *A Theory X management will not be able to transform an organization's IT capabilities because the hierarchical control mentality will prevent the necessary employee involvement in system design and use.*

If one examines failures of IT implementation, one finds specific patterns that not only explain the failure but suggest certain interactions that, even if successful in the short run, would be destructive to the organization's long-term capacity to innovate and adapt. These interactions, shown in Table 7.2, involve specifically the cultural assumptions around participation and control.

The various IT visions are shown down the left side and the two cultural extremes with respect to participation and control are shown along the top. These can most easily be characterized in terms of McGregor's Theory X and Theory Y, especially as these apply to the CEO or senior management as individuals.

The specific hypotheses embedded in Table 7.2 have been stated above. The logic behind the first one derives from research on automation, especially the research of Larry Hirschhorn, which shows that workers in highly automated plants become anxious because of their high level of responsibility and the absence of supportive bosses. And they become highly dependent on complex technology they often do not understand.[19] This combination of dependency and anxiety can lead to psychological denial and the inability to manage a crisis. That is, when the system sends alarm signals, the anxiety level is so high that workers assume that the information must be wrong and ignore it.

The scenario underlying the second hypothesis, which has been played out in a number of organizations, is potentially the most dangerous because the subculture of IT plays directly into the assumptions of a control-oriented Theory X management. In the short run, there is the illusion that the IT system has given management the perfect and ultimate control tool, especially if the system designers can also be categorized as Theory X. If control-oriented designers are working with control-oriented managers, one is bound to get an organization that will look perfectly controlled but that will sooner or later fail for lack of employee commitment and involvement. And certainly there will be no motivation or capacity to innovate.

Evidence for the third hypothesis comes from Zuboff's study of the paper mill that dramatically increased its productivity as workers learned the logic behind the automated system they were using and discovered that they could run the plant perfectly well without lots of managerial control. But managers were not willing to give up this control; they started to order workers to do things they already knew how to do and to take credit for some of the improvements, leading workers to abdicate in resentment and consequently to underutilize the system.

What is important to note is that the same system implemented with a Theory Y management (based on idealism about human nature and a belief in collegial, participative decision making) would have entirely positive results because the managers would be happy for workers to exercise more control and take over the system.

[19] L. Hirschhorn, *The Workplace Within* (Cambridge, Mass.: MIT Press, 1987).

The fourth hypothesis is self-evident, in that the Theory X organization will not have transformational visions in the first place and will not be able to elicit an innovative capacity.

In summary, the capabilities of IT in combination with a control-oriented management will produce negative results in each of the IT visions, though those results may not show up initially. If the designers of the system are also operating under assumptions of hierarchical control, we have the potential of great harm to the organization in terms of its long-term ability to innovate and to adapt to changing circumstances.

The implication is that the cultural assumptions around employee involvement, the importance of hierarchy as a principle of control, the prerogatives and rights of managers, and the nature of authority are the critical ones to examine in any IT project, because the potential of IT as a force for innovation will not be achieved if those assumptions are too close to Theory X.

Summary and conclusions

We can summarize the hypotheses about IT by stating that an organization's capacity to innovate will increase to the extent that it has:
(1) the capacity to connect everyone;
(2) the ability to open and close channels as needed;
(3) the ability to filter information in the channels;
(4) multiple channels into and from the relevant environments and to the relevant decision centers;
(5) the capacity to use the most advanced IT systems;
(6) at least one fully functioning advanced IT system;
(7) a Theory Y management that will use the IT applications appropriately and sensitively.
We noted that culture will constrain the ability to implement IT solutions, but IT can surface and unfreeze cultural assumptions.

If the IT capacity is present and if the cultural assumptions favor innovation, the organization will develop processes and structures that will increase the likelihood of members inventing and implementing the new ideas that will make the organization more adaptive in a rapidly changing environment.

The crucial point of this analysis is to note that if such technological and cultural conditions are not present, it is pointless to work on organizational processes and structures. People will simply resist the kinds of changes that may be necessary. Only if we can create the appropriate synergy between culture and IT capability will we get the long-range benefits we are looking for.

The interweaving of cultural and technological factors is the essence of the sociotechnical model of organization design. I hope that the above hypotheses can stimulate thinking about how to increase the probability of innovation and can serve as a kind of diagnostic grid to assess a group's degree of innovativeness. Above all, I hope that by focusing on culture I have made it clear why resistance to change and the desire of organizations not to innovate are entirely normal and understandable.

8 | A relational view of learning: how who you know affects what you know

ROB CROSS, LISA ABRAMS, AND
ANDREW PARKER

Think about how you are likely to get information that helps you learn and be successful in new or existing projects at work. Are you more likely to (A) Type in a few words on a search engine and get what you need or (B) Seek out people who have done something similar, either learning from them or going on to people or to documents they suggest? If you fall into category A, information that matters to you is readily attainable through technical means. If you fall into category B, you might end up getting information from a database, but the way in which you find the information and deem it credible is heavily intertwined with your social network. By a show of hands, who would typically follow path A? How about B?

WE have posed this question in more than fifty presentations over the past four years to executives from a wide range of industries, government agencies, and nationalities. In our interactions with thousands of people, we have yet to see more than a lonely hand or two pop up in response to option A. Despite the explosion of information, and the increasingly sophisticated technologies that provide us with easy access to this information, it seems that even the most technical of us learn primarily from other people. This is not all that surprising. Our heavy reliance on other people for information and learning is one of the most consistent and robust findings in the social sciences.[1] It also matches our intuition and lived experience in organizations: other people are critical to our ability to find information, learn how to do our work, and develop professionally.

[1] T. Allen, *Managing the Flow of Technology* (Cambridge, Mass.: MIT Press, 1977); J. S. Brown and P. Duguid, "Organizational Learning and Communities-of-Practice: Toward a Unified View of Working, Learning, and Innovation," *Organization Science* 2 (1991), pp. 40–57; E. Rogers, *Diffusion of Innovations*, 4th edn. (New York: Free Press, 1995); E. Wenger, *Communities of Practice* (Oxford University Press, 1998).

152

Despite this, most organizations invest little in developing effective human networks, almost always choosing instead to build ever larger, faster, and more accessible databases. While you might hear executives talk about the importance of social networks, it is rare to hear them discuss concrete actions for nurturing and supporting rich, vibrant networks of employees, apart from developing communities of practice or struggling to get employees to use some collaborative tool. We have been involved with more than sixty organizations in the past four years that have participated, at one time or another, in research programs at the Institute for Knowledge-Based Organizations. Our specific interest has been with a technique called social network analysis, which can help managers better understand how to promote learning and information flow via effective networks in organizations.[2] In this work we have consistently found that better-connected people in networks enjoy substantial performance, learning, and satisfaction benefits.

Here we want to offer two ideas in relation to such networks. First, the composition of your network – in other words, whom you get information from – has a significant impact on your learning and decision-making. This matters not only in solving specific problems but also in learning about new career opportunities or engaging in personal development. In the first part of this chapter, we offer specific ways to promote personal networks that are better for learning.

Second, the quality of your relationships also has a great deal to do with the extent to which you are likely to learn from those around you. Specifically, the degree to which trust exists in a relationship determines in large part how effectively you can learn from that person. In a trusting relationship, we are likely to listen to and believe more firmly in what the other person is saying; that is, we trust the person's competence and will allow him or her to influence our thinking. Such relationships also give us the freedom to ask questions that reveal our lack of knowledge because we trust the person's benevolence. More than just a nicety, building trust in networks has a great deal to do with one's own learning and the ability of an entire organization to

[2] R. Cross and L. Prusak, "The People Who Make Organizations Go – or Stop," *Harvard Business Review* (June 2002), pp. 104–114; R. Cross, N. Nohria, and A. Parker, "Six Myths About Informal Networks – and How To Overcome Them," *Sloan Management Review* 43 (2002), pp. 67–76.

learn and improve. The second part of this chapter, which is based on interviews we conducted in twenty organizations, will describe ways people successfully promote interpersonal trust.

Uncovering learning biases in personal networks

Providing employees with a means of developing their personal networks is a very powerful way to promote connectivity in organizations. It can allow employees to spot biases in their networks and help them understand where they might invest in developing certain kinds of relationships instead of others. For example, is a person getting information only from employees at a certain hierarchical level and thus not learning from those lower in the hierarchy? Alternatively, is a person leveraging only colleagues who are physically close, or in the same functional unit, instead of reaching out to different people in order to benefit from diverse perspectives? Given the extent to which people acquire information and learn how to do their work from others, these are important considerations in assessing the effectiveness of one's own network.

There are many ways to assess the composition of your network and its impact on what you are likely to learn over time. For example, sociologists commonly look at the way in which similarities among people on socially important dimensions such as age, race, education, and gender create clustering in networks. Reflecting on the list of people important to us from an informational or learning point of view often reveals the homogeneity of our networks. We have an extremely strong tendency, known as homophily, to seek out those who are similar to ourselves.[3] This of course has a striking effect on what we learn and the views we come to hold.

But this profile of our network does not always illustrate the more subtle means by which the people to whom we are connected affect our learning. In many coaching sessions with managers at all levels in organizations, we have found at least six dimensions of personal networks to be important.[4]

[3] P. Lazersfeld and R. Merton, "Friendship as a Social Process," in M. Berger (ed.), *Freedom and Control in Modern Society* (New York: Octagon Books, 1964).

[4] Here we are bypassing purely structural properties of networks via the well-established structural hole measure (R. Burt, *Structural Holes*, Cambridge,

Vertical dispersion. Quite often networks can be biased if people rely too much on others in certain hierarchical positions. Managing relationships with those above, at the same level, and beneath you is a hallmark of a well-rounded social network. Connections with those above you in the hierarchy can be critical for making decisions, acquiring resources, developing political awareness, and being aware of happenings that are beyond your immediate purview. Those at the same level are generally the best for brainstorming and providing specific help or information based on similar work they are doing. And those beneath you are often the best source of technical information and expertise. In general, balance here is important, and people's networks seem to fall out of balance when they do not maintain enough relationships overall, focus too heavily on those higher in the organization, or miss the technical expertise that can frequently be gained from those at lower levels.

Horizontal dispersion. People in organizations are generally motivated to pay attention to, interact with, and learn from those in their home department. Human resource practices such as hiring, orientation, training, evaluation, and compensation all tend to promote interaction within, and not across, various departmental boundaries. Compound this with certain leadership styles, cultural values, and unit-level performance metrics, and there is little wonder that people have few relationships with those in other organizations or in other departments within their own organization. Particularly as one moves up in the hierarchy, such bridging relationships become more and more important to ensure effective learning and decision-making. Yet time constraints tend to decrease the number of these relationships precisely when they are needed most.

Physical proximity. The likelihood of collaborating with someone decreases substantially the farther you are from that person. Distances of just a few feet, let alone floors in a building or even buildings

Mass.: Harvard University Press, 1992) because this metric provides little clue as to what one should do differently. We also are not focusing here on communication media, though understanding biases in reliance on face-to-face interaction, telephone, e-mail, and instant messaging can, on occasion, show executives how their use of various media constrains (or enhances) their ability to learn from others.

themselves, often prove to be critical fragmentation points in networks. While certain collaborative tools can bridge such gaps, such
as e-mail, instant messaging, and videoconferencing, proximity still
frequently dictates people's networks. With executives, this problem
often results in their not understanding the needs of those in different
locations, such as field or non-headquarter sites, and so making poor
decisions.

Intentional interactions. Does your network promote serendipitous
learning and innovation? Look at almost any manager's Day-Timer
or Palm Pilot: it is not uncommon to see back-to-back meetings from
7 a.m. to 7 p.m. or beyond, day after day. The critical question from a
learning perspective is whether the people who are your primary conduits of information are appropriate for the task-relevant information
you need or whether they are simply built into a schedule. Quite often
we hear executives recount poor strategic decisions they made that met
nothing but heated resistance – all as a result of not getting the right
information from the right parts of the organization. A large culprit in
these scenarios was schedules that permitted only certain voices to be
heard.

Time invested. Do you invest enough time in maintaining relationships
that are important to you? It is not uncommon to find people spending the most time and effort maintaining relationships that need little
investment or those that are antagonistic and of little benefit. People
have finite time and energy to put into relationships – managing these
investments wisely can yield substantial performance and learning
benefits.

Time known. Finally, is there diversity in your network in terms of the
length of time that you have known people? Again, we are inclined to
believe that balance is best here. If you have known too many people for
too long, you are most likely to be hearing things you already know
or, more insidiously, knowingly or unknowingly using other people
to get your own opinions confirmed. It is generally good to see new
people cycling into (and out of) a person's network as his or her job
changes. But, of course, having too many new people in a network
often indicates a lack of sounding boards or confidants with whom
one can discuss personal or inflammatory issues.

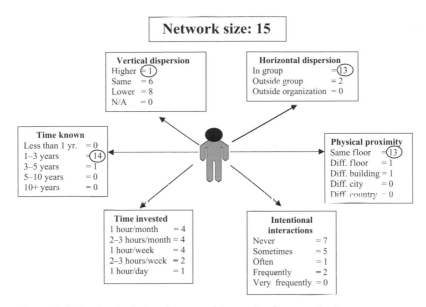

Figure 8.1. Lack of relationships reaching up in the organization.

Combining these dimensions to assess your overall network can provide powerful insight into relationships that need more investment and those that need less. For example, consider two different profiles of executives, each reflecting different biases in personal networks. Both networks were the same size (each executive listed fifteen people on whom he relied for information). However, the composition of each network reveals some striking differences between the executives.

First, Figure 8.1 shows a senior executive in a major electronics organization. Having recently been promoted to this position, he found that the bulk of the people he relied on at this point in his career were new to him. While he was pleased with this network from an informational perspective, he was a little less comfortable with the extent to which he could trust these people to discuss and brainstorm tough organizational issues. One implication of this assessment for him was a need to rekindle relationships with two past mentors who could be distant advisers.

Additional biases existed. For example, he was concerned with his excessive reliance on people lower in the hierarchy and on those in his own group. While he had set out to build relationships with his employees in order to be an effective leader, it was clear to him that he had

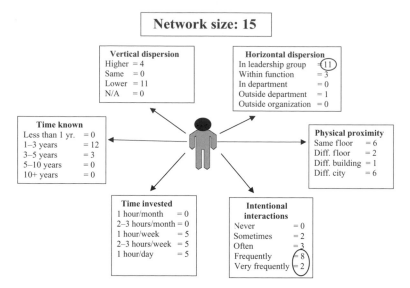

Network size: 15

Vertical dispersion
Higher = 4
Same   = 0
Lower = 11
N/A   = 0

Horizontal dispersion
In leadership group = 11
Within function   = 3
In department   = 0
Outside department   = 1
Outside organization = 0

Time known
Less than 1 yr. = 0
1–3 years   = 12
3–5 years   = 3
5–10 years   = 0
10+ years   = 0

Physical proximity
Same floor   = 6
Diff. floor   = 2
Diff. building = 1
Diff. city   = 6

Time invested
1 hour/month   = 0
2–3 hours/month = 0
1 hour/week   = 5
2–3 hours/week = 5
1 hour/day   = 5

Intentional interactions
Never   = 0
Sometimes   = 2
Often   = 3
Frequently   = 8
Very frequently = 2

Figure 8.2. An over-reliance on people from the same group.

not established sufficient relationships with those higher in the organization. As a result, he often missed opportunities to leverage resources or knowledge that existed elsewhere in the organization, and he was less able to obtain buy-in on initiatives he wanted to pursue. Finally, he was also surprised to note his heavy reliance on those physically near him. The network analysis showed him that relying too heavily on spontaneity and not reaching out systematically to those in different locations were biasing the information he had to work from. To fix this imbalance, he began to structure time into his calendar for people he might not necessarily bump into in the halls or cafeteria.

Now consider Figure 8.2, a profile of a government executive brought in to manage a critical division of an agency after the September 11 hijackings. This person was relatively new in his role and had spent a great deal of time in his first year meeting and establishing shared goals with his extended leadership team. The concern here, in his eyes, was an excessive reliance on this group of people. While he was turning to those higher in the agency, the remainder of his informational relationships tended to come from his leadership team. A critical step for him was developing relationships deeper within the agency to get a ground-level view of happenings as well as outside of the agency to ensure fresh perspectives. He was also concerned with his heavy reliance on people who were built into his schedule. Upon reviewing his overloaded schedule, he quickly noted that the amount of time he spent with the same people led to comfortable relationships but likely did nothing to help him develop new insights or perspectives.

Assessing the composition of these executives' networks had strong implications for both of them in terms of their own learning and development. We have outlined in an appendix to this chapter a very simple personal network diagnostic and encourage you to take a few moments to apply this perspective to your own network. On a personal level, such assessments can be a very powerful means of promoting an ability to learn and develop professionally. They can also be a critical way to develop rich, vibrant networks within an entire organization. Several organizations we have worked with are embedding this diagnostic approach into their career development processes. In these settings, annual development goals include both content-related learning and network development objectives. Structuring this kind of development process into the work of an entire organization can have dramatic effects on the connectivity of strategically important groups of people.

The importance of trust

A second important consideration for learning in networks lies not with the people you are connected to but with the quality of the connections you have. Through a separate phase of research at the Institute for Knowledge-Based Organizations, we have found trust to be critical in effective learning relationships. Our findings are based on surveys of 138 people in three global companies with headquarters in three different countries. Two types of trust are especially relevant to knowledge-sharing. One is benevolence based trust, what most of us mean when we talk about trust. It focuses on vulnerability: I trust that you will not harm me if given the opportunity to do so. Trusting someone in this way allows you to expose your own lack of knowledge with the confidence that the person will not ridicule you or, worse, tell others that you are not very smart. As a result of this kind of trust, people

	High competence-based trust	Low competence-based trust
High benevolence-based trust	High learning and social opportunity	Low learning opportunity but high social opportunity
Low benevolence-based trust	Potential learning opportunity	Low learning and social opportunity

Figure 8.3. Trust and learning opportunities.

are more forthcoming about their expertise and much more likely to be creative and learn what they need to in order to do something better or differently in their work.

The second type of trust our surveys showed to be critical to learning is competence-based trust. This focuses on ability: I believe that you know what you are talking about; I am confident that you have the correct information. This is a prerequisite to a person seeking information from another. Just as important, people end up learning more from a person whose competence they trust because they are much more likely to listen to and absorb what that person says. Particularly in ambiguous situations or for important projects, one's willingness to let another person influence his or her thinking, and thus actions, is intertwined with a belief that the person knows what he or she is talking about.

These two types of trust may exist independently. For example, I can trust that you would tell me the truth if you knew it (benevolence) but not trust that you know what you are talking about (competence). Conversely, I can believe that you are knowledgeable (competence) but not be sure that you will tell me the truth (benevolence). We have summarized the effects of having both, one, or neither type of trust in Figure 8.3. As you can see, a lack of both types of trust will make learning unlikely, but if there is a lack only of benevolence-based trust, learning is likely to take place. Of course, both types of trust will have a positive effect on the opportunity for learning.

Competence-based trust matters especially in exchanges in which the knowledge sought is tacit or complex. If what I need to know is not written down anywhere or is difficult to evaluate, I will have a hard time verifying it. In this context, I must be confident that the person who gives me information knows what he or she is talking about. I have to trust his or her competence.

Trust-building behaviors

To understand how people promote trust in their relationships, we conducted a series of in-depth interviews in twenty companies. We discovered significant consistency in what people look for when determining whether someone else can be trusted. Our research concentrated on trust between two people when one person (the knowledge seeker) needs information from someone else (the knowledge source) in order to complete an important project. We asked people how they determine whether others are trustworthy in this context. Our respondents identified six behaviors that signal trustworthiness.

First, people who are trusted indicate both what they know and what they do not. Expertise inspires trust, but so does admitting the limits of your knowledge. If I know you will not pretend to know something, then I am more likely to trust the accuracy of what you tell me. In addition, a wrong answer is worse than no answer at all because incorrect information presented as truth can lead the seeker down an expensive and time-consuming path. Employees who are clear and open about what they do and do not know are also a boon to managers because they require less monitoring.

Despite the benefits of acknowledging the limits of knowledge, admitting ignorance is taboo in some organizations. In those environments, employees feel pressure to know or to appear to know the answer to any question. But organizations concerned with learning and effective knowledge-sharing should work to change that cultural norm. One way is to encourage people to recommend others whom they believe to be more qualified in a particular subject area. As with all the suggestions for encouraging trusting signals, it is not enough to tell people to do this. Managers have to model this behavior and reward people who follow their example.

Second, people who are trusted deliver information clearly and consistently. One potential source of ambiguity is the use of jargon, the "private" vocabulary of particular groups or professions. When a knowledge source responds to a request from someone outside his or her group with jargon, the answer is likely to be useless or worse, and the seeker's trust in this source might decrease. But the problem of misunderstanding goes beyond jargon because even common words can have different meanings to different groups of people. A "project plan" and "on time" can mean one thing to one group and something very different to another. A trusted knowledge source knows what needs to be explained and how to translate the language of one group into the language the seeker understands.

Honesty and completeness go hand in hand. Leaving out crucial information can very quickly be perceived as dishonesty. A co-worker who gives you information to help you prepare a sales pitch but neglects to mention that the client hates PowerPoint presentations will not be trusted again. Similarly, it may be true that "we are merging with ABC Corporation," but a manager who fails to add, "so there will be layoffs" will lose employees' trust. And timing is crucial. Finding something out days or weeks after your manager knew about it, too late for you to respond to the news, is a trust breaker. People may hate to deliver bad news, but putting it off can result in resentment, the loss of an opportunity to find a solution, and a loss of trust.

Third, people who are trusted display consistency between actions and words. This may sound almost too obvious to mention, but fully 75 percent of our interviewees identified this as an important trust signal that many people in their organizations did not display. This may be as much or more about managing expectations in a reasonable way as about dishonesty. Just as we may be tempted to answer a question whether or not we really know what we are talking about, so we may be tempted to say, "No problem. I can handle it" to almost any request. No matter how good one's intentions, not meeting deadlines may cause problems for people who rely on that work getting done. Although an individual may have "honestly" intended to get the work done on time, the result of failing to deliver on that promise will be a loss of trust.

Fourth, people who are trusted respect others' vulnerability and confidential information. This also seems obvious, but many interviewees identified the failure to live up to this behavior as an important source of distrust. Even when you are not the direct victim of an indiscretion, you can lose trust. People will talk about sensitive subjects only when the person they confide in has demonstrated that he or she will not pass on the information inappropriately. A norm of keeping confidences helps create a safe environment in which people are willing to expose potential weaknesses, ask questions, ask for help, and reveal sensitive information. Maintaining a safe environment goes a long way toward building trust and credibility.

Fifth, people who are trusted broaden the conversation beyond work. Getting to know one another, even a little bit, outside of work-related topics contributes to the formation of trusting relationships. Discovering similarities (we both have adopted children, we both like *The X-Files*, we both water-ski, we both read historical novels) contributes to trust. Note that we are talking about a reasonable and appropriate amount of personal discussion, not full disclosure of the details of private lives. A co-worker who tells you more than you want to know about his or her life outside the office shows poor judgment that may reduce trust rather than build it.

A conversation about personal experiences of the workplace unconnected to current work can have a similarly positive effect on trust. Experts in negotiation say that trust often develops more quickly in a discussion unrelated to the topic of negotiation. In addition, non-work related communication in organizations pays dividends by helping people understand each other's backgrounds and motivation, and, often, by demonstrating co-workers' ability to maintain confidentiality.

Finally, people who are trusted recognize and share what is valuable. A trusted knowledge source will share genuinely valuable knowledge and give time to the seeker, not just do the minimum needed to respond to a request. In most of the organizations we worked with, time, tacit knowledge, and access to personal networks were the most popular tokens of value given to people who were trusted. Of course, a willingness to share valuable knowledge requires trust in the seeker. One interviewee described what she called "trust tests." She would trust someone with information or time that was not crucial but was still valuable to the recipient. If the knowledge seeker used that information in a trustworthy way, she would increase what she felt comfortable giving. Sharing contacts and social networks poses a special risk to the knowledge source. Our own relationships and reputation can suffer if the knowledge seeker does not treat the contact appropriately. So reciprocal trust is especially important in sharing anything as valuable as a contact.

Improving networks within organizations

Although networks are hidden from view, managers can influence them in ways that make the organization more effective. Instead of trying to improve communication among everyone in the organization, however, it is more productive to build and improve networks at specific points where collaboration matters. Three levels of intervention can help in this pursuit. First, as the bulk of this chapter has outlined, we can strengthen employees' personal networks so that they have access to more diverse sources of information. Second, we can build relationships and networks within groups or departments. Third, we can alter various aspects of the organizational context in which a network sits in order to promote effective collaboration where appropriate. We have summarized some interventions at each level in Table 8.1.

Despite, or maybe because of, the explosion of information and technology over the past decade, most people still find information and learn through their personal networks. We are much more likely to get information that affects what we do at work from other people than from the Internet or databases. While we might ultimately draw on information from a database or document, how we find and place credibility in that information is intimately intertwined with referrals from people we know. This seems to become more pronounced and have greater organizational and personal impact as people take on more senior positions within organizations. Yet most executives do little to assess or develop networks that can effectively support their learning, development, and work.

Here we have simply proposed two aspects of personal networks worthy of attention. First, characteristics of the people you are tied to can strongly influence your learning and development, for better or worse. Simple assessments can help establish awareness of learning biases as well as plans for development of more effective personal networks. Second, the quality of the relationship you have with another person affects the extent to which that relationship is effective for learning purposes. Very simple behaviors can promote interpersonal trust and have substantial implications for learning and development over time.

Table 8.1. *Individual, departmental, and organizational network improvements*

Individual improvements
(1) Cultivate contacts outside your group and outside the organization to avoid insularity in your network.
(2) Develop a global perspective by having people in your network who are in different cities and countries.
(3) Maintain an even number of contacts with juniors, peers, and seniors to avoid hierarchical bias in your network.
(4) Create a dynamic personal network. Rather than relying on friends and colleagues you have known for several years, create new contacts.
(5) Ensure that high-maintenance ties are rewarding. If not, reallocate some of your time to making new connections.
(6) Establish new ties that are grounded in both benevolence- and competence-based trust.
(7) De-emphasize old ties that are lacking in competence-based trust.
(8) Reinvigorate old relationships that are high in competence-based trust but low in benevolence-based trust. For example, trust can be enhanced through discussion of a shared interest that is not related to work.

Departmental improvements
(1) Where possible, work should be structured as a collaborative endeavor rather than with an eye solely to individual accountability.
(2) Leaders should actively encourage collaboration in group problem-solving so that all voices (even the most junior) are heard.
(3) Leaders should involve people on the periphery of networks to get actively involved in projects rather than just relying on a chosen few.
(4) Managers should celebrate collaborative accomplishments rather than only individual accomplishments.
(5) Face-to-face forums should be held that encourage people to meet others and learn their expertise.
(6) Specific roles (e.g. knowledge managers) or pieces of roles (e.g. modified staffing coordinators) should be created to help people within the department connect with others as necessary.
(7) Managers should encourage a trusting working environment by example. For instance, they should be willing to admit a lack of knowledge when they turn to others for information.
(8) Managers can establish a trusting environment by supporting employees. For example, people will be more likely to go out on a limb in a meeting if they know they have their manager's support.

Individual, departmental, and organizational network improvements
(*continued*)

Organizational improvements

(1) Demonstration of collaborative behaviors should be a meaningful component of people's performance-evaluation processes.

(2) In general, people should be promoted on the basis of both individual accomplishment and collaborative endeavors.

(3) The organization's recruiting process should screen for people who have actively demonstrated collaborative behaviors in past work.

(4) In general, training should be conducted in a group setting (rather than sending individuals to customized programs) that allows content transfer as well as the development of relationships with people engaged in similar work throughout the group or organization.

(5) Orientation practices should help new people develop an awareness of who does what in the organization. This will allow people to know whom they should turn to when faced with a specific problem or opportunity.

(6) Staffing mechanisms or procedures should be in place to ensure that when projects are initiated, the employees with the most relevant expertise are utilized (rather than those whom a given leader might know and like).

(7) Communities of practice should be supported in the organization in a way that helps integrate networks by creating relationships across functional, physical, or hierarchical boundaries.

(8) In general, transparency and fairness in decision-making, especially with regard to salary, evaluations, rewards, and promotions, will create a more trusting environment within an organization.

Appendix: Proforma for conducting a quick assessment

Step 1: Write down the names of people you rely on for information or problem-solving to do your work. These people can come from any and all walks of life.

Names	

Step 2: For each person identified in step 1, please answer the following questions (e.g. vertical dispersion) about your relationship to them.

	Vertical dispersion	Horizontal dispersion	Physical proximity	Intentional interaction	Time invested	Time known						
Name of person with whom I network.	Please indicate each person's hierarchical level relative to your own. 1 = higher than yours 2 = equal to yours 3 = lower than yours 4 = not applicable	What part of the organization does each person work in? 1 = within same group 2 = within same business unit 3 = within same division 4 = within same organization 5 = different organization	What is each person's physical proximity to you? 1 = same building 2 = different building 3 = different city 4 = different country	To what extent are your interactions with this person structured into your job? 1 = never 2 = sometimes 3 = often 4 = frequently 5 = very frequently	How much effort do you put into maintaining this relationship? 1 = 1 hour or less per month 2 = 2–3 hours per month 3 = 1 hour per week 4 = 2–3 hours per week 5 = 1 hour or more per day	How long have you known each person? 1 = less than 1 year 2 = 1–3 years 3 = 3–5 years 4 = 5–10 years 5 = 10+ years						

Step 3: List the number of relationships that fall into each response category for all of the major descriptors below (e.g. vertical dispersion).

Vertical dispersion
1 = higher than yours
2 = equal to yours
3 = lower than yours
4 = not applicable

Horizontal dispersion
1 = within same group
2 = within same business unit
3 = within same division
4 = within same organization
5 = different organization

Physical proximity
1 = same building
2 = different building
3 = different city
4 = different country

Intentional interaction
1 = never
2 = sometimes
3 = often
4 = frequently
5 = very frequently

Time invested
1 = 1 hour or less per month
2 = 2–3 hours per month
3 = 1 hour per week
4 = 2–3 hours per week
5 = 1 hour or more per day

Time known
1 = less than 1 year
2 = 1–3 years
3 = 3–5 years
4 = 5–10 years
5 = 10+ years

Step 4: Take a look at the composition of your network and identify biases that may affect how you do your job. For example, do you have a tendency to go only to people who are accessible to you rather than to those who may have more relevant information?

Strength/bias	Implication/action

9 | *Improved performance: that's our diploma*

WENDY L. COLES

HAT does it look like when an organization is learning? How do we know when learning is occurring? Educational institutions use tests, grades, and diplomas as indicators, but what are the indicators outside traditional educational systems?

I cannot say that I knew what learning at General Motors would look like when I first joined the organization in 1978. But I was pretty sure it was not learning I was seeing when I witnessed the plant training coordinator first reading the GM instructor's manual verbatim to a group of us new employees, then reading to the class the corporate lecturette, and, finally, "augmenting" our lesson with a video that offered only a simulation of the lecturette's key points. As I looked around the classroom of freshman foremen, I realized we were all bored and offended by this antiseptic presentation sent down from headquarters. It seemed very much removed from the pain and grime of our manufacturing lives.

Even so, the other foremen frowned with disbelief when afterward I shut down my manufacturing line and took my department into the cafeteria to teach them how all the parts they were making would be assembled into throttle body injectors. Their disapproving stares all seemed to ask the same question: "Didn't I care that I had a production quota to make?"

With a PhD in education, I had expected to be placed in the education and training department when I arrived at GM. What a relief it was not to be there. It quickly became apparent to me that that was not where the major learning initiatives should originate. But that was twenty-five years ago, and since then GM has aggressively moved forward – perhaps not in the spirit of intellectual curiosity or a commitment to helping people grow, but in the spirit of leapfrogging the competition in cost and quality improvements. And that is a challenge we could not have begun to take on in an organization that was not deeply interested in learning. I will share with you what I saw in that learning lab.

The GM story

GM is committed to learning about learning. The company is ever increasing its understanding of the similarities and differences between individual and organizational learning, and how organizational learning contributes to corporate performance.

I have overheard people in the field of organizational learning express frustration that organizations and their leadership do not care about learning. I cannot say that about the leadership of GM, as they have always expressed a belief in the relationship between learning and performance. I submit that the challenge is not convincing leaders about the importance of learning but helping them understand the conditions the organization must establish to promote learning.

My goal with this chapter is to demonstrate how GM has invested in learning about learning and to show the strengths and weaknesses of some of the company's methods. My hope is that through GM's example, you will gain both an increased understanding of what promotes organizational learning and some respect for the complexity of making it happen.

Learning is for life

Human beings are either growing – hence learning – or dying. We are thinking creatures. Learning is the fuel of life. Learning and discovery give meaning to our lives. Learning lets us do things we could not before. We can see that learning has occurred when there is a change in behavior. These definitions of learning hold true for any human entity, be it an individual or a group.

In my quest to understand some of the key ingredients of organizational learning, I found it helpful to draw on examples outside of GM. Here are a few that illustrate the concepts of individual and organizational learning. Let us begin with individual learning.

Example 1

W. Edwards Deming was a statistician sent by the United States to Japan after World War II to help revive the economy there and get the industrial base up and running. He taught statistical process control and the concepts of effective management to the Japanese. The Japanese government was very appreciative of Deming's work and in

1950 created the Deming Prize to recognize companies that show the greatest quality improvements.

It took Deming's success in Japan to awaken the US to his teachings. In the early 1980s, there was a television program, *If Japan Can, Why Can't We?* In response to this challenge, GM asked Deming, who was then in his eighties, for help. He agreed to work with GM and other US companies because he was committed to helping the US auto industry regain its footing as a competitive international force.

So Deming traveled every week to Detroit in his eighties and early nineties to counsel and educate leadership on issues of quality improvement. At his request, his hotel room in Detroit was equipped with a fluorescent light over the desk, and he sat at this desk every night before he went to bed and pulled from the breast pocket of his suit jacket the wad of business cards and bits of paper he had collected during the day. While reviewing them, he thought about his lecture for the following day and how what he was learning at that moment might fit in. He then modified his lecture notes to incorporate his new insights. Deming believed there was still much for him to learn and maintained the discipline to do so, the discipline to capture ideas, reflect on them, and adjust his behavior on a daily basis. Deming was an individual who was learning continually, even at age 91.

Example 2

Sarah Little Turnbull is founder and director of the Process of Change Innovation and Design Laboratory at Stanford University and is one of America's most influential designers. In the 1950s, she created freezer-to-oven Corning Ware for the Corning company, finding a new use for Pyroceram, a material previously used on missiles because of its ability to withstand intense heat and freezing cold. Later, she worked with such agencies or companies as NASA, General Mills, and 3M – even helping to develop suits worn by astronauts.

On a visit to her office at Stanford, she greeted me in her signature black tunic and turban, the tunic absolutely plain except for the face of a clock meshed into the fabric on her chest. The clock faces upward so that Turnbull can always see the time. She pulled open her four long filing-cabinet drawers and said, "This is my life view. This reflects how I see the world. And, by the way, it's constantly changing."

She also told me about her love of travel – not for the joy of visiting new places but for the delight of returning. She receives six newspapers a day. After she's been away, she lays them out and, starting with the most recent day and going backward, she looks at how the major stories have unfolded. She is engrossed in examining the events changing our world and how they are communicated. At age 82, she is studying the patterns of how we view emerging issues, and, by so doing, she is continuing to gain insights while enhancing what she shares with her students. In other words, she is still learning.

Turnbull and Deming show us that adults can learn at any age. Furthermore, they demonstrate that even with individual learning, specific behaviors are necessary: discipline, a search for patterns, and an understanding, over time, of the importance of these patterns. These attributes of individual learning are prerequisites to organizational learning.

Learning within organizations

Just as individuals benefit by learning from experience, so do organizations. Learning allows organizations and individuals alike to improve productivity and seize new opportunities. But organizational learning does not happen in a vacuum; the process must be supported and encouraged by individuals within the organization who can clearly see the relationship between learning and improved performance. The following examples illustrate that relationship.

Example 1

We are in a courtroom, and the jury is listening to the defense lawyer presenting her final argument in support of her client. Is she convincing the jury of her client's innocence? Were her witnesses credible? Is she covering all the important issues in her closing argument? The jury recesses to discuss its verdict: guilty or not guilty.

Actually, this is not an ordinary court scene. This is a mock court created and paid for by the attorneys to test the mettle of their defense. A friend of mine is the psychologist who orchestrates this type of exercise. He aims for as much realism as possible, randomly selecting the jury just as it happens in the actual process and setting up the chambers to look just like they do in a real courthouse.

This process helps lawyers learn how to argue cases by giving them insight into how juries will perceive their arguments. This is learning through experimentation, and for these lawyers it clearly results in improved performance.

Example 2

My twenty-four-year-old son is a high-school teacher in Big Rapids, Michigan. Using a schoolwide network of information, which he can access through a computer in his classroom, he can learn about each of his students. Are there two parents in the home? Are they at home most of the time or do they have occupations that take them elsewhere? How has Mary done in previous years? How is she doing in her other classes this year?

What's more, every eight weeks, the school's guidance counselor calls together all of the teachers to discuss each freshman and answer such questions as, "How is this student doing in her classes? Does anyone have tips on the most effective methods for helping this student learn? Are there any collective actions we should be taking to help this student?"

The guidance counselor also keeps detailed records of all students through the high-school years and into college and beyond to get a sense of whether or not the school is making a difference in their lives. This information is shared with the teachers, not to show that one instructor is doing a better job than another but to help all of them understand the collective impact of their work. They use this information to reflect on what they are doing in their classrooms and whether their actions are indeed positioning students to lead productive lives. This is an example of an organization being clear on its purpose (success in adulthood) and establishing a tracking system in the larger environment to feed back information on how well the organization is fulfilling that purpose. This can be called a "learning loop."

Example 3

In 1990, GM (and you thought we would never return to GM!) began systematically to promote organizational learning.

GM is a complex company, with up to sixty program teams world-wide designing new vehicles simultaneously. Our past is filled with examples of one team not knowing what another team was doing, and hence missing opportunities to learn.

A senior vice-president laid the foundation for change when he said to one of his program leaders, "It is not enough for you to build a quality car. I want the other programs to learn from your efforts." Consequently, this program leader was held accountable for monthly reviews on what he and his team were learning and how they were sharing it with other teams. An observer was assigned to help the leader document and analyze what the team had learned.

That particular team was experimenting with a radical new vehicle design, accelerated timing, and manufacturing in Mexico. Six months later, another team was in Mexico, preparing to build a vehicle there, so, in the spirit of inquiry and efficiency that GM's management had begun to foster, the person in charge of planning this initiative contacted her counterpart from the first team and asked if there was anything she should know before proceeding. Did she get an earful! In fact, he and his team had almost blown it – and manufacturing had not even begun.

This first team had been in Mexico for several weeks, interacting with the folks in the plant without realizing that they had been disregarding all protocol. They had failed to initiate the project by first spending time with the senior managers at the plant, who were so deeply offended that they called the program off for several weeks. So the planner, because she had connected with her counterpart on the first team, was tipped off early enough to build the proper relationships with the senior management team in Mexico.

This example demonstrates that a leader can set the tone for organizational learning by establishing clear expectations that people are responsible not only for capturing their own insights but also for finding out what others can teach them.

Experimentation, discipline, feedback loops, and a clear mandate for learning are only a few of the organizational characteristics necessary for learning. GM continues to experiment in order to learn about learning. Let us look at some of those initiatives.

How GM learned to learn

GM's process of learning might look easy, but I can assure you that in the frenzy of execution, leaders are, more often than not, scrambling to act without pausing to learn. Multiple interventions are required to reshape the behavior of any organization if it is to learn continually.

Organizational learning does not happen on its own – it takes discipline and an infrastructure. I became convinced of this after years of hearing people at GM say, "We are a learning organization. We make more vehicles than any other company, hence we have more opportunities to learn. We can be smarter than any other company."

But getting smarter did not happen automatically for GM. Learning is not one-dimensional, as any of you who have children or have dealt with school systems will know. People have individual learning styles (some learn by reading, while others rely on observing, talking, or learning by doing, for example). And each subject, each lesson to be learned, needs to be approached in its own way.

When I talk about learning at GM, I am not talking solely about individuals getting smarter. I am talking about an organization getting smarter. And I am not talking about the classes offered by GM University. I am talking about making cars better than we ever did before. The reward comes in improved performance. That's our diploma. It requires a change in mindset, a change in behavior, a change in roles and responsibilities, and a change in work processes.

Let us look at some of the methods used to promote learning within GM.

Method 1: Learning leaders

Before an organization can learn, its leaders must be capable of effective inquiry, which means more than just finding out "Who done it?" A learning leader is someone who can ask the questions that invite employees to reflect, to step out of the fast pace of their day-to-day existence and look for the patterns in performance.

This is a very difficult cultural challenge for many organizations. In our John Wayne environment, we are expected to know everything and to be self-sufficient. In reality, though, a John Wayne type is not a learning leader. A learning leader is one who can say, "I don't know everything. What can I learn from others?"

At GM, all leaders are expected to become learning leaders, who model continuous learning. It may not come naturally, so training sessions are available to help leaders develop the skills and behaviors that promote learning within themselves and others. Executives are taught how to understand that we all have different mental maps, that there's a difference between advocating a position and listening to others. This is tough stuff, but these are lessons used extensively by GM to help key leaders be more effective.

Much of GM's thinking has been influenced by the work of Peter Senge, Peter Scholtes, Fred Kofman, Chuck Wisner, and Chris Argyris.[1] Their teachings on "ladders of inference" (tools to discern the difference between assumptions and observed behavior), "the left-hand column" (a tool that helps people understand the difference between what is said and what is thought), and "conversations without toxic waste" (tools that help people say what they are thinking without offending others), have helped many senior leaders understand the value of shifting the dynamics so that people interact with one another in new ways. GM designed and delivers numerous training programs that bring to life the values of a learning leader.

I could literally feel the difference when I walked into a room of senior executives who had invested several years learning these communication skills. Their dialog was pointed and honest, without the political one-upmanship one sees too frequently in large organizations. The leaders of our program teams, internally called vehicle line executives, are extensively trained in these skills and take semiannual refresher sessions. Program team members are also trained, thereby providing a variation of team-building that specifically addresses how to improve communication among team members.

In those areas where leaders have built learning into the culture, the openness and healthiness of dialog and collective understanding have resulted in more effective decisions. Regrettably, leaders who truly understand the value of effective conversation skills are still a rare breed.

Method 2: Visual information display

Decision-makers are more likely to keep in mind the multiple variables that go into a decision when the breadth of information is displayed – either on paper or electronically – on the walls of a conference room. Information displayed in this way helps employees see the complexity

---

[1] Much of what we teach is based on the tools described in P. M. Senge, C. Roberts, R. B. Ross, B. K. Smith, and A. Kleiner, *The Fifth Discipline Fieldbook: Strategies and Tools for Building a Learning Organization* (New York: Currency/Doubleday, 1994).

of decision-making and understand the multiple impacts of any decision. The goal is to ensure that decision-makers have easy access to all pertinent information, while keeping in mind how the upcoming decision will affect other decisions.

This concept has been applied to several areas of GM. For example, GM's marketing, sales, and service organization has Collaborative Decision Centers in each of its five regions in the United States. The centers are linked to accommodate live video and audio feeds, and shared data. GM's product development organization also uses this concept, in the guise of Operations Rooms, which are electronically equipped with all the information about specific vehicle programs. When a product team meets in the Ops Room, members have easy access to everything they need to track their program and make decisions.

For both organizations within GM, displayed information helps facilitate immediate decisions, but of course there is much an organization can learn from studying past decisions, their impact over time, and how current decisions may influence future ones. GM is looking to experiment with using the decision centers as learning laboratories, to help groups improve not just the decision of the moment but the entire decision-making process.

In an effort to experiment with decision-making in context, GM Powertrain has developed a model with four levels of decision-making and has identified the information required for each level. Each executive is required to review the information monthly and update any for which he or she is responsible. This online information lets all leaders see the outcome of their decisions and the state of their business within the context of the larger system.

Method 3: Visible work processes

Making work processes visible has been a prerequisite for much of the learning within GM. How can a process be improved if there is not a collective understanding of how it currently works? A great deal of effort has been put into mapping how we design our vehicles, how we administer personnel policies, how we interact with our supply community. Once these processes are made visible, it is easy to see where to establish feedback loops for continual improvement.

For example, the engineering organization uses technical integration engineers to monitor the engineering process, look for variations from the standard process, search for the root cause of the variations, and implement changes when better practices are confirmed. GM also documents how manufacturing engineering and product engineering work together.

In one instance, the manufacturing and product engineers met to discuss the door for one of GM's new trucks. Together, they went online and saw the work process whereby product engineering specifies the product requirements and then gives them to the manufacturing engineering team, which in turn designs the process to manufacture the door. Before the conversation had proceeded very far, manufacturing engineers told the product engineers they needed a particular type of seal on the door. After some discussion, everyone realized that the seal was not a requirement but a familiar solution. The real requirement was that they needed to be able to assemble the door in a certain way, and they needed to make sure it would not leak.

Because they had been able to "see" the work process, both sets of engineers had been able to refine their understanding of that process and uncover the assumptions that threatened to disrupt it. Through this experience, they found a new way of working together, thereby reducing the risk of confusion, lost efficiency, and poor quality.

Method 4: Information taxonomy

Thinking about how to organize information is a key element of creating a learning environment. How does one easily access what is known? Given a workforce of 400,000, how does one provide each employee with the most current information he or she needs on the job?

Here is an example of how bad it can get. In the past, GM collected information about its customers according to division. The Buick division collected information only about Buick customers, Chevrolet collected information about its customers, Cadillac knew the Cadillac customer, and so on. No one in the company had a picture of the whole.

GM has since made a major effort to compile information in one spot, organized by household. Now, for example, we understand what percentage of a family's garage is GM and what percentage of that is Chevrolets. We can ask ourselves, "Do families that purchase SUVs tend to have Chevrolets as well?" and answer the question with confidence. Imagine the importance of these new insights for marketing and selling.

So, how do we create information systems that give us the flexibility to look at things differently? Currently, each function in GM is exploring various answers to this question by assigning information technology experts and cybrarians to organize the information that feeds into work processes. GM's goal is to provide a personalized home page for all employees so that when they turn on their computers each morning, the basic categories of information they need to do their jobs will appear on the screen. This will enhance productivity enormously. However, there are some concerns.

For one thing, there is a scarcity of people who are schooled in how to think about the work to be done and the information required, how to display what is known, and how to integrate ongoing learning into the process. There are very few American universities providing such an education. Also, we are concerned about developing an information system that reinforces silos – segmented sections of the company that operate independently. US companies are only beginning to recognize the importance of cross-functional processes. We must be careful that information systems do not reinforce a segmented perspective of the business.

Method 5: Social networks

Creating situations conducive to sharing is critical to organizational learning. How do you get people in the company with similar interests to share what they know with one another? How can they find out who else in the company may be interested? How do you get people to slow down long enough to share what they know? Without formal situations built into an organization's practices, the sharing of learning does not become a priority.

An example of this can be seen in GM's focus on alliances with other automotive companies, a major strategic issue and a complex proposition. To meet the challenge of building strong, healthy partnerships with its strategic partners, GM assembled a team to address the issue. Although the team comprised seasoned executives, none had much experience with partnerships. Each executive was assigned to a specific partnership, and it soon became clear that without some sort of formal intervention, each executive would focus solely on his or her assigned alliance and not on the larger questions about these partnerships. So a major effort was made to connect the executives in a monthly telephone conference call so that they could share their experiences and insights and learn from one another, while enabling the central office to document their insights.

Many of the executives resisted this monthly forum. They saw it as just one more time-consuming activity instead of as a vital contribution to the company's knowledge base on building alliances. It required a formal intervention, something as simple as a teleconference, to shift behavior from individual endeavors to learning and sharing as a group, thereby improving the performance of the whole. GM also had to formalize social interactions when it was implementing its global Order to Delivery System, which was designed to reduce the time between an order and the delivery of the vehicle. Monthly telephone conference calls connected the North American team with teams in Europe and South America. During each call, the group was asked, "What issues are you facing?" and, "Is there any team that may be able to shed some light on these issues?"

In one case, North America was having difficulty calculating delivery dates to the dealer. Europe offered to share its method on the next call. Because Europe has a longer logistics supply chain, it is more difficult to pinpoint delivery dates. Consequently, the European team had developed a statistical method for calculating delivery dates and tracking them along the logistic chain. Although the precise formula could not be applied in North America, the method itself was applicable and was very useful for the North American team.

This particular situation illustrates an important concept: teams cannot always assume an explicit transfer of knowledge; that is, a team cannot expect to be able to adopt outright another team's practices. Instead, we encourage teams to look for the principles that underlie another team's actions and decisions, a tactic that gives everyone even greater learning possibilities.

While the above cases might sound trite, it is too often the case that organizations fail to grasp significant insights because they do not create opportunities for people to talk and discover, through their interaction, insights that may be crucial to their jobs, and to the organization's performance.

Method 6: After-action reviews

This helpful intervention is one that we at GM learned from the US Army. It is composed of five simple questions:

- What was the intent?
- What actually happened?
- What can we learn from this?
- What action is required?
- Whom do we need to tell?

The US Army asks these questions after all military events – anything from an invasion to a public address. We introduced this technique at GM not as a mandate but in the spirit of giving everyone one more tool that is easy to use. I have seen it employed by leaders eager to debrief after a key meeting, engineers wishing to assess the merits of a vehicle test drive, and personnel executives hoping to pilot a new vacation policy. It has no administrative overhead, and it can take as little as thirty minutes to implement. But, like most learning methods, it still requires discipline.

Method 7: Learning observers

This intervention is built on the belief that we are all too busy to learn. We introduced this concept into the busiest part of our operation: new vehicle design and development. Leading the development of a new vehicle is overwhelming – it involves juggling lots of events, coordinating the stakeholders, and keeping to a tight schedule. Even with all of these responsibilities, a program leader also has an obligation to figure out what her team has learned so that she can pass this knowledge on to other teams.

To help the process, GM developed a special team of analysts to perform the role of learning observers, who capture observations, feed them back to the team, sort out the implications, and recommend changes where appropriate. Those best suited to the role are middle managers on their way up the ladder, who will gain new insights by studying the system but are seasoned enough to understand the fundamentals of the operation. Being a learning observer is not an easy task; it requires working like a journalist, knowing the subject well enough to describe accurately what is going on, and having the analytical skills to dig deep into the situation – all the while describing it in an objective

fashion. This role was instrumental in helping the organization understand the difference between the ideal way to develop a vehicle (the way
that looks right on paper) and the way vehicles are actually made.

Method 8: Global task teams

This concept brings together potential executives from various organizational functions and regions for a two- to three-month assignment.
The team's charge is to learn more about the company and to explore
each member's leadership potential while developing a recommendation regarding a complex, strategic issue.

For example, one team was asked to deal with the issue of what
vehicle GM should introduce into India. Given the Indian economy,
GM believed at first that there might be a market for a village fleet, a
mixture of vehicles sold to an entire village. Learning in this particular
case happened in two phases. First, the team explored the alternative
scenarios that might lie behind what was presented as the issue (how
to increase vehicle sales in India); then, they defined the problem (how
to provide low-cost transportation while meeting customers' cultural
needs). Our eight-member team had access to all the information and
experts in the company, so they could easily discover what GM already
knew about the subject. They also traveled to India with a facilitator
to further define the problem.

Their findings? Even though there is little money in India and large
extended families, most people wanted to own a vehicle. Our team
returned with a very specific recommendation to design a vehicle that
would be smaller than current vehicles but larger than a bicycle.

This process, known as "action learning," requires a specific problem plus access to what the company already knows, coupled with
a process that promotes creativity and learning. Action learning has
been successful at GM because it provides senior executives with high-
quality recommendations and gives future leaders a broader understanding of how the company functions. In our experience, both sides
have been pleased with the process.

Method 9: Decision-making

GM has also experimented with learning through decision-making,
using Russ Ackoff's Management Learning and Adaptation Model,
which shows the components of decision-making, their interactions,

Organizational learning, adaptation, and management

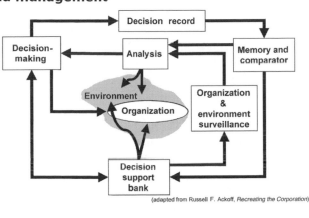

(adapted from Russell F. Ackoff, *Recreating the Corporation*)

Figure 9.1. Russ Ackoff's Management Learning and Adaptation Model.

and how to learn and adapt while implementing the decisions. Key to this model is a leader who wants to improve decision-making and has the discipline to monitor the execution of decisions, as well as an environment where there is no fear of reprisal should it become clear that a decision was less than ideal.

This model requires capturing the details of a decision when it is made: the names of the decision-makers, the underlying assumptions (those variables outside the control of the implementers that could affect implementation), the deliverables, and the time-frame. The model also requires monitoring the implementation and the impact of the decision. It is only with this sort of system that leaders can truly understand the impact of their decisions and thereby gain insight into how future ones can be more effective.

GM has experimented with Ackoff's model in marketing and product development. The marketing division, for example, tracked the impact of incentives on vehicle sales. Does creating sales incentives actually increase the number of sales or does it simply pull ahead sales that would have occurred at a later date? By capturing multiple decisions to add incentives and then monitoring the impact on sales, leaders gained greater insight on the number of pull-ahead sales versus sales that would never have been made without the incentive. In another example, monitoring the decisions made during the development of new vehicles revealed to the vice-presidents how their reluctance to choose a location for the plant and decide which powertrain to use often delayed the programs. This documentation enabled the senior leaders to see that their need for flexibility in decision-making was not compatible with the discipline required by the vehicle execution process.

Conclusion

Ten years after adopting these learning methods, GM's performance has improved significantly. No single factor is the cause, yet few would quibble that a focus on continued learning was a major contributor.

Beginning in the mid 1990s, the change in operating performance at GM has been nothing short of phenomenal. Improvement rates in key areas such as employee safety, product quality, and organizational productivity have been 20 to 60 percent per year. According to many metrics, GM is now the best in the industry. Without the spirit and understanding of learning, along with the attendant structure, process, and discipline, these improvements would not have been possible.

As I move on from GM, I am convinced that a great deal of learning occurs within the for-profit sector. GM is driven by the need to improve its performance continually. It understands the relationship between learning and closing performance gaps. Yet I am concerned that more educational institutions are not stepping up to help develop processes for learning in the business sector. There are still many questions that must be answered to foster a dynamic learning environment.

For instance, what would an organization look like if it truly modeled a vibrant, ever learning company? The organizational qualities Arie De Geus describes in *The Living Company* come close, but do we really know how a company should be organized to support learning?[2] I have outlined some of the things we tried at GM, but I have to acknowledge that we are remiss in not being able to lay out for a CEO a blueprint for creating an information system that supports organizational learning.

[2] A. De Geus, *The Living Company* (Boston: Harvard Business School Press, 1997).

Also, who owns the learning process within an organization? Do CEOs give much thought to the systems by which their companies continue to get smarter? Should they? If not CEOs, who?

Where are the resources that help organizations establish a taxonomy of information to support organizational learning? Yes, there are information technologists to set up the technology, and these people will happily share an opinion on the taxonomy, but where are the unbiased conceptual experts who understand the dynamics of learning and how to organize information for a large organization?

Which information technology is right for which learning situation? In some cases, there is one correct answer, and in others, a worker needs a breadth of alternatives from which to choose. When is the cost of information technology worth the return in learning and when is it a distraction? The computer age has provided the opportunity for accelerated learning, but we must continue to experiment to learn how to use it most effectively.

GM is committed to continually learning, continually getting smarter, continually improving its performance. Its commitment to human safety and vehicle quality is based on rigorous experimentation and testing. GM does not rehearse its plans in a courtroom, nor does it have the luxury of reviewing a simple set of notes each night or reconstructing its story from end to beginning. But we do study trends, we do have leaders with the discipline to document and learn from our past, and we do have a spirit of inquiry that drives experimentation.

Learning is a complex, dynamic, multidimensional process that includes information technology, learning methods, and business and leadership processes. Business is a complex, dynamic, multidimensional process that requires efficiency and effectiveness.

The worlds of learning and business must move closer together. I can only hope that out of this will emerge an academia that engages with industry to look at learning, business, and information technology not as separate entities but as entities working together. A more conscious effort by academia to bring the diverse tools and methods for learning into the business world can only increase our efforts to discover the most effective and efficient methods of continually improving the quality of services for our customers.

10 | *The real and appropriate role of technology to create a learning culture*

MARC J. ROSENBERG

Y O U may have heard that classroom training is dead, that learning through technology is faster, cheaper, and better. Forget the classroom – just plug in and learn, anytime and anywhere. I hear that all the time. But I also hear that the era of technology-based learning is over, gone with the bursting of the high-tech bubble. Which of these pronouncements is true?

The truth lies somewhere in the middle. Managers and trainers alike have long hoped that technology could be a panacea for organizational and business problems. Just the availability of new learning technology is often seen as a reason for using it. But as we all get more comfortable and experienced with technology, we have come to understand that it is a tool for organizational learning, not its solution. Simply going from classroom training to online learning or from a personal coach to an online information repository does not guarantee more or better learning. In fact, when used inappropriately, technology can be a hindrance – and a costly one.

Yet there is a myriad of appropriate and highly beneficial roles for learning technology. To understand how technology can be used to facilitate learning, it is important to look beyond traditional classroom-training perspectives. As important as training is, it is just one way to facilitate learning, and just one way to use technology in that effort.

This chapter looks at ways to use learning technology by examining how people learn, every day, and the tools they use to facilitate their learning. It introduces a framework for creating a learning enterprise supported by five interdependent pillars: training, knowledge management, communities of practice, performance support, and talent alignment. All of these pillars are essential for maintaining an open learning culture. To ignore even one is to impair individual and organizational performance. And technology, used appropriately, strengthens each pillar, imparting integrity to the entire structure, like rebar in concrete.

The successful use of technology in creating a learning culture depends less on employing the latest bells and whistles of hardware and software, and more on addressing the learning requirements at hand. The future of learning technology is full of promise and uncertainty. Charting its trajectory is not easy, though, as we can see from its shaky past.

Some historical perspective

Although computer-based training has been around in various forms for more than thirty years, business leaders, as well as corporate training leaders, have always considered it marginal. For the most part, training organizations and a few programs in higher education institutions have experimented with new hardware and software, putting out an occasional course that promised to revolutionize organizational learning only to find that compensating for different operating systems – and different versions of those systems – required multiple releases of the same product. Furthermore, the content of these courses needed to be updated continually, and development cycles were long. But even more important, the use of technology for learning represented a radical departure for the people making the decisions – who had all been trained in a more traditional way and had no experience with learning technology. Thus, funding and resources for training, including personnel and facilities, were focused overwhelmingly on recreating the school environment within the corporation. So, in light of the technological hurdles and the shortage of success stories, demand, and role models, it is no wonder that classroom training continued to dominate the learning landscape.

Then the Internet was born. All at once, interoperability issues disappeared; all you needed was a browser. And because programs could be updated instantly, online training could keep up with the pace of change. This created a great economic incentive for organizations to get into e-learning, and training organizations followed suit. Investment flowed into dozens of companies that built libraries of thousands of courses. Learning management systems became the essential tool for training organizations eager to do with online training what they had done with classroom training: become a one-stop shop for training needs throughout the enterprise. The same organizations that once touted their classroom offerings now wanted to put much of them online. Some companies put all or part of their operations in the hands of third-party suppliers. Content was purchased by the bucket-ful, loaded onto servers, and made available to all. Everyone operated on the assumption that if a little online training was good, more must be better.

After the economic boom of the 1990s, economies around the world began struggling, which caused training budgets to be slashed and gave rise to deeper concerns. For the first time in more than a decade, organi-zations were questioning not only the value of technology-based learn-ing but also the value of training in general. Some companies eliminated or outsourced entire training departments. Others cut them back so severely that they have become, in effect, inoperative. Of course, many companies have maintained their commitment to training in all forms. But there is no doubt that the overselling of learning technology, com-bined with new economic realities, has dealt the training industry a severe blow.

What is the proper role of technology in learning?

Now that the giddiness over learning technology has subsided, corpora-tions – not just training departments – are asking, what next? Nobody assumes that learning is inconsequential or that technology does not have a role to play. But more sober and clearer thinking may make this a great time to reconsider its role.

Slowly, but certainly, four new realities are emerging that are funda-mentally changing the learning landscape:

(1) *Believing that face-to-face classroom training is disappearing is as misguided as thinking that the Internet is a passing craze.* The class-room will continue to be critical to any learning strategy. It provides a place where people can interact, experiment, collaborate, and create. And while all this is possible online, the classroom's (or laboratory's) unique nature provides a great environment for these activities. In addi-tion, there will always be times when a live, expert instructor is essential to explain, observe, guide, and give feedback.

(2) *Technology-based learning is here to stay.* Technology enables orga-nizations to conquer both time and location in the delivery of skill and knowledge. It allows constant content updating and facilitates

the connectivity of people separated by time zones and organizational boundaries. Thus, both traditional and online training will play significant roles in the future of learning. The key, of course, will be determining when each should be used.

(3) *Justifying the expense of learning technology is no longer a cakewalk*. Even the argument that technology can save money in the long run may not be enough if the performance results are not there. These concerns will shift the criteria for success from educational results ("Did they learn?") to performance results ("What can they do and how will that help the business?").

(4) *Organizational learning is facilitated through strategies and techniques that go far beyond training*. The learning needs of individuals and organizations have never been fulfilled by training alone. Learning and learning technology belong not just in the classroom but in other workplace settings, as well as at home, in hotel rooms – anywhere people do their work.

The surety of hindsight enables us to see the wrong steps we have taken in the past, and these four realities enable us to see the future in a new way. The role of technology in learning requires us to rethink the nature of organizational learning itself.

Learning and training are different

Face it. Training cannot fulfill all learning needs. Sometimes we learn in a classroom, but we also learn in many other ways. Learning and training are not synonymous. Think about it this way: the average employee spends about ten days a year, less than 4 percent of his or her work time, in formal training. How do employees learn during the other 96 percent of the time they are on the job? They learn informally by talking with other people and watching them perform. They also learn from documents and online information, from the news media, and from simple trial and error.

   If we think of training and learning as one and the same, we tend to see learning technology as a reflection of the training or instructional model. Classroom courses become online courses. Distance learning classes often look the same as traditional classes. Trainers become focused on computer-based training, complete with lessons, modules, tests, and grades. This drives our thinking about learning management and brings issues of enrollment, tracking, and completions to the top of our to-do list. We focus on that 4 percent of formal training and, unfortunately, abdicate our responsibility the other 96 percent of the time.

But learning and training *are* different. Learning is an *internal* process whereby we take in information and then translate it into knowledge, skills, and capabilities. It is something we all do all the time, like breathing. Training, on the other hand, is one of many ways to facilitate learning, an *external* experience we go through using a structured approach called instruction. In addition, training has generally focused on specific job or task-based skills, like typing a letter or welding, while education – another way to facilitate learning – has broader aims, focusing on long-term, enduring capabilities. If we can decouple learning and training – if we can see training as just one way to learn – then the opportunities for learning technology increase substantially, and its role changes dramatically.

The learning enterprise

Beyond the differences between learning and training, there are also differences between individual and organizational learning. Traditionally, learning efforts have focused on individuals. Now we must expand our focus to include the whole enterprise.

A learning enterprise is a high-performing organization with a culture that allows knowledge to grow and flow freely across departmental, geographic, and hierarchical boundaries so that it can be shared and made actionable. It is an organization in which this knowledge is systematically and efficiently applied for valued purposes, such as business growth, operational improvement, product development, new market entry, defense against competitors, customer satisfaction, and the enhancement of employee performance, as individuals and as teams.

There are also important distinctions among the places where learning takes place. Certainly, the classroom is an important venue, but we can no longer view it as the sole bastion of learning, and we can no longer view learning technology as applied only to training settings. In a learning enterprise, technology must be able seamlessly to cross the line between formal and informal learning every day, for everyone.

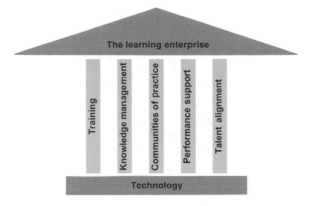

Figure 10.1. The five pillars of the learning enterprise are strengthened by technology to support both individual and organizational learning, anytime and anywhere.

With the recognition that learning is more than just training, that individual learning is less effective without organizational learning, and that more learning goes on in the workplace than in the classroom, the stage is set for establishing the proper role of technology.

A framework for examining the role of technology in learning

A learning enterprise is supported by five pillars: training, knowledge management, communities of practice, performance support, and talent alignment. All must work in harmony to create a learning culture. To understand the proper role of technology in support of learning, we will examine how it is applied across this framework (Figure 10.1).

Training

Mention the word "learning" to most businesspeople and they will immediately associate it with training. Use it with academics, and they will likely focus on school. If the promise of a learning culture is to be realized, and the contributions of technology to that culture are to be meaningful, this perspective needs serious rethinking. Yet there is no denying that as one of the major and most familiar pillars of the learning enterprise, training – online or in the classroom – plays a major role.

As I have already noted, formal training accounts for only about 4 percent of an employee's total work time. But it is by far the most common and recognizable way to facilitate learning. It seems appropriate, therefore, to tackle the role of training first so that once this 4 percent is done well, we can address learning during the other 96 percent of the employee's work life. Online training can reach people who are dispersed geographically, and it allows very large numbers of people to participate in a course through an automated, self-paced (asynchronous) mode. This can markedly improve the efficiency of training, enabling more instruction to be delivered to more people at a lower cost. Furthermore, being able to reach more people quickly can be a significant strategic advantage. Many companies have not been able to train their sales force, customer service representatives, product developers, and others quickly enough to meet ever changing competitive threats or consumer needs, or to take advantage of innovations.

When the workforce can learn at a far faster pace through technology, the competitive advantage, in the form of a shorter time to competency, is self-evident. And the ability to update asynchronous training the moment the content changes increases the organization's ability to meet the needs of dispersed people who rely on accurate content to do their jobs. Using technology to deliver a consistent instructional program to all who need it can ensure that no critical content falls through the cracks.

Here is a good example. When the US government had to train tens of thousands of airport security personnel for the Transportation Security Administration, it required broad reach, near impossible speed, the ability to update the learning as new procedures were developed, and a highly consistent instructional program. Online training was the only way to go.

Even more interesting, technology provides an opportunity to depict more authentic scenarios in a training situation. From the days when film and video were introduced into the classroom, we have known that it is possible to bring the outside world into the training environment. Now, new learning technologies enable us to increase that benefit manyfold. Through the power and creativity of simulations and the ubiquitous nature of the Internet, we can create scenarios that rival the real world, making learning more relevant, more effective, and, in many cases, more fun. Finally, we are getting better at using technology to observe students' performance and provide, electronically, the kind of high-quality feedback and coaching that often seem more valuable than the course content itself. A hotel chain, for example, chose to train its front-desk personnel, in the critical area of customer service, not through a lecture or even an online course. They chose a creative, game-based simulation in which individual scenarios are presented to the learner, who earns "applause" for choosing the right solution. And if the system detects inappropriate selections, an online coach appears with additional, reinforcing content.

Of course, technology is not always applied well in training. Building technology-based training is hard and complex. If the message of the lesson is not clear, there is no instructor to clear up the confusion. A greater variety of questions and reactions from students must be anticipated and built into the product, and more effort must be made to focus on learners' specific interests and needs.

And technology is not always applied to the right training need. Learning technology applied to the wrong need can inhibit rather than accentuate learning and may in fact be responsible for the perception that technology does not work. Organizations that rush to put all training on the Web risk weakening the overall training program in the name of cost savings (which may be elusive if job performance or business results suffer). Think about employee orientation, for example. One argument suggests that orientation programs are ideal for online training. The content is fairly stable and relatively simple. And since most new hires will need some form of orientation, the audience may be large enough to justify it. A brewing company, for example, put a lot of their new-hire orientation online, enabling people to get up to speed faster than if they had to wait for an orientation class. In fact, some orientation materials were sent to prospective employees' homes so that they could get a sense of a life of making beer. This resulted in some prospects dropping out early, before the company had invested much in them.

But a counterargument is just as powerful. Leave orientation programs in the classroom (the brewery might argue, "How can they understand the business if they can't smell the beer?"). There is validity in the need for employees to bond with their peers and begin working together as a team. Here is a story from the consulting industry. A professional services firm that recruited dozens of MBAs from around the country used classroom-based orientation training so that new hires could build relationships that would help them survive the somewhat nomadic life of a consultant. Years later, many employees still rely on other members of their "start class" for advice and counsel even though they may see them only a few times a year.

Synchronous instructor-led training, delivered over the Internet, can allow people to "attend class" at a distance, decreasing costs and expanding reach. Of course, there are times when more traditional classroom solutions are best. For example, when the content is so unstable that only a few people know it, it may be best to put those key "teachers" in the same room as the people who need their knowledge. In addition, live instructors can do more than just deliver content. In the traditional classroom mode, they can also observe performance and offer corrective feedback. They can facilitate in-depth discussions, set the stage for experimentation, and help learners deal with failures and risk. Thus, in most training situations, the optimal solution will certainly be a combination of online (asynchronous and synchronous) and classroom instruction.

So now we have accounted for the 4 percent of the work year when people are in training. This is where discussions on learning technology often end. But what about the rest of the time, when people are on the job? How should learning technology be used in call centers, on the factory floor, at the customer's location, in the executive suite, or at home?

If we believe that learning takes place all the time, in all roles, functions, and locations where work is performed, then we must look beyond training for approaches that fit these situations. This brings up another crucial point. Until now, I have referred to technology-based training as "online training," not "e-learning," as has become common practice. The reason is clear: if learning extends beyond the training function, then e-learning must also. E-learning is more than online training, or "e-training." It includes online training but goes way beyond to include three additional pillars of a learning enterprise: knowledge management, communities of practice, and performance support.

Knowledge management

Knowledge management is the creation, archiving, and sharing of valued information, expertise, and insight within and across communities of people and organizations with similar interests and needs, the goal of which is to build competitive advantage. Essentially, it is getting information from those who have it to those who need it. It enables organizations to codify their intellectual capital and store it in a way that allows people to find and make use of it. But more than that, knowledge management also focuses on creating opportunities for collaboration between individuals and teams. This helps organizations get a better handle on the critical questions, "Who is doing what?" and "Who knows what?"[1]

Here is a good example of knowledge management in action. A telecommunications company was competing for a global contract from an international bank. A team of nearly a hundred of the most experienced technical specialists and salespeople was assembled and deployed worldwide. These people were already well trained – the best and brightest in the organization. But they needed accurate, real-time information about products, competitors, and the bank. By knowing more, they could be faster. And by being faster, they could win the contract.

The company recognized that information, available to the right people at the right time and in the right context, would provide a competitive advantage. They turned to knowledge management. A small group of product and industry specialists established a "knowledge center" at corporate headquarters. From there, updates on products and competitors, along with news about the industry and the bank, were sent to the field teams twice a day. So good and so timely was the information that, in many cases, salespeople knew more about the bank's business than the bank did. They were able to respond to product and pricing objections because they had good intelligence on competitors' activities and product updates. In addition, everyone on the global team fed raw intelligence back to the knowledge center on a daily basis. This knowledge was edited and reformatted according to pre-approved standards and templates, and then turned around within a day and sent back to the field The result was a successful sale, after which the bank commented on how thoroughly the sales team "knew" the organization.

Knowledge management helps build a learning enterprise. Knowledge repositories become its collective intelligence – and memory. In the preceding example, knowledge management facilitated learning in a way no training strategy could have. Updates were almost

---

[1] Communities are an essential component of knowledge management but are also important on their own. Therefore, they are treated here separately, immediately following the knowledge management section.

instantaneous, so everyone had accurate information. Teamwork was fostered as all the salespeople and technical specialists submitted and accessed information in the same way. Knowledge-sharing was rewarded. Response time was significantly reduced, people learned what they needed to learn fast, and business was secured.

Of course, the information strategy had to be carefully thought out. Although the sales team did not use an overly elaborate knowledge management system, it did employ technology as an integral and critical part of its approach. E-mail and secure websites were the main vehicles for information-sharing across the globally deployed sales team. While templates were used to create content, they were fairly simple and easy to use. Even that old-fashioned technology – the telephone – was used to keep everyone in touch. Based on this success, the company's knowledge management system was scaled up and enhanced so that it now contributes substantially to the learning of everyone in the sales organization. Classroom training still plays a major role, and online training is growing significantly, but there is a fundamental recognition that beyond courseware, technology can help people learn though direct, timely access to essential information. In fact, a large part of the training program is designed to teach employees how to use and rely on the knowledge management system.

For anyone who has worked with huge binders of outdated documentation and has tried to keep up with color-coded page updates, new knowledge management approaches have been nothing short of a revolution in information management and distribution, as well as a revolution in learning, because of their ability to update a broadly distributed workforce, and keep content up to date in real time. When information is easier to find and more accurate, more people will use and learn from it. We all know this from our daily use of the Internet. We learn from a host of websites when we shop for a car, seek medical advice, make investment decisions, and more. And although we do not think about it, we favor the sites where knowledge management technologies and practices help us gather information more easily and with greater confidence.

Communities of practice

We do not learn just from courses and information repositories; we also learn with and through others. When training and knowledge

management are implemented in ways that allow everyone to participate, the effect is to democratize knowledge in the organization, creating a culture that supports more collaborative work and collaborative
learning.

We have been pretty successful at making training more interactive
and collaborative. But what happens outside the classroom? In conference rooms, at lunch, over the phone, and in many other ways, people
collaborate. This is nothing new; working together is not only good
business, it is human nature. When people get together to solve a problem, accomplish a task, evaluate a situation, or formulate a plan, they
learn from each other. They take these experiences to their next meeting
or project – and learn even more as they go along.

Sometimes, one group of people does not know what other groups
are doing. Another team – across the hall or around the world – might
be doing the same work, perhaps better or perhaps worse. The work
that one group sets out to do may have already been done, even implemented, and nobody in the group even knows. This redundancy of
effort slows innovation, adds cost, and puts the organization at a business disadvantage. Online collaboration tools help organizations eliminate redundancy by overcoming time and distance. They make the
benefits of water-cooler or lunch-table conversations available more
quickly to more people, improving everyone's awareness of what is
going on.

If we encourage and facilitate collaboration across the business,
we can enhance organizational learning tremendously. Of course, this
requires the leadership and culture that allow knowledge and idea sharing to flourish. Collaboration often takes the form of one or more
knowledge networks, which are usually informal associations of people who come together for the purpose of sharing specific information.
It is not uncommon to hear an employee say something like, "I have
three people I can call when I have a problem doing X," or, "Whenever I want to know the latest information about Y, I can e-mail these
two people." However, if the relationship is more formal and involves,
perhaps, membership in a group of practitioners, or when a group is
formed to achieve a specific and shared objective or to develop specific
knowledge, a community of practice is born.

Communities of practice provide opportunities for people with similar interests and needs – wherever they are – to work with and learn
from each other. Such communities can be vertical or horizontal, and

people are often members of more than one. Vertical communities often reflect organizational charts, or subsets of organizations. Sales and IT departments are examples of vertical communities. In the sales organization, for instance, the vertical community might include the sales vice-president at the top, the branch managers, the sales force itself, plus all the support people in the sales organization. These might include sales-specific IT support staff, customer service representatives (if part of the sales team), technical specialists who support account executives, secretaries, trainers, and others.

Horizontal communities reflect more of a professional affiliation or interest. Within a company, all executives – or all scientists, programmers, and account executives – might form horizontal communities of practice. For example, a decentralized global bank operated with a regional organizational structure, so there were, in a sense, a variety of vertical communities within this structure. Each region, for instance, had its own IT staff. It soon became apparent that each IT group was reinventing the wheel, or creating "one-off" solutions that, while useful in one region, were useless in the others. The bank did not want to abandon its regional structure, but it did want to help everyone understand what everyone else was doing. By establishing horizontal communities of practice around programming, IT support, and project management, it became far easier for similar people in different regions to communicate with one another about their work. Over time, redundancy was reduced and teamwork increased.

Sometimes, horizontal communities extend beyond the walls of a company. Java programmers from many companies meet through javasoft.com. The site, from Sun Microsystems, provides training, knowledge repositories, communities of practice, tools, and other resources for Java developers, wherever they are. So powerful and popular is this site that one company abandoned its efforts to create an internal community and instead began referring people to the javasoft site. E-learning professionals can experience a similar horizontal community through the E-Learning Guild.

Communities are sometimes permanent, giving members an opportunity for long-term collaborative work and learning. However, there are many situations in which communities of practice might form for a short-term purpose and then dissolve. In the earlier example of the telecommunications company, the sales team was assembled to pursue a specific business opportunity. When the deal closed, that community of practice was dissolved.

In the health arena, online communities have always been important to people who need to share information on medical issues, especially those that affect small groups in the general population. Consumer support groups can form online, and information about new treatments can be shared quickly. Companies are also gathering their customers into communities of practice in order to provide special services, allow people who own similar products to share ideas about new ways to use them, and solicit in-depth feedback.

Collaboration technologies like e-mail, chat rooms, and discussion boards are important, but they are not sufficient to establish a successful community of practice. Online communities need tools to manage membership and access to community content. Establishing a community of practice must be easy enough to warrant the effort, but not so easy that too many are formed and they cannot all be managed. If someone wants to form a community of practice that will be of value to the organization, they should be able to do it fairly easily, without so much work as to discourage them. But no organization can manage hundreds of communities if they are too similar to one another, making it hard to discern the specific value of each. This balance is hard to achieve, especially if the idea of communities "takes off" in the organization, but it must be maintained.

Furthermore, the content associated with the community's work should either reside within the community or be easily accessible. It makes little sense for people to be part of a community of practice that allows them to collaborate in a secure, semi-private, or exclusive way if the content they create and work with is not under the community's control. Security is also an important issue, as many communities are formed to work on special or proprietary projects that may require an added layer of access protection. Finally, and perhaps most important, communities need enough participation and valued content to encourage people to join and contribute. Designating a community leader or facilitator, either from within or outside the membership, to monitor and keep the community engaged, is critical.

New community-building technologies that focus on communications, membership management, and document- and application-sharing foster collaboration across time and distance. They enable people to share insights and ideas faster than before. Innovations and best practices that were once hidden are more readily discovered and, over time, are codified into the knowledge base of the organization. In the learning enterprise, this cycle of collaboration, best practice development, and broad knowledge distribution makes for powerful learning.

Essential to the success of any knowledge network or community of practice, and to knowledge management and training efforts in general, is the availability of experts and expertise. We constantly rely on the expertise of others, whether they are in the next office or on the other side of the world. Sometimes our own social network is all we need. But many times, we do not know who really is an expert and who is not. We do not know where the best experts are or how to reach them. Most important, our level of confidence in what we hear often varies with our personal level of trust in the source.

Access to experts and expertise can be more formal. In a community of practice, experts are likely to emerge either as resources or community leaders. They may be elected or appointed, but in almost all successful communities, they become collaboration facilitators, and they may also become knowledge "gatekeepers," who certify content before it is disseminated to the rest of the group. Thus the expert can be not just a knowledgeable person but a knowledge leader.

If there were no experts, nothing of value could be accomplished, and learning would be very difficult. Even if we know who the experts are, they may not have time to help us. And some people who are indeed experts either do not know that they are or shy away from identifying themselves because they fear they will be inundated with requests for help. Anyone who has ever tried to develop a course or write a technical document knows how hard it is to find and hold on to a true subject-matter expert.

Technology is offering some solutions. Online directories containing more than just contact information help people identify the right person to talk to. The ability to use knowledge networks and communities of practice to disseminate expertise makes it easier to support larger numbers of people who need help. This is why, in the e-commerce world, many companies use knowledge bases and frequently asked questions to help customers, instead of asking them to call the help desk and wait on hold – sometimes for hours (which is also more expensive). When you equip an online expert database with enough content at the right level of detail, and make it easy enough to use, most people will *prefer* to consult it, seeking out the author only as a last resort. However, if the content of an expert knowledge base is so robust that users have to search too many levels of detail or so simple that they cannot get their questions answered satisfactorily, or if it is not organized the way users think about the content, they will likely abandon it. So knowledge structures, navigation, and searching take on additional importance.

The idea of experts and expertise does not stop with simply providing explicit business or technical knowledge. Expertise is also manifested in coaching and mentoring. In these roles, experts are more than a source of knowledge; they are also advisers who are charged with providing guidance, corrective feedback, and performance assessment. Even more challenging is providing the tacit knowledge that comes not just with expertise but also with experience. The ability of experts, coaches, and mentors to put an experiential context around the knowledge they share often increases its value significantly. Here, online storytelling and case studies might be combined with old-fashioned personal interaction.

Technology-supported expertise within a learning enterprise will likely be a combination of access to the right expert person or group and to a well-designed knowledge base authored by experts. It may also include emerging tools that scan documents and communications, such as e-mails, to discover hidden expertise. But none of this will matter if experts do not step up and identify themselves. Do they have the time to serve in this role or are they told this is just one more responsibility on top of their already heavy workload? Are they appropriately recognized for doing it? Are there negative consequences for doing this, such as being blamed if their advice does not work? These issues should not be dismissed lightly. For all the benefits of learning technology, a learning culture can be stopped dead in its tracks unless people see something positive in it for them.

A knowledge network or community of practice succeeds because the people involved believe that collaboration, either informal or formal, helps them do their jobs better and more easily. But the likelihood of success is enhanced even further when peer interactions are augmented by access to experts and when an incentive program is in place that encourages not only membership but also active participation and contribution.

Performance support

Many people still think they need the help of a tax expert to file their returns. But look at the millions of people who are filing their returns without hiring a professional. How do they do it? TurboTax, Tax Cut, and other similar tools guide users through the tax return process and make it easier in many ways. They hide unnecessary information unless or until it becomes necessary. They do the math behind the scenes. They ask questions and try to anticipate users' problems. They provide more logical ways to navigate the process and translate tax jargon into language that's easier to understand. Automatic links to specific websites ensure that the software is updated if the tax code changes (without requiring the user to read the tax code!). Finally, users can work on their returns in one sitting or sporadically over a few months, and, of course, at any time of the day, making the process not just easier but also more convenient and accurate.

That is an example of performance support, the fourth pillar in the learning enterprise framework. The idea is that with the right support, people can perform at a higher level than they would have been capable of on their own. Performance support has been around for a while, in the form of job aids and trouble-shooting guides, for instance. But the advent of technology has enabled more complex tasks to be handled through an electronic performance-support system (EPSS). These systems run the gamut from end-user software, like TurboTax, to complex manufacturing systems (enabling one skilled operator to run an elaborate process), customer care and customer relationship management (CRM), and project management systems that can change the very nature of how a job is done or how an organization works.

Is EPSS a learning technology? Some argue that if performance support replaces human performance by doing the task for the user, learning does not occur. If performance is what matters, and there is improvement without learning, that is okay. In fact, from a productivity perspective, it may even be better.

But others claim that learning is an outcome of using performance support. TurboTax may hide the complexities of the tax return process, but it provides a more detailed analysis of the filer's financial state in some ways, embedding the expertise of the professional tax preparer in the software. Thus, different and perhaps more valuable learning occurs; as people learn more about their finances, they can take more appropriate actions to mange them.

In business settings, such as customer care, representatives cannot know everything they need to know about a company's products, prices, features, and promotions. So this information is embedded in an EPSS. Certainly, representatives have to learn to use the system, but because the system improves productivity, they have time to master new skills, such as upselling or providing a higher level of service.

In a learning enterprise, complex tasks that are well defined and well tested, or tasks that have become repetitive or menial, are great candidates for performance support. If workers have access to performance support for such tasks, they will have more time to learn new things. Then the process begins anew. For example, early versions of word processing software included computer-based training to teach people how to use it. But as the programs have become easier to use, the amount of training required has dropped considerably and has been replaced by better help systems and other tools that can automate key functions. This can reduce the need for training or perhaps redirect the excess training capacity to higher-level skills, such as helping people become better writers. Thus, performance support is about continually reinventing how work gets done and shifting learning resources toward new and likely more complex opportunities.

Talent alignment

There is no value in training, knowledge management, communities of practice, or performance support if these tools are not targeted to the right people, at the right time, for the right purpose, and at the right depth. Training that comes too late or is inappropriate for the audience is wasted (what would happen if advanced technical training was given to salespeople who did not have basic technology skills?). Knowledge resources that are too detailed or not detailed enough will be useless to those who need the right information, right away (how would executives react if they asked for a product briefing and got 200 pages of technical specs?). While communities work well when they attract people with common interests, they are a disaster if members do not know who is or should be in the community (would members of an R&D team really want to share their research if they did not know or trust the people who would have access to it?) or if they themselves do not know which community to join. If the experts who teach courses, create knowledge, or facilitate collaboration do not know whom they are serving, they are apt to miss the mark in terms of how much information to provide (ever ask a simple question and get an answer that was so complex you could not use it?). And although performance support systems can mitigate the need for training, they cannot be of much value if the users are not competent enough to use them (ever notice what PowerPoint presentations look like when designed by people who do not understand the fundamentals of visual communication?).

For all of these tools to work, they must be aligned with the people and groups using them. This means knowing a lot about the people in an organization. Most companies have lots of information about their employees – information from when they joined the organization, about their careers and competencies, about the training they have taken, the work they have done, performance reviews, certifications, etc. The problem is that this knowledge is often siloed in the HR organization, making it difficult for a complete picture of the individual to be formed. In other situations, the information may be tucked away so deeply in a personnel file that it is difficult to find and woefully inaccurate. Because of this, it is no surprise that people are often assigned to jobs they are not qualified for, or are too qualified for. The inaccessibility and the inaccuracy of this information also makes it very difficult for individuals to nominate themselves or volunteer for new and unique assignments, or to serve as expert resources. And, perhaps most important, the inability of an organization to understand strengths and weaknesses as they relate to the capabilities and readiness of its workforce almost always leads to rising costs, a misallocation of resources, and a loss of competitive advantage.

Organizations that strive to achieve a learning culture must, therefore, establish strong and informed links with the talent that is in them. Advances in human resources technology have been helpful. Almost everyone agrees that it is important to understand the skills that people bring to the job so that resources can be aligned to support them. In the past, employees' competencies, usually in the form of résumés or lists of skills, were detailed in large binders that were almost never opened, primarily because they were too massive and difficult to use, and because they were often out of date before the ink was dry. Today, employee capabilities are online, can be easily updated, and can be integrated into training plans so that each individual can have a personalized learning path. More than ever, technology is helping companies develop more accurate profiles of their people and the internal organizations for which they work. This employee intelligence helps the organization position its talent in the most appropriate, high-value roles and deal more effectively with performance gaps.

Knowledge management and community tools can be designed to "read" these profiles and provide the right level of content or point to the right community of practice. Of course, such profiles can provide only a macro view of an individual. Ultimately, it is still the role of the manager or supervisor to assess a person's readiness for a particular job or role as well as his or her level of performance. For example, electronic résumés have provided organizations with a more efficient first-level screening process, but no selection decision should be made on the basis of this process alone. So while technology can help identify and sort people according to skills and other factors, it cannot do this alone. Understanding this limitation will help human resource and line organizations use these technologies appropriately.

Using technology to integrate talent information with the other pillars of a learning enterprise has other important advantages. In recruiting, an organization can better determine when to hire skilled people and thus reduce the need for training and other resources, and when to hire less experienced individuals and invest in the learning components they will need. In staffing, a learning enterprise will have a much better view of the capabilities of its employees and its internal organizations, enabling it to be more responsive in deploying – and redeploying – these resources. In succession planning, a learning enterprise will be able to assess more confidently its "bench strength," increasing its ability to deploy talent to areas of the business that are weak. This coordination of talent and learning adds value by increasing the precision with which learning resources can be applied.

Of all the aspects of building a learning culture, talent alignment may be the least recognized. Yet without it, investment in the other pillars of the learning enterprise can yield lackluster returns, and the learning culture may stagnate. The technology within evolving human resource and performance management systems will do little if the information is not used to make sure people are matched with the resources they need.

Synchronization is the key

No single pillar of a learning enterprise – not training or knowledge management, or any of the other tools – can support a learning culture independently. It is the combination, or synchronization, of these resources, and the synchronization of the tools and technologies they use, that add the greatest value.

We can begin with training, using technology to enhance the authenticity of the content and the efficiency of its delivery, and then use knowledge management to keep people current for the fifty weeks a year they are not in class. We then put a more human aspect on all of this through communities of practice, in which people share what they know, anytime and anywhere. Technology can also help identify and provide access to experts, who not only develop content but also serve as coaches and mentors for individuals and teams. In a learning enterprise, authoring a course or creating other forms of intellectual capital is highly regarded, and these products are "signed" by the person who created them. This, in effect, says, "I wrote this and am willing to answer questions about it." As new performance-support tools come online that mitigate the need for instruction, we can shift our training and knowledge systems to new or more important areas. Finally, talent alignment systems, practices, and tools that touch everyone, such as recruiting, staffing, performance management, and career development, can use technology to make sure that learning needs are matched with the right resources, at the right level of detail, and precisely when they are needed.

Conclusion

Technology is essential to building and sustaining learning in today's large and complex organizations. It improves the quality and expands the reach of learning products and approaches of all kinds. But equally important, it enables these resources to work in harmony, creating a far more valuable solution. Most organizations approach learning challenges as training problems, and most efforts to create a learning culture end up primarily with a training culture. We know the two are not the same. We know that learning is a basic human activity that takes place everywhere and every day. We also know that every role or function within an organization has a learning component and that everyone who works there is a full-time learner. So the development of a true learning culture transcends the training function. It involves a variety of approaches, including knowledge management, communities of practice, performance support, and talent alignment, to support the culture. And now, with the advent of new, ubiquitous, and easy-to-use technologies, we can extend this culture across time and place so that individuals and groups learn on their own schedule, according to their needs and preferences. Technology enables us truly to bridge individual and organizational learning. We can provide a single, personalized gateway, or portal, to all learning resources for each individual while maintaining a singular organizational perspective. This is true "blended learning." It's what builds learning enterprises – places where learning cultures thrive.

11 | *The agility factor*

EILEEN CLEGG AND CLARK N. QUINN

O RGANIZATIONS must be able to adapt quickly, shift contexts, and make informed choices in a world in which information, relationships, technology, and organizations themselves are in constant flux. In light of this environment of relentless change, organizations today are particularly susceptible to falling behind in efforts to increase what we call "the agility factor," the characteristics and behaviors that enable individuals and organizations to interact successfully with extreme change, to survive in a world in which the rate of change is increasing and unexpected events are becoming more radical in nature.[1]

Some people are responding to the lack of predictability in the world around them by taking more personal control. For example, we see more college students choosing multiple majors, an increasing number of workers opting to start their own businesses, individuals becoming more active consumers, and people looking to their personal networks instead of outside institutions for social context. New possibilities are emerging for deeper creativity and collaboration, which many people are embracing – and others are forced to accept – to retain some personal stability in a continually changing environment.

But while certain individuals have the capacity to adapt to extreme change, as do many small and highly focused businesses, larger organizations – which must rely on planning and systems – are by nature slow to react. Is it possible for an organization to build systems that create a capacity to anticipate and react quickly to extreme change? We think so.

Research for and review of this chapter were provided by biologist Julia Willsie, Kevin Wheeler, president of Global Learning Resources, and Robert Stephenson, director of the Harvey Project.

[1] R. Mittman and E. Clegg, *The Future of Global e-Education* (Menlo Park, Calif.: Institute for the Future/Vivendi Prospective, 2001).

Learning from nature's extremophiles

A learning culture that promotes agility and emergent knowledge is fundamentally different from a system that rewards adherence to the status quo. Effective leaders understand this and may try to update their organization's approach to education and training, but an entirely new model is needed. It is not possible to think strategically about how to cope with an uncertain future within a framework that presupposes the continuation of old systems. We need an entirely fresh look at the question of what kind of learning culture supports constructive interaction with extreme change.

We can gain insight into this question by turning to the field of biology, in which we find "extremophiles," nature's most adaptive organisms. These microorganisms can provide an apt framework for thinking about a future characterized by sudden as well as gradual change, and for learning about systems that allow successful interaction with change.

Extremophiles, which were named for their love of extremes, have characteristics and behaviors that enable them to live in environments too hostile for other organisms. They were discovered fairly recently (the term is only thirty years old) in such places as deep undersea vents at temperatures well above boiling, in Arctic seas at subzero temperatures, in highly acidic environments, and even in salt lakes, where other life forms cannot exist. Scientists have developed understandings about the internal mechanisms of extremophiles that allow them not only to survive but even to thrive in the harshest conditions on Earth and possibly on Mars.

Sometimes these microorganisms adapt instantly to changes in the environment, but many of the characteristics that allow them to survive in conditions that are deadly to other organisms have evolved over millennia. These characteristics have counterparts in a set of behaviors and systems that can be invoked by individuals and organizations, enabling them to be more resilient, more adaptable, and more agile in the face of change. The following is an overview of some characteristics that account for extremophiles' ability to survive in harsh environments and a brief introduction to what they can teach us about human learning systems, which we will discuss later in this chapter.

Strong ionic bonds. Proteins are essential for life. When they collapse, the organism can no longer survive. Extremophile proteins have more and stronger ionic bonds – bonds that have positive and negative charges. This suggests that strength is the result of internal cohesion, which often comes from the tension of opposites. It also suggests that integrating people with diverse ideas and approaches through a shared mission leads to organizational fitness.

Environmental monitoring. Certain extremophile behaviors occur in direct response to changing conditions. For example, the brine shrimp, although it is not technically an extremophile, has an extremophile response of releasing embryos in a dormant rather than live state if conditions are poor. This suggests a continual monitoring of outside conditions, a tight coupling between environmental changes and organizational response.

Heat-shock proteins. These special proteins are created or released only when an organism is on the brink of death, its proteins denaturing. Heat-shock proteins are released to restore the other proteins. All organisms have heat-shock proteins; they are activated at a higher temperature for extremophiles. The implication for organizations is that empathy helps people recover from trauma.

Equilibrium. Extremophiles have two ways of coping with external threats. One is to pump out potentially toxic substances; the other is to manufacture a substance that is compatible with the threat. This suggests a rapid evaluation of the environment and explicit decisions about whether to incorporate or exclude particular ideas.

Symbiosis. Some extremophiles are able to live in hostile environments because they form symbiotic relationships with others; for example, deep-sea extremophiles can live on inorganic matter and therefore are able to feed their host/protectors, giant tubeworms. This suggests radical approaches to strategic relationships.

Extremophile learning cultures

Exploring the mechanisms of nature's super-survivors helps jump-start thinking about learning that is appropriate for an environment of extreme change. We can infuse what we know about extremophiles into the learning framework and see what existing educational approaches, theories, and technologies support the agility factor. We can then extend the framework by hypothesizing new approaches. This framework is still in the early phases of development; the goal at this point is to help people and organizations see new patterns and raise questions. Consistent with the extremophile analogy, this framework must remain open to new ideas and interpretations.

To help move the imagination from the biological to the human version of an extremophile, anthropomorphic exercises are helpful. One can identify "extremophile type" people as those who, when plunged into challenging situations, come up with surprising and successful solutions. They may not be people who stand out in ordinary times, but they rise to the challenge of extraordinary times with wisdom and intelligence. Examples include Rosa Parks, who launched the civil rights movement by refusing to move to the back of a bus, and Winston Churchill, who was not a particularly noteworthy figure until he rose to lead the Allies in World War II.

When conditions change and people must mobilize, there is usually someone who is out in front, someone who is highly adaptive to a new set of conditions, just as in nature, organisms with certain "preadaptive" characteristics are most likely to succeed. Such people may at first appear nonconforming, but they are leading the way to a new direction. Most of us know one or two extremophiles among friends and co-workers – the mild-mannered person who becomes superhuman on deadline or the seemingly disorganized colleague who comes up with a stunning innovation in the middle of a crisis. In schools and workplaces everywhere right now, instructors and managers are finding that at times of pressure, those who have the most relevant contributions are not necessarily the straight-A or corporate ladder types. We no longer can measure an individual by his or her ability to conform to previously set expectations. It seems that the ability to assess and adapt quickly to new situations is becoming more valuable. But we do not have a deep understanding of how to encourage this behavior. Nor do we know how to assess whether students and workers are developing adaptive behaviors.

Already, most organizational leaders and educators have a strong sense of the need for agility, but they lack a systematic way of thinking about it. Biology has given us a model. What can it tell us? The following are ways that extremophile characteristics map to implications for learning cultures.

Encouraging stronger links

Biologically, it is clear that the strong ionic bonds of extremophile protein are a feature of a resilient organism. Organizationally, the corollary is cohesiveness. For extremophiles, the protein's structural integrity depends on the polarity of the bonds: opposites attract. The extremophile's characteristic of having a dense network of ionic bonds translates into an image of an organization that values diversity. The positive and negative charges connote opposites: opposing learning styles, opposing ideas, opposing cultures, opposing personalities, opposing values. Some management experts talk about "managing polarities"; that is, allowing conflicting views to coexist.

The adaptive value of diversity is demonstrated not just in microbiology's ionic bonds but in population biology's genetic diversity ("hybrid vigor") and, on the human front, in "super-copers," people who are capable of thriving under stress. Santa Barbara psychologist Betty Frain found a positive correlation between this capability and the ability to bond with a variety of people.

Inclusiveness is a point of strength for learning cultures, increasing the agility factor by providing more opportunities for interacting with the unknown. People who work cross-culturally have observed how subtle differences in perception can be brought together to create an "interculture." People who manage groups with highly diverse skills and personalities have noticed that products and services are more successful when many different kinds of people contribute to the creative process.

The talk about diversity is superficial, however, unless substantial efforts are made to dig down to a level where similarities are found and bonds are created. Understanding differences enables people not just to recognize and appreciate but to interact with – and take advantage of – cultural, learning, and personality preferences. It is not enough to gather different people together. It is essential to explore and discuss their differences, find complementarities, and define the bond that unites people – for example, corporate values or educational goals. Already the term "learning disabilities" is being dropped in favor of the notion that there are different learning "strengths." Similarly, the dominance of Western values will change as people are encouraged to define and express their own cultural values. As those values blend, learning cultures will become stronger, not with "multicultural" but with "intercultural" learning.

Sensing context

To survive, nature's extremophiles have a primitive way of reading their environment that prompts them to invoke certain behaviors. This suggests the need to see shifts that are under way or are likely to occur. In light of today's information glut, it is critical that people see the "big picture" if they are to make the best decisions about what actions to take. This requires recognizing the contextual filters that are constantly being thrust on individuals in ordinary communication – in the classroom, through the media, and in casual social relationships.

We are already familiar with the problem of "not seeing the forest for the trees." Empirical experiments in attention demonstrate that too strong a focus on task can interfere with the ability to detect unusual occurrences.[2] Part of the role of education is to help people, as the Apple Computer slogan goes, "think different" so that they will be able to see the gorilla in the room before it is pointed out by someone else. Staying attuned to the larger context involves information gathering and information disassembling, intentionally turning ideas upside down. With digital libraries making possible a more granular level of information, one can get data without the interpretation. And information is increasingly breaking "out of the box" and becoming embedded in the environment. Learning cultures of the future will encourage people to discover their own patterns in these increasingly ubiquitous data, using tools like exploratory data analysis and data mining.

Expressing empathy

One of the most startling and inspiring extremophile responses is the heat-shock protein that is released when the organism is near death. In anthropomorphic terms, this can be thought of as a "care-giver" protein because it is activated for the sole purpose of "healing" other proteins.

[2] Professor Daniel Simon, University of Illinois, created a series of videos showing this phenomenon.

Human counterparts are recognizable in most organizations – their loyalty tends to be more toward other people than to the organization. They can be the water cooler crowd, the e-mail jokesters, the people who will lend an ear without parlaying the talk into office politics. In education, they often are the mentors, coaches, and nonjudgmental support people. Empathy is increasingly recognized as a factor in effective management and teaching. It is not something that can be manufactured or faked but is an essential element in reducing fear and creating a "safe zone" in which learning and productivity thrive.

In times of crisis, successful companies, departments, classrooms, and networks often are the ones in which an empathic person takes on the role of looking after those whose spirits and productivity are flagging. When close colleagues are being laid off or other such threats encroach on daily activities, it does not work to declare business as usual. People are not productive or innovative in an atmosphere of fear. But the human heat-shock protein can help stabilize the organization, lift spirits, and keep everyone focused on the task at hand. These individuals need identification, recognition, and nurturing.

Inoculating

When there is a threat in the environment, the extremophile has two options for maintaining equilibrium: pump out the threat or find a way to live with it. The first uses up a lot of energy. The second involves developing internal characteristics similar to those of the threat. For example, sodium chloride outside causes a halophile (salt-loving) extremophile to generate potassium chloride inside, which is an equally effective and less reactive salt. In the human environment, this is the phenomenon best known as, "If you can't beat 'em, join 'em." Successful learning cultures are those that help organizations and individuals recognize threats – often in the form of new ideas – early on and start embracing instead of fighting them. Adopting new ideas and approaches in an organization is easier when people are already familiar and up to speed with the change. Thus forward-thinking employees should be encouraged to identify and develop connections outside the organization so that they can bring in new ideas, preparing the organization to face other, potentially more threatening ones. Note that there must be explicit, conscious evaluation of new ideas, and they must be customized to fit the organizational environment to be useful. The idea is not only to adopt new ideas but also to adapt them and to ensure that individuals are equipped to incorporate them into their work.

Think of the many developments that would have seemed threatening as recently as a decade ago: employee flextime, working at home, employee involvement in high-level business decisions, open airing of conflict, blurring social and work lives, sharing intellectual property, customer input into manufacturing and business processes, outsourcing critical business functions. These new approaches could be damaging if suddenly imposed on a company that is not prepared to adapt to them. However, they have enhanced the success of companies where they are implemented compatibly with organizational values.

Exploring new partnerships

Biological symbiosis has as its organizational counterpart the growing practice of mergers and acquisitions, outsourcing and partnering. The extremophile example involves tubeworms, which can live in the absence of organic nutrients if they ingest extremophile microorganisms that live on inorganic matter. This suggests that large companies can benefit from the innovations possible only in small, agile companies. The most apt example is large companies outsourcing R&D and other strategic functions to more nimble players.

New issues arise in a world in which businesses come together and break apart, in which large companies absorb and then use or destroy small businesses. How are new ideas and products assimilated in a culture that did not create them? What characterizes companies when they are defined less and less by a specific goal or product or service or location? Agile companies are those that have built-in strategies for ingesting – or being ingested by – another company, including making values and strategies explicit. A familiar unsuccessful scenario involves the small company that meets its demise after being acquired by a larger company that does not understand the cultural or strategic approaches that led to the smaller company's initial success. If all parties clearly communicate their culture and strategies, they can analyze in detail how to leverage their similarities and differences to support a successful symbiotic relationship.

Five extremophile strategies

The activities described above represent some ideas about how the biological inspirations of extremophiles can play out in an agile organization. The agile learning culture is one with a strong and appealing internal identity that has successfully identified and incorporated diversity. The culture is tightly coupled to the external environment and encourages the continual monitoring of events and ideas. It identifies and nurtures empathic types who help maintain the community within the organization. There are mechanisms whereby good ideas – whether from inside or outside – are valued, tested, and disseminated, and internal practices can be quickly modified, as well as mechanisms for developing valuable partnerships with other organizations.

Although the extremophile approach is fundamentally different from the current paradigm in management and education, there are innovations on the horizon – social and technological – that map to extremophile characteristics. Here are five strategies that organizations can consider to increase their ability to interact with change.

Leveraging human complexity

Building bonds strong enough to enable an organization to remain cohesive through extreme change involves deep understanding and sophisticated communication among a diverse group of people. Diversity within an organization protects it from external threats. The more types of people within, the more likely an organization is to have the collective ideas and skills and other resources to meet unexpected challenges. But those resources must be identified, celebrated, and expressed. In many organizations, competencies may be identified, but understanding the larger scope of factors that characterize individuals provides greater strength and opportunities.

Using technological tools for learning-style and competency assessments, personality profiling, value articulation, and work-style identification, individuals can get a highly granular look at their abilities, and organizations at their component parts. Whereas in the past it was traditional to call on language translators, in the future organizations will know how to communicate in different learning media and for different personality types to reach a larger audience. Good technological solutions are available now – and excellent solutions are coming in the future – to the problem of identifying and understanding the unique qualities and needs of individual workers.

Historically, the problem with managing polarities has been that people at different poles did not understand one another – introverts versus extroverts, visual learners versus text learners, brainstormers versus action-oriented workers, engineering versus marketing, people from different cultures divided not just by language but also by deeply embedded contextual cues that are hard to identify, much less translate. However, now there are explicit models that can explain the motivations of different types and "translate" one to another. Once people know their learning style, personality inventory, and cultural biases, they can be encouraged to develop knowledge-based (not just kindly motivated) tolerance. Groups can explore ways to bring different types together to create more effective meetings, processes, and teams. It is true that people like people whom they are like and tend to cluster around similar types, but the benefits of incorporating differences are clear. Understanding how different types contribute to the complete enterprise helps cement the shared contribution.

Beyond identifying the basics, such as one's interests, profession, preferred learning method, and demographic niche, individuals can be encouraged to explore and define the more elusive aspects of themselves – understanding nuances of their artistic selves, intuitive knowledge, and unique personality characteristics. Such in-depth personal understanding can sharpen both the individual and organizational extremophile response. For the individual, deep self-understanding enhances creativity, which is essential for acting when there is little time to prepare and often no prescribed response to change. For the organization, promoting individual self-knowledge and creative expression enables access to human resources in the deepest and broadest sense of the term. This in turn brings about the "hybrid vigor" characteristics described earlier.

Developing "wise" information technology

Just as extremophile organisms thrive by dynamically responding to their environment, success for most organizations will depend on ongoing, accurate context-sensing. Two components of this are access to relevant data and the ability to arrange the data to create unique solutions. Beyond the "smart" technology that responds to its environment independent of human interaction, information technology is increasingly becoming "wise" by sorting through knowledge to help people find creative solutions.

The amount of available information is increasing exponentially. The challenge for business is finding and leveraging the information that addresses specific challenges. Technologies on the horizon, such as the Semantic Web, promise to deliver information labeled and organized so that it can be accessed by intelligent agents (technologies that can adapt information to an individual's or organization's specific needs) even before the individual or organization knows what it is looking for. Technology is also being developed that will personalize content according to the individual's knowledge, needs, learning style, and particular problem. For example, a person would not need to read an entire book to find specific ideas if "books" were published in response to a person's needs and conditions. This would be possible by creating content in small chunks, each one richly described and tagged with meta-data in standard ways, thus capable of being easily found and rapidly assembled to create personalized "books." Many organizations are working on the requisite standards and specifications, and some models are available for envisioning how to break apart and arrange information for easiest access. Once the critical mass of content is available in this granular, well-described, and standardized way, technologies will be able to provide the "invisible hand" to reassemble truly personal and relevant information.[3]

The other aspect of "wise" technology is a collection of methodologies enabling people to see a larger landscape. Multimedia approaches, such as visual interpretation of information designed to stimulate different parts of the brain, can open the mind.[4] Research and futures firms have been using visual information-mapping techniques for decades as a way to "see more." For example, timelines juxtaposing different categories of events, visual "landscapes" depicting movement of information, and mind maps that show relationships among ideas that may not appear to be connected. More elaborate visualization techniques are being developed through simulations that are becoming more sophisticated with built-in scaffolding. Beyond the how-to

---

[3] H. W. Hodgins, *E-Learning World Congress Summary* (Saratoga Springs, N.Y.: The Masic Center, 2002).
[4] K. H. Woolsey, *Vizability* (Boston: PWS Publishing Company, 1995).

aspect of simulations are the new online "worlds" in which people can not only learn but also talk with others who are learning. For example, Active Worlds is an online center where conferences, classes, and simulations are available to teachers and students who "go there" and take on the form of avatars (virtual people who appear three-dimensionally, representing the participants in shared spaces). As individuals are increasingly required to think in terms of dynamic interactions, these new multimedia tools support fresh perspectives.

Encouraging always-on cross-mentoring

Relentless change can leave workers reeling, sometimes rendering them ineffective if they are confused about how to shift directions. Learning from the extremophile's heat-shock protein, it is necessary for agile organizations to have a repair mechanism that can be activated during stress. This means building empathy into the organizational system. For example, IBM has for years assigned mentors to employees – specifically, mentors who are not in the same department or otherwise in competition with the person they are mentoring. The sole purpose of the relationship is to provide guidance and support.

Mentoring in the extremophile learning culture goes beyond the senior-to-junior model of support. Readiness for change can be enhanced by the availability of a suite of mentors. The practice of reverse mentoring (for example, when corporate executives shadow researchers in the lab to understand the R&D process – the opposite of the usual mentoring scenario, in which the researcher learns about management) is already on the rise. As people become more adept at identifying their own and others' complex offerings, they will be in a position to help one another in a variety of ways. Typically, mentoring is task-oriented, but it can also be based on culture or style. The empathic type, who exhibits characteristics similar to the extremophile's ability to release heat-shock proteins, may be a mentor to someone who has difficulty with change. A person identified as having a highly organized approach to work might be a mentor to someone who is more disorganized. Someone who is an expert in a content area or has a specific skill-set would work with people lower down on the learning curve. Cross-disciplinary work would be easier if people could access colleagues with overlapping interests. These kinds of pairings occur

already among people who recognize – and are not afraid to acknowledge – their strengths and weaknesses.

Leveraging human complexity for mutual aid requires not just identifying and celebrating differences but also communicating one's offerings and needs. With everything from smart materials that can "beam"
information, to local area networks that allow instant information
exchange, it will be possible to locate people who may have the right
information or skills at the right moment. If we leverage technology to
share information about ourselves, we will increase the likelihood that
people who need our unique capabilities will be able to find us. For
long-term or onetime mentoring relationships, technology is increasingly available to support intimate and immediate communication.
Instant messaging was just the beginning. Now people can exchange
real-time photos, interactive simulations, video clips, and a variety of
data types that will be all the more available in the coming era of
relevant content.

Mentoring can move beyond person-to-person support through
technology that allows experts to offer customized learning from a
distance. It is possible to bring the world's best role models into one's
living room or classroom to lecture or demonstrate a skill in a prere-
corded DVD or a live holographic performance. For practice and peer
feedback, simulations allow people to build, communicate, and critique in an online environment. And information technology systems
can track and represent a learner's actions as a basis for reflection.

Tapping social and value networks

If organizational equilibrium means turning outside threats into internal opportunities, and if agile organizations are those that monitor
the environment and evaluate new ideas, then it is critical for companies to identify and leverage the social networks of their employees,
especially their relationships outside the organization. Scholarly and
popular literature on social networks has become so prevalent that
one magazine, *Wired,* actually created a social network map of the
social network research. But beyond the intriguing research into how
and why different people and ideas connect with one another, there is
practical value to mapping relationships inside and outside the organization: to discover links to organizations that have embraced ideas
that looked like threats in order to learn from their experiences.

There are several network-mapping tools available, but they assume that information is available to plug into the tool. Even organizations that recognize the value of understanding internal and internal/external links puzzle over how to identify them. There are tools that can search e-mail to find out which employees are working on which topics and who is communicating with whom, but of course this practice raises privacy concerns and requires massive investment for uncertain results.

Effective leaders of groups, business units, or classrooms are likely to know their employees or students well enough to recognize the "connectors" and other key links within the organization, and to know their external affiliations. Employees and students will be more inclined to share this information – and contribute to network maps – in learning cultures where diversity and connectivity are valued; that is, in innovative organizations where people are urged to go "off campus" and "out of the office" for new experiences.

Strategic community-building

The organizational equivalent of extremophile symbiosis is the establishment of relationships. At an individual level, relationships are about the social network. At an organizational level, relationships are about strategic partnerships. To achieve maximum value from symbiotic organizational relationships such as partnerships, mergers, acquisitions, and outsourcing, knowledge and information must be shared across organizations. There are several aspects to this imperative: data exchange must function seamlessly, tacit knowledge should be made explicit, and organizational identity must derive from something other than a company's products or processes.

Mechanisms to build symbiotic infrastructures are becoming increasingly sophisticated, allowing new partners to work together with customers. These include buy-side systems (such as electronic data exchange and electronic marketplaces), sell-side systems (such as customer relationship management programs and electronic dialogs), and enterprise-wide systems (such as enterprise resource planning systems, which integrate buy-side, sell-side, and internal systems). New interfaces and programs are being developed to help manage the complexity of seemingly simple transactions.

Similarly, knowledge repositories are becoming more complex. The challenge, as often happens, comes with the use of the technology. A study by the Delphi Group found that the largest segment of corporate knowledge resides in employees' brains (42 percent), followed by paper documents (26 percent). Only 20 percent of corporate knowledge is contained in electronic documents. In order for companies to function smoothly while entering into various partnerships and alliances, it will be necessary to find ways to identify, tap into, and record tacit knowledge in a way that can be transmitted quickly to new partners.

Effective management of data flows and knowledge is essential to smooth functioning, but the more elusive form of organizational glue – culture – also must be managed in a way that allows even disparate organizations to work together. Culture analysts are using anthropological tools to identify the distinguishing characteristics of an organization. The resulting profile can help with mutual understanding during mergers and acquisitions, and with developing a unique description of the company's "personality." This becomes increasingly valuable as organizations compete for market share and top talent. A company with a resonant "meme" (a powerful phrase or idea that functions as a social gene, diffusing far and wide with ease) can have an advantage. For example, most businesspeople seem to know instinctively the meaning of "The HP Way," and indeed Hewlett-Packard's innovation-rich, employee-sensitive culture became a dominant force in the new economy.

Conclusion

Nature's extremophiles provide inspiration for a framework integrating a variety of different areas of research into a coherent approach for developing a future-oriented learning culture. This framework, which must be continually refined within each organization, suggests new ways to assess and leverage talent, information, communication, and relationships in a world in which the rate and degree of change are increasing.

Organizations will need to view individuals in new and complex ways so that their skills and ideas can be quickly accessed, assembled, and activated for a variety of unanticipated circumstances. Highly flexible and personalized technologies are emerging to support these extremophile responses, but they will work only to the extent that the adaptive mechanisms are in place before the conditions change.

Rather than an infrastructure feature, agility is a capacity that is woven into the fabric of an organization. There is no prescription for creating this capacity. It develops through an emergent process based on radically new assumptions about individual learners and organizational principles. Developing this capacity will enable an organization not only to survive turbulent times and unexpected outcomes, but also to capitalize on changes that provide opportunities. The result is a more nimble, more successful organization: an extremophile organization.

12 | Tools and methods to support learning networks

DORI DIGENTI

T
o learn as individuals and to foster a learning culture in our organizations, most of us end up looking outside our organizations
for knowledge and information. We take courses and attend conferences, where we meet people and share our ideas and experiences.
Afterward, however, we may find that the valuable learning that has
taken place outside does not change anything inside the organization.
The problem is that we have not mastered the organizational skills
and practices that would allow us to take full advantage of external
learning opportunities. And we have only a scattershot approach to
choosing which external opportunities to pursue. If we do attend a
particularly inspiring conference, we can share what we learned easily enough by posting a summary on the organizational intranet or by
sending e-mails to potentially interested parties, but most of the new
ideas do not get used because there is no internal social process for
making sense of them.

These gaps in organizational capability are the motivation for creating a learning network, a group of people who come together in
an informal and experiment-based association that bridges organizational boundaries in order to share information, learn about a topic,
and create knowledge using mutually agreed learning strategies and
collaborative tools and methods.[1]

I would like to thank the members of the C3 LearnNet and the COSP
Network, Professor Edgar Schein of MIT, and the American University/
NTL master's course in Organization Development.

[1] The definition and theory of learning networks used in the chapter are
drawn from the work of Edgar Schein on what he calls learning consortia. See "Learning Consortia: How to Create Parallel Learning Systems
for Organization Sets," Working Paper 10.007, Society of Organizational
Learning, 1995; as well as from the author's work on collaborative learning
networks, see "Collaborative Learning: Real-Time Practice for Knowledge
Generation," *Systems Thinker* 11 (2000), pp. 1–5.

Why do I write about "learning networks" and not "communities of practice"? From my perspective, here are some of the differences between the two. First, a community of practice includes members who share a certain practice, such as accountants or trainers across a global organization, whereas a learning network is more a community of interest, in that the members may not engage in the same sort of work but want to learn together about a specific field or topic. A second distinction is that a community of practice is typically *within* an organization, whereas a learning network crosses organizations. In fact, the boundary-spanning character of a learning network is part of what creates its value. It provides member organizations with a more systematic means of pursuing external learning opportunities than relying on the happenstance of courses and conferences.

Organizations that attempt to create learning networks often select and adapt the technology and tools that will support the network on the basis of the members' knowledge, the availability of the tools, and other factors. This chapter will explore several tools and methods that support learning networks, and how they have been used in two learning networks with which I have been involved: the Cross-Company Collaboration Learning Network (C3 LearnNet), an association of for-profit corporations focused on improving collaboration among their organizations, and the Community-Science Partnership Network (COSP Network), a community-driven network focused on national environmental issues. The comparison between a corporate and a civic learning network is intended to show that there is no one set of tools that fits each and every situation. This chapter will explore the software and Internet tools these learning networks use as well as the methods that support the effective use of these tools. The distinction between tools and methods is somewhat arbitrary, but these two classes of "technologies" must be used together for each to be used effectively. They must be integrated as an organizational capability for a learning culture to take root in the learning network and in the members' organizations.

About learning networks

Each learning network is unique in size, configuration, and goals, but they all share several characteristics. First, a learning network is based on peer-to-peer communication. Unlike employees in a business or other organization, members of a learning network assume that participation consists of each member contacting other members directly, without any hierarchy or chain of command. The advantage of this approach is that multiple parts of the organization can be in touch simultaneously instead of having knowledge filtered by individual experts, managers, or gatekeepers. This does not imply, however, that learning networks are completely self-organizing (see the subsection "Skilled facilitation" below).

Second, a learning network is motivated by a desire for new knowledge and learning that can be applied within each member's home organization. The issues that move organizations to develop learning networks have to be tied to process improvement, new approaches or projects, or best practice exchanges, over a medium- to long-term period. For example, in C3 LearnNet, members participate in monthly sessions in which an organization gets feedback from other members on one of its key best practices. In the COSP Network, the sharing of information and experience with technical advisers, and the capture of that information in stories and a database directory, form the focus of annual and teleconferenced quarterly meetings.

Third, participation in learning network activities presupposes that members have a certain amount of time to pursue external learning. The classic example is 3M's 15 percent rule, which lets employees allocate 15 percent of their time to enrichment, learning, or skunkworks activities that will help them become better contributors to the organization. In addition to granting such time, the home organization must visibly value the network activity and the learning that results.

Finally, learning network activities, which by definition link organizations across geographical distance, are wholly dependent on the accessibility of network communication links. It takes experimentation and reflection to discover which communication media work best for a given learning network.

The big picture: how to choose and combine tools for learning networks

Before laying out the specific tools that can be used to support learning networks, it is helpful to draw back the lens and consider some of the bigger learning and communication issues. Each learning network

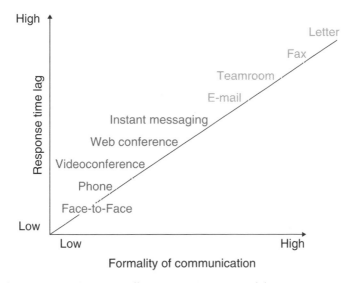

Figure 12.1. Dennis Rozell's communication model.

is unique, but they all share the basic need for supporting tools that provide familiarity, impact, and flexibility.

Asynchronous and synchronous tools

One of the most important distinctions in tool types is between synchronous tools, which people use to communicate at the same time, and asynchronous tools, which people use to access information at their own pace and time. Synchronous tools include face-to-face meetings, telephone conversations, videoconferencing, Web conferencing, and Internet chat. Asynchronous tools include instant messaging, e-mail, teamrooms, broadcast media (audio recordings, videotapes), and databases or document management systems. The key to using both synchronous and asynchronous tools is to understand the best use of each mode and to consider the formality and lag time associated with each (see Figure 12.1). Synchronous tools result in more consistent participation than asynchronous tools. Also, groups reach decisions more easily using synchronous tools. Synchronous tools create "live energy" by engaging the senses more fully and bringing immediacy to the interaction. The limitations of synchronous approaches include the need for extra documentation and scheduling and time demands, especially for face-to-face meetings.

   Asynchronous tools have become increasingly popular since the mid-1990s as a solution to the limitations of synchronous communication. The convenience of asynchronous participation, which can take place after hours, from remote locations, and in short bursts of time, is compelling. Keep in mind, though, that relying too much on asynchronous modes of communication can lead to apathy and disconnection among the learning network members.[2] A balance between regular face-to-face meetings and periods of asynchronous communication maintains energy and the flow of communication. C3 LearnNet members, for instance, found it difficult during periods of restricted travel budgets – in the late 1990s and immediately following September 11, 2001 – to sustain a face-to-face meeting schedule, and so they became dependent on asynchronous tools. This dependency meant that when there were naturally slow periods in postings, members were compelled to make emergency "prime the pump" postings to get communication flowing again.

Push or pull?

The right balance must be found in the learning network between "push" methods of communication (e-mail, phone, print) and "pull" methods (websites, scheduled events, conferencing). Each type of endeavor will require a different balance. In the activist-oriented COSP Network, push methods have been welcomed as a way for members to keep each other informed of their activities and for scientists to be included in activist projects. For the business-driven members of C3 LearnNet, however, push methods have been used only to request participation in pull events. Excessive push activity would be construed as internal spamming and would backfire on the sender very quickly!

---

[2] On the other hand, there is a danger in assuming too much about a period of inactivity in asynchronous communications. While it may be true that a problem exists, it could be equally true that members are all traveling at the same time or are extremely busy with other tasks. The only way to find out what is causing a lull in communications is for the facilitator or leader to ask, and typically picking up the phone and calling a few key members will quickly supply some answer as to why things are quiet.

Creating a rhythm

Only through learning by doing does an individual learning network find the best balance between push and pull technologies and between synchronous and asynchronous modes of communication. One of the most important factors in finding that balance is creating a rhythm for communication, no matter what form it takes. Members of the COSP Network expect to receive an electronic newsletter every month, so they look for it in their inboxes. C3 LearnNet's monthly teleconferences have become a major communications focus, with many planning phone calls and e-mails leading up to the formal session. So, no matter what combination of tools a network chooses, network members or leaders must pay attention to the rhythm of their use.

Archiving

Many of the tools available to learning networks allow for extensive archiving, so there is a tendency to save everything. This is very useful for new members of the learning network, but it is a burden on the person or people maintaining the archive. Again, the nature and purpose of the network are highly relevant. In the case of C3 LearnNet, members decided that it makes sense to maintain only a sixty-day archive of threaded discussions. The COSP Network, which works on much longer-range issues involving government regulated activities, found value in discussions from five years ago. If the network chooses a minimalist archiving strategy, digested documents or some other way of experiencing the learning network's evolution can help new members. This can take the form of annual reports, a learning history, or selected papers or meeting proceedings. Whatever the decision, a long-term network member can help new members fill in the gaps in the archive, revealing the context and tacit knowledge behind the words.

Co-evolution of tools and learning network practices

Members of learning networks develop their supporting tools as the network itself is evolving, thus there is a "co-evolutionary" relationship between a network and its suite of tools. There are two aspects to this co-evolution. The first is that members may start out using one set of tools and move to a different configuration of supporting tools as the network evolves. This evolution does not always go from the simple to the more complex. For example, the COSP Network began its network-building activities with an e-mail distribution list but found that it was too fragmentary and intermittent, so they replaced it with a monthly newsletter. Similarly, C3 LearnNet found that Web conferencing, while providing many advanced features, was not preferable to a predistributed presentation with a teleconference.

The second aspect to this co-evolutionary process is that learning networks may change their use of a tool over time, exploiting different features as the needs and capabilities of the network mature.[3] This can take the form of engaging new capabilities of a specific tool or dropping the use of a certain feature. In C3 LearnNet, some members experimented with graphics features embedded in the teamroom software, but most members did not use this feature and so over time it was used less and less. There was no moment when a decision was made not to use the graphics capability; it just naturally faded away as members focused more on text-based asynchronous tools. This is a critical point to consider in the learning network and its interactions with tools, because there is the danger of particular learning styles – in C3 LearnNet's case, the traditional text-driven exchange of information – becoming dominant in the network and excluding other learning styles. As we will see, the facilitator plays a critical role in this regard, making sure that network members are aware of the range of tools available and raising members' awareness when a tool falls into disuse.

The next section explores specific tools and their uses in learning networks, and refers to the "big picture" issues discussed above. The exploration below is again based on two specific learning networks; other groups may have very different experiences using these tools.

Specific tools for learning networks

Face-to-face meetings

There is often a temptation in learning networks to idolize the face-to-face meeting and regard communication over any distance as a poor

---

[3] W. Orlikowski, "Using Technology and Constituting Structures: A Practice Lens for Studying Technology in Organizations," *Organizational Science* 11 (July–August 2000), pp. 404–428.

substitute. There does seem to be general agreement that if a business or organizational decision must be made, a face-to-face meeting is the place to do it most efficiently and effectively. But everyone has had the experience of attending a face-to-face meeting, whether for one hour or three days, and emerging from it saying, "Now, what was that all about? What did we decide?" In other words, the face-to-face meeting is not a lost art over which we must continually express our regret.

For a learning network, face-to-face meetings are a luxury and have more to do with building social networks than does a typical face-to-face meeting within a single organization. Distance communication can force us to be more precise, more conscious of time, more accommodating, and more attentive than we are in live meetings. In the learning network context, the question is not how to make distance communications make up for their shortcomings but how to blend distance and face-to-face, synchronous and asynchronous communications, so that the network can form the social and intellectual bonds that support genuine learning.

To give one example, C3 LearnNet began with annual face-to-face summits, and after one year the group decided to meet twice a year, once in the fall and once in the spring. The members found a good balance between the semiannual face-to-face meetings and the monthly teleconferences and Web discussion in the teamroom. In 2001, however, several member companies found that their travel was limited because of the combined effects of terrorist threats and budget cuts, so videoconferencing was substituted for the fall meeting. Members experienced a fair amount of dissatisfaction with this medium, and in spring 2002 the group again held a face-to-face meeting. There was strong feeling in the group, based on tradition and experience, that the semiannual face-to-face meetings were critical to the network's existence, despite the often good results from distance communication media.

E-mail

E-mail is the still the most popular communication technology in most organizations, and we do not need to review its general uses here, except as they relate to learning networks. The advantages of e-mail for a learning network are accessibility, ease of use, and familiarity. However, members of learning networks that are just being formed can mistakenly assume that everyone has e-mail access. In the COSP

Network, for example, some members in remote parts of Alaska do not have e-mail. And consider what could happen when a member is traveling or residing in a country with limited Internet access or speed. Therefore, learning network members need to be mindful of relying too much on e-mail.

The e-mail access issue may be temporary or rare in a corporate-based learning network but is quite prevalent in civic networks. While it is easy to imagine access challenges in parts of Alaska, there are also network members in the lower forty-eight states who do not consistently use e-mail to communicate, either because of lack of access, lack of funds, or lack of basic computing skills (and sometimes just because of stubborn refusal). Learning networks can thrive in these circumstances by using various strategies:

- maintaining a list of those without e-mail and sending hard copy to them;
- periodically downloading information to a CD for those with computers but no Internet access;
- finding Internet access at a local library;
- pairing members who have Internet access with those who do not;
- relying more on synchronous tools such as teleconferencing.

The bigger issues with Internet access in civic networks go beyond the scope of this chapter, but a crucial point to keep in mind is that members without Internet access do not know what they are missing, and so a strategy must be worked out to disseminate the "menu" of available information and encourage these members to participate fully.

Tales of e-mail abuse are rife in the media and in organizational lore. In a recent study by Christina Cavanagh of the University of Western Ontario, 80 percent of those who receive more than fifty e-mails per day said that e-mail is out of control.[4] Much wasted time is spent sifting, filtering, and deleting unwanted messages. Many organizations are poised to send in the e-mail SWAT team to curb e-mail offenders, but often the change effort is temporary, and we creatures of habit return to our old ways.

E-mail is particularly poor for managing processes that occur in stages or in multiple versions over long periods, because the flow of

[4] "Researcher Questions Usefulness of Email in the Workplace," press release from the University of Western Ontario, March 8, 2001.

decisions and documents is difficult to track through a linear series of messages. In one case with C3 LearnNet, two members spent a lengthy telephone call trying to track a sequence of e-mails, the outcome of which had led the two members to opposite conclusions.

This problem is particularly serious in a learning network, because members must account not only for communication misunderstandings within the network but also for differences among organizations in their e-mail environments. This is especially true if members use e-mail with attachments as a document-sharing device. The problems that occur with attachments include lack of firewall permission, incompatible software, faulty attachment processing, and a simple failure to notice that the attachment is there. Likewise, everyone configures his or her e-mail archiving scheme differently, so there is no standardization on document handling. If a member leaves the learning network, no one will be able to access that person's e-mail repository, which could result in critical gaps in knowledge. Copying everyone in the network on every communication only makes matters worse. C3 LearnNet members discovered that the more people copied on an e-mail, the less responsibility each person takes for replying to it. In short, e-mail can become a serious impediment to the development of a learning network if it is relied on for all asynchronous communications.

Teleconferencing

The humble telephone emerges as a hero for the support of learning networks. Now that user-led teleconferencing with advanced features is possible, other media cannot rival the nearly universal accessibility and ease of use of the teleconference. First, even without the availability of the latest features, teleconferencing allows the energy and immediacy of real-time interchange with virtually no need for a learning curve, no intrusiveness of the technology, and no worry about organizational firewalls or protocols. Beyond the simple multiparty phone call, advanced user features allow recording for later playback by calling an 800 number, recording onto CD-ROM, direct private links with the operator, and participant muting, among other features.

In the COSP Network, national public-access teleconferences are used to give leading scientists an opportunity to make presentations on important issues in the field. The conferences last one hour and consist of a ten- to fifteen-minute presentation, followed by forty minutes of discussion and five minutes of wrapping up. Participants have experienced no technical difficulties (except in a couple of cases when they forgot the phone number) and were pleased to hear from the speaker and make contact with other communities struggling with similar problems. C3 LearnNet uses teleconferencing on a monthly basis to share best practice case studies. These conferences are also one hour and are accompanied by a PowerPoint presentation or short document or graphic distributed to members in advance.

Videoconferencing

In the 1990s, videoconferencing was a breakthrough technology that offered real-time visual and audio connections with any point on the globe where the technology was available. In many corporations today, standing videoconferenced meetings with branch offices or partners are a way of doing business. In the learning network environment, the creative use of videoconferencing can add to the feeling of connectedness between members. Unlike the standard business use, however, which is typically point-to-point conferencing, the learning network by definition is almost always multipoint (three or more videoconferenced locations linked together). In the multipoint scenario, the complexity of videoconferencing can detract from the experience because of the need for careful facilitation, extra fees for a bridging service, the increased possibility of lost connections, and varying levels of equipment capability.

For the COSP Network, videoconferencing has not been a possibility because most communities lack access to equipment. In the case of C3 LearnNet, videoconferencing has been used when face-to-face meetings are not possible, but with mixed results. Some members have objected to the cost of the videoconferenced sessions, the difficulty of scheduling the videoconferencing room, the need to focus on the medium and not on the content of the meeting, and sometimes poor picture quality. But videoconferencing does allow document-sharing and spontaneous discussion, and if facilitated properly can accommodate real interchange among peers instead of lectures by a talking head.

Web conferencing

Web conferencing has taken the business world by storm. The technology offers sessions that allow each participant, while sitting in his or her office, to view a presentation, participate in sidebar chat, and hear a live presentation over the telephone. Participants who miss the session can access an archive that sequences the presentation slides with the audio presentation and includes a transcript of the sidebar chat. These tools are undeniably powerful and engaging, and they are being used extensively by training departments, human resources departments, and other parts of organizations to link branch offices together for presentations, thus saving money and avoiding the need for "road shows" and training lag time.

For the cross-organizational learning network, however, there can be snags. Members of C3 LearnNet have found that even when firewall barriers are said not to be a problem, they are. Also, the spontaneity of some of the monthly meetings has been compromised because of the need to upload presentations two to three days before the Web conferencing session. Many members like to tweak their presentations at the last minute, and Web conferencing does not allow that. For Web conferencing to take place in a home, there must be two lines, one for the teleconference and one for the Web-based presentation. Web conferencing works best at high bandwidths, so there is a *de facto* need for a broadband connection and a phone line. While some members can parse the chat, presentation, and teleconferenced input very nicely, others have found the chat window distracting. There is also a cost for Web conferencing and for the teleconferencing connection, and those costs have continued to increase despite the drop in long-distance costs over the same period.

For these reasons and more, after using Web conferencing steadily for about six months, C3 LearnNet members decided to share their presentations on the teamroom, from which everyone could download the material, and then have a teleconference. This method was found to be much more flexible, and members ended up spending less time paying attention to connectivity and tools, and more time paying attention to content. They did lose the ability to access the audio and presentation archive, also an additional cost, but most found that the summary notes and the presentation were sufficient.

Teamrooms

Teamrooms are Web-based, secure collaborative spaces that enable a team or network of people to communicate by posting messages and documents that can be accessed at any time from any place with

Internet access. Teamrooms host a suite of features, including threaded discussions, shared documents, chat, calendars, application sharing, and project management tools.

Teamrooms can complement and in some cases replace the use of e-mail. That is, members can engage in threaded discussions in the teamroom rather than sending out e-mail messages to the entire learning network. The advantage of this approach is that everyone has access to the space and can see the sequence of messages free of other e-mail traffic. Also, anyone entering the discussion can instantly see the earlier contributions. For document-sharing, the teamroom is vastly superior to individual e-mail archives, as mentioned above.

However, to make the teamroom work as a central collaborative space for a learning network, several factors need to be in place. First and foremost, teamrooms require broadband access to work effectively. This means that community groups like the COSP Network will not use a teamroom because the access is too slow over a dial-up line (some teamroom designs include an "offline" version, but these often do not capture the entire teamroom content). For corporate members, the challenge is the agreements, incentives, and sanctions that the network puts in place around teamroom participation. Returning to the "push-pull" question, members can default to visiting the teamroom only when they receive an e-mail reminder to do so. But this system can be a trap, undercutting the "pull" nature of the teamroom and subtly encouraging members to revert to using e-mail only.

C3 LearnNet members have tried various strategies to encourage teamroom use: e-mail reminders, incentive systems, invitations broadcast and narrowcast, and others. In looking over three years' use of teamroom technology, members concluded the following:

- The teamroom did become the central collaborative space, and it was relied on for information on the network's activities.
- The frequency and individual participation numbers never reached the level that members desired.
- There were intense periods of interchange, which were exciting and helpful, and long periods without activity.
- New members could browse the teamroom and find a lot of useful information.
- Access and firewall issues would arise with some frequency but were usually resolved without too much hassle.

- Once the teamroom became the source for information, complaints about its shortcomings lessened; in other words, acculturation took place.
- The chat feature was never really used, nor were graphics (except presentations) or fancy text features. In effect, the teamroom was used like an e-mail and document repository.

Websites

As the Internet has evolved, the fundamental functions of global connectivity – to disseminate and share information – have gotten a bit lost in the onslaught of marketing, pop-up ads, spam, and flash animations. However, in the case of the learning network, a website is a powerful tool for dissemination and orientation for new and prospective members. A public website can act both as a repository for accumulated knowledge in the network and as a place to refer those who are curious about the network's activities.

There is a mysterious inverse relationship, however, between the cumulative value of a site – how it grows and evolves – and the frequency with which members visit it. In short, the website can become invisible to the network unless there is a facilitator who continually reminds members that it exists. In a similar vein, network members or those interested in network activities will not find all the great things posted on the website unless they know that those items are there. The learning network will need a "what's new on the website" process, but it is not useful to have such information solely on the website (since long-term members visit the website less and less). In the case of C3 LearnNet, links from the teamroom to the website, and occasional reminders during teleconferences, have been used to call attention to new website features. The COSP Network notifies members in a monthly electronic newsletter about new website content, and in some cases the newsletter has been sent in print by postal mail and new website content can be accessed only at the local public library or by downloading new documents and pages to a CD-ROM.

Expertise locators and knowledge management agents

Expertise locators and knowledge management agents are a class of search, filtering, retrieval, and people-linking software that delivers content and connections to a personal portal. Knowledge management agents allow organic and automated connections to be made on the basis of people's expertise and areas of interest. Knowledge management agents are now being integrated into suites of tools comprising enterprise information portals (EIPs) or knowledge portals.[5]

While this new class of tools is being adopted and used inside leading corporations, none of the vendors has yet come up with a cross-organization application that would be useful for learning networks. In the near future, however, expertise locators and affinity "bots" may help learning networks form. A possible scenario would feature a highly secure, privacy-protecting website (run by a professional society for its members, for example) that would collect the interests of members by bots that comb their e-mail repositories. Then, the natural affinities of these society's members could be "discovered," and new working groups or learning networks could be formed. There are many technical leaps that would need to occur to make this scenario a reality, but the more we understand that the knowledge we need may lie outside our own organizational boundaries, the more interest and potential profit there will be in creating cross-organizational "agents" to discover that knowledge.

Methods for learning networks

Learning networks, in order to be effective, must have structures that support their work. For want of a better word, let us call these structures "methods." One could just as easily use the term "learning environments," but no matter the term, we are trying to elicit a complex whole that combines the right physical "stuff," psychological environment, and streamlined virtual tools that allow diverse groups of people to access their collective knowledge across distance and benefit from the exchange. Most learning networks struggle initially with which tools to use and only later realize that two other aspects – the physical space in which members work, either collectively in face-to-face meetings or individually in homes or offices, and the development and facilitation

[5] D. McDonald and M. Ackermann, "Just Talk to Me: A Field Study of Expertise Location," in *Proceedings of the 1998 ACM Conference on Computer Supported Cooperative Work* (New York: ACM Press, 1998), pp. 14–18.

of learning goals – are the key to making any tool effective. There may not be any way to avoid that initial period of experimentation with various tools, but if one member can focus the group on the broader aspects of the environment in which the learning network can or should gather, the network can evolve more quickly and successfully.

Collaborative spaces

A learning network that operates using a set of collaborative tools must be able to generate and inhabit "collaborative spaces." Whether these spaces are physical or virtual, without them as background and as container, the collaborative tools cannot be used effectively, and learning will be limited.

An effective physical collaborative space provides the mobility, flexibility, light, air, positive tactile aspects, and audio-video capabilities that enhance any face-to-face learning experience. We might think that we know a good collaborative space when we see one, but perhaps it is more accurate to say that we know when we *don't* see one. After a two-day meeting of C3 LearnNet several years ago, which was held in a corporate meeting room, a member commented that he felt as if he had been in a sensory deprivation tank. The room was wonderfully wired for every kind of virtual and video presentation, but there was no natural light, and the ceiling was low and dark. The net effect was a feeling of total disconnection from the outside world and from nature. This member's comment shocked the hosts, who felt their facility was a state-of-the-art meeting space and a good collaborative space, and it highlighted the difficult balance we need to strike between the wires, electronics, and screens we seem to need and the light, air, and natural materials that we actually do need. The COSP Network had its own experience of a poor physical collaborative space when it held a gathering in a hotel meeting room that a keynote speaker described as a bomb shelter. In this case, the room had neither the infrastructure for audio-visual presentations nor natural light. Participants empowered themselves to deal with the room by bringing in greenery, posters, and uplit torchiere lamps, demonstrating that even the worst spaces can be moderately improved through creative efforts.

Virtual collaborative spaces play the same role as physical spaces. If the learning network's success is based on peer participation and the electronic exchange of knowledge, then the virtual space in which this occurs needs to be inviting and engaging. An early teamroom used by C3 LearnNet had a deep blue background that many users found to be cold. It was replaced by a sunnier color scheme and button-driven menus. There are legions of guides and research papers on building virtual collaborative spaces, many of which are accessible through various professional groups.[6] The best guide to a good collaborative space, though, is the constellation of members that form the learning network, who should work for consensus and periodically revisit the virtual environment question. In the future, we may have learning environments that can evolve with social and learning practices, in other words, "spaces that learn," but for now, learning networks will need to build their own best environments.

Skilled facilitation

There is no substitute for skilled facilitation in the learning network, especially if the network is relying on distance learning tools for communication and connection. Skilled facilitation includes managing the knowledge repository; prompting members for participation in teamrooms, meetings, or projects; introducing new tools; monitoring network activity; and designing and facilitating network interactions. The facilitator must maintain a neutral position: his or her every action should be focused on balancing the needs and goals of individual members with those of the network as a whole.

While learning networks form with specific goals, memberships, tools, and activities in mind, these initial frameworks evolve over time. Much of the facilitator's job is to highlight this evolutionary process and work for consensus on emergent decisions. For example, if a tool is no longer being used, the facilitator needs to notice this lack of use and question it. What are everyone's assumptions? Are the members dissatisfied with the tool? Do they have access issues? Do they find it less useful than other tools? Has it outlived its usefulness? As the learning network evolves, its use of tools will evolve, and the facilitator's job is to note when those changes have occurred and encourage discussion and decisions.

[6] See, for example, the Association of Computing Machinery's Special Interest Group on Computer–Human Interaction (SIGCHI), http://www.acm.org/sigchi/.

The facilitator's role in balancing interaction modes and revealing hidden barriers to learning can mean the difference between the success and failure of a network. Unfortunately, the facilitator often becomes overwhelmed with detailed maintenance tasks – archiving, prompting, organizing – and loses sight of what the network needs for its next stage of development. Just as our sophistication in using learning network tools needs to evolve, so does our understanding of the central role of the facilitator.

Conclusion

Just as each organizational learning culture is unique and requires individualized interactive tool-sets, so does each learning network need to find its own right mix of tools and methods. By definition, each network must start with a best guess of the tools that will be accessible and usable by its members, and then agree to revisit the tool-set composition often and make adjustments accordingly.

As a result of my experience with learning networks in the corporate and civic environments, I have concluded that when choosing tools, networks would do well to observe Ockham's razor, a principle attributed to the fourteenth-century logician and Franciscan friar, William of Ockham, which states that when there are two competing theories (in our case, tools that support learning networks), the one that is simpler is the better. Be aware that, whether the tools initially chosen to support the network are simple or complex, their use will evolve with the development of the learning network, and so the cost, maintenance, and time spent on learning to use the tools must be considered. Facilitators can keep an eye on how the tools are supporting the goals of the learning network. And the types of collaborative spaces in which the tools are used is a critical success factor in the network. A focus on the "latest and greatest" tools without consideration of the spaces in which they are used and the interactions they create will be unlikely to result in a sustainable learning network.

Illustration © Eileen Clegg

13 | *Envisioning a learning culture: history, self-governing citizens, and no dancing elephants*

BROOK MANVILLE

EVERY learning project or initiative launched in the modern organization quickly devolves to one fundamental question: How can we create the culture that will support the transformation we need? Anyone who has ever taken up the challenge knows that, for all the leverage of technology, programs, or innovative new processes, the fulcrum is always the culture of the organization. Where does the culture of a learning organization come from? What does it look and feel like in the best possible example? How does the culture relate to all the other pieces that seem to be required for a true "learning organization"? This chapter proposes an answer quite outside the current boundaries of discussion, using an unusual case example drawn from the early history of Western civilization. It is not intended as a handbook but as a thought experiment – to visit a way of working and learning that is largely foreign to what we expect today and has everything to teach us about the future.

Dancing elephants

Before beginning that experiment, we need to paint some picture of the "current boundaries of discussion." Let us start with a recent business bestseller. At the end of 2002, Lou Gerstner, the retired CEO of IBM, published his story of the successful turnaround of that computer conglomerate, which he led through the 1990s, and the book soon joined the ranks of must-read management tomes. The title of Gerstner's volume borrows from a well-known change management study by

---

This chapter was developed with debt to my recent book (co-author, Josiah Ober), *A Company of Citizens: What the World's First Democracy Teaches Leaders About Creating Great Organizations* (Boston: Harvard Business School Press, 2003). See also B. Manville and J. Ober, "Beyond Empowerment: Building a Company of Citizens," *Harvard Business Review* (January 2003), pp. 48–53.

James Belasco from a few years before, *Teaching the Elephant to Dance*.[1] The metaphor suggests that both Gerstner and Belasco share an assumption about large organizations today, one not unlike that of most people who struggle to create major change – that any large entity requiring transformation is ultimately clumsy, intractable, and even a bit dull witted. Big companies are like big elephants that can be made to move gracefully and artfully, and indeed to "perform," only through the most clever or authoritarian strategies.

Not surprisingly, the elephantine assumption frames most beliefs and developmental approaches of those seeking to create a "culture of learning" in organizations today; and similarly, those assumptions tend to frame debates about how to achieve that goal. Let us be honest: creating a learning culture in a business that is large, set in its ways, and has little history of or understanding for building human capabilities is no small task. Inevitably, the solution that is offered up involves some kind of top-down mandate and prescribed behavioral change: one must create a daunting combination of threatening imperatives and soaring incentives to (a) get people to share knowledge, invest in training, or otherwise take action to generally improve themselves, and/or (b) get managers to support training programs, install learning tools, initiate communities of practice, or whatever. In the best cases, leaders will also personally model the desired new behavior, visibly (and authentically) engage in particular training and professional development programs, and experiment with new ways of working with colleagues. And let us be clear: there are various successful examples of elephant-like companies that have, eventually, in some sense of the word, been made to dance the learning dance. Let us give Lou Gerstner some credit at IBM, and of course also Jack Welch at GE, John Brown at BP, and all the other usual suspects, who are well chronicled in books, articles, and conferences devoted to training, HR, knowledge management, and related industry disciplines.

I take nothing away from such heroic accomplishments, and my purpose in this chapter is not to belittle the dancing elephants. Circus trainers have their virtues, and no one should make light of leaders

---

[1] L. Gerstner, *Who Says the Elephant Can't Dance? Inside IBM's Historic Turnaround* (New York: HarperBusiness, 2002); J. Belasco, *Teaching the Elephant to Dance. The Manager's Guide to Empowering Change* (New York: Plume, 2002).

who successfully lead major transformational change. But such cases, at some level, often represent only incremental innovation. These are stories of rigid, siloed, and distrusting organizations that through force of will and threat of punishment became more open and oriented to cross-boundary learning and some kind of linkage between learning and performance. In most cases, the "culture of learning" is being layered onto something that already exists. At its best, that kind of program improves the situation, but the organization never seems to reach an optimum state; and more often than not, the "transformation" falls short of enduring change. Consider, here, another metaphor: the stand-alone automotive air conditioners in the 1950s that were bolted on to a car. They did cool the vehicle, but they were expensive, noisy, inefficient, and a serious drag on engine performance.

A more radical approach

Suppose, instead, that we wanted to envision a more radical solution for creating a learning culture, one that did not begin with the assumption that we are constrained within the fundamental industrial structure of a hierarchically organized, CEO-directed company, with a set of command-and-control incentives and restrictions, and with people who are considered replaceable parts. Can we envision a learning organization of the future, starting with some fresh assumptions, and look to discover a model in which learning is not just "layered onto" the status quo but is deeply embedded in the fundamental values, structures, and practices of the culture and community of the organization? What would that be like? How could we begin to understand that?

In pursuing such a vision, I am respectful of many others who have already asked a similar question. In the last decade, many portraits of the "learning organization" of the future have been sketched with the aid of various evocative metaphors, ranging from biological ecosystems to particle physics.[2] Here, too, I am happy to acknowledge the value and creativity of such explorations, though I would argue that

[2] The literature on the learning organization and "organization of the future" is vast; important recent contributions that have influenced me include P. Drucker, *Post-Capitalist Society* (New York: HarperBusiness, 1993), and "The Future of the Company," *Economist* 22 (December 2001); T. Davenport and L. Prusak, *Working Knowledge: How Organizations Manage What They Know* (Boston: Harvard Business School Press,

in envisioning what is fundamentally a human organization, images of beehives, rainforests, fractals, and sub-atomic pieces of matter can take us only so far.

My purpose here is to suggest a vision of the learning organization of the future and to describe a very vital and real culture of learning through the case study of an actual human organization in the past. I offer up a model based on what was arguably the Western world's first "learning organization": the democracy of self-governing citizens of ancient Athens. This was the city-state you learned about in high school, the community that flourished in the fifth and fourth centuries BC and produced some of the world's greatest art, literature, and other cultural and military achievements. This was Athens, the world of Sophocles, Pericles, Thucydides, Plato, and Aristotle. At its height, its 30,000 citizens ruled over a vast – the equivalent of many billions of dollars – empire of tribute-paying subjects, reigned supreme with a powerful navy, sustained war after war with resilience and determination, and lasted more than two hundred years, while producing astonishing innovations in multiple spheres of human endeavor. It was indeed not only a learning organization but a "high-performing organization," and the linkage was not accidental.

Like all case studies, and organizational models derived from such, this one requires some leaps of faith to make the relevant comparisons. It also requires some patience to adjust for obvious differences between the actual case and the future application of its design principles and practices. Yes, ancient Athens was a political community and not a business or even an explicitly not-for-profit enterprise; no, the Athenians did not have computer networks, intranets, or Kirkpatrick levels of learning impact. And were it not for the fact that they spoke the Hellenic language fluently, I would be the first to admit that things like "ROI" or "systems thinking" would have sounded positively Greek to them. If we can put aside, for the moment, all the reasons not to make this kind of modern–ancient comparison, I can offer an explanation

1998); C. Leadbeater, *The Weightless Society* (New York and London: Texere, 2000); J. Kluge, W. Stein, and T. Licht, *Knowledge Unplugged: The McKinsey & Co. Global Survey on Knowledge Management* (New York: Palgrave Macmillan, 2001); E. Wenger, R. McDermott, and W. M. Snyder, *Cultivating Communities of Practice* (Boston: Harvard Business School Press, 2002); and M. Wheatley, *Leadership and the New Science* (San Francisco: Berrett-Koehler, 1992).

for why looking back at this community might yield some particularly interesting insights. So what, then, would the designer of the future learning organization have to learn from Athenians in the golden age of Greece?

From modern to ancient

The case begins with certain fundamental trends in today's workplace, trends that will almost surely accelerate in the future. The study of the Athenian experience also addresses some fundamental dilemmas that any builder of a learning culture ultimately faces.

The first trend to note is the increasing "democratization" of the workplace and of society in general.[3] For years we have been witnessing the "flattening of organizations" as managers increasingly are forced to rely on the judgments, creativity, and experience of knowledge workers, giving up traditional control and authority to those who have the real expertise and are creating the real value of a business. Add to this the increasing spread with which information is transported via rapidly evolving communications technology and the corresponding expectation of all of us for greater transparency in our dealings with one another, transactional or otherwise. Knowledge workers expect greater autonomy, freedom, and access to information about the world in which they live and work. Our own political system is driven by polling, our shopping by disintermediation and instant access to product information and price comparisons, and our healthcare is increasingly characterized by better-informed patients, challenging the paternalistic role of authoritarian doctors.

The second trend is the importance of values and the search for community. Surveys and studies continue to suggest that workers in today's

---

[3] Here again, the literature is vast. Some useful starting points: F. Fukuyama, *The End of History and the Last Man* (New York: Free Press, 1992); R. Ackoff, *The Democratic Corporation* (New York: Oxford University Press, 1994); C. Manz and H. Simms Jr., *Business Without Bosses* (New York: John Wiley & Sons, 1995); R. Purser and S. Cabana, *The Self-Managing Corporation* (New York: Free Press, 1998); P. Slater and W. Bennis, *The Temporary Society: What Is Happening to Business and Family Life in America Under the Impact of Accelerating Change* (San Francisco: Jossey-Bass, 1998), pp. 1–23; V. Postrel, *The Future and Its Enemies: The Growing Conflict Over Creativity, Enterprise, and Progress* (New York: Free Press, 1998).

knowledge economy are keen to align themselves with organizations whose values match their own, that stand for something they believe in, and in which they can align their activities and labor with certain principles shared by the other members.[4] Consider, for example, some of the basic shifts in workers' assumptions. In the industrial age, work was exchanged for money; in the knowledge age, work is exchanged even more for meaning. In the industrial age, a company's brand was merely a marketing image; in the knowledge age, brand is personal and both flows from and adds to the identity of those creating and sustaining it. In the industrial age, workers assumed that executives were elite, different, and had their own code of behavior; in the knowledge age, we hold our leaders to high standards and do not want to follow people whose ethics or behaviors are at odds with our own. To use an increasingly common phrase, workers today are no longer "employees" but are more like "volunteer investors" – choosing with whom and where to invest their skills and experience in ways that make some kind of difference and in contexts that reinforce and develop their own sense of personal values and identity.[5]

A third trend, indeed the focus of this volume, is the importance of learning in the workplace. Knowledge workers today look for organizations that can give them the opportunity to grow continually, and more and more leaders have come to understand that the company that develops its people and generally learns faster than the competition will fare better than others.

Despite such trends, there remains a fundamental misalignment in today's workplace: between, on the one hand, knowledge workers' aspirations, professional goals, and contributions and, on the other, the culture of industrial age thinking that is still the norm in most corporations. Though many elephants have been taught to dance, they are still mostly elephants – big, awkward, and dumb. Most people in organizations are still ultimately underappreciated for the value they create, are told what to do, have little opportunity to develop themselves in

[4] See, for example, A. Wolf, "The Final Freedom," *New York Times Magazine* (March 18, 2001), pp. 48–51.

[5] For good discussion of new language reflecting such changes, see T. O. Davenport, "The Human Capital Metaphor: What's in a Name?" *Learning in the New Economy e-Magazine* (Spring 2001), http://www.linezine.com/4.2/articles/tdthcmwian.htm.

ways that benefit both them and the organization, operate in work-places characterized by less-than-full transparency and questionable or inconsistent cultural values, and often live with a good dose of fear. Though the last thirty years have seen much "empowerment" for working people, the freedom and equality implied in that term are still relatively limited. There are indeed examples of democratically man-aged companies.[6] Most managers, however, would tell you that if there is democracy in a business, it must be carefully limited and that any large-scale attempt to let people govern themselves will yield a vastly inefficient or even chaotic environment that cannot meet the demands of today's rigorous, intensely competitive marketplaces.

Similarly, learning in most organizations today operates as a discon-nected function: a training program here, a training program there, perhaps an intranet of information to choose from when needed. But none of it is central to the strategy of the company, nor is it rewarded or encouraged with the same fierceness, say, as staying within one's budget or hitting one's revenue quota. Even more important, few companies can truly claim to have a culture of learning grounded in the deepest DNA of what their organization is all about. The "learning organiza-tion" and the "democratic company" are seen either as unreachable ideals or as impractical and difficult models. And most managers will see no obvious connection between organizational learning and the processes of decision-making implied in self-governance.

Athenian genius

The genius of the ancient Athenians, and the reason they merit study as a model for the learning organization of the future, was their cre-ative solution to exactly the kind of dilemmas discussed above: how to give people the freedom and autonomy they demand but still find ways to align their efforts and interests for the good of the whole and thus create knowledge that scales. And perhaps more important than the solution *per se* were the results that it delivered: massive organiza-tional performance. To achieve the astonishing things that they did, the Athenians began with the premise that there would be better results, motivation, and indeed "results-oriented learning" if every member of

[6] References in Manville and Ober, *Company of Citizens*, p. 187, n.3.

the community had a real stake in making decisions.[7] They designed
their organization believing that every process and structure of the
community had to reinforce the value of building and contributing
knowledge to the common good and to provide the means for every
individual to make himself better at the same time. Instead of seeing
their state as an elephant that had to be made to dance by some king or
tyrant, they envisioned and created an organization in which there was
a fundamental unity between individual and society; an organization
whose values were founded and cultivated by the members themselves;
an organization that governed itself and thus accepted full accountability for its decisions; an organization in which public participation
and dialog created active, real-time learning, and aligned that learning
with the needs of the overall community. They created a company of
citizens, and indeed citizens of a very special kind.

It is difficult to grasp, on any kind of emotional or intellectual level,
the essence of the ancient Athenian citizen culture. Before discussing
its constituent elements, some comments at the whole-system level and
some basic comparisons of modern and ancient assumptions might be
helpful. The modern organization (e.g. corporation) typically exists as
an abstract and formal entity; it is usually some kind of legal structure,
owned by either proprietors or shareholders, with managers in charge.
Workers are paid to play well-identified roles, and if someone leaves
or needs to be fired, another is found to replace him or her. If a certain
skill is needed, it is hired in; if that is not possible or feasible, existing
people are trained. The company exists and operates independently of
the employees, who are ultimately fungible.

---

[7] A common criticism of Athenian democracy was its limitation of citizenship to adult males; and indeed beyond the 30,000 or so citizens of
Athens, there were thousands of noncitizens in the form of women, children, resident foreigners, and slaves. This is not the place to engage in the
moral debate about the rightness or wrongness of the "citizen elitism"; it
is likely that the eventual downfall of the community was exactly because
of the Athenians' inability to extend citizenship more widely. My purpose
in advancing the Athenian model as a "learning organization" should be
distinguished from the ancient prejudices about who could or could not
be a citizen; and readers should not accept this discussion, or my reference
to Athenian citizens with masculine pronouns, as a judgment on what
should be in any given "community of citizens." The model proposed is
not intended to be taken in all literalness from the historical record. For
more discussion, see Manville and Ober, *Company of Citizens*, pp. 149ff.

By contrast, the Athenian democratic community was a member organization. No privileged individual or elite was in charge – just the members themselves. Citizens were born and died, but with every change, the community itself changed. The community prospered on the basis of the growth of every individual, both alone and as a member of a collective body. Leaders came from the body of citizens, and everyone had to learn how to rule and be ruled in turn. There was no separate class of managers, no legal abstraction or impersonal corporation. Nobody got trained, but everybody was learning all the time. Learning was living in the community, and the community by its nature and organic life was a constant and insistent teacher.

So how did they do it? How did the ancient Athenians build a culture of learning grounded in the fundamental assumptions and processes of the organization? It is a complicated story, spanning hundreds of years, but the essential principle, as we have already suggested, was the powerful linkages these people made between learning and democracy and between individual and community. At its core, their culture of learning was a culture of democratic citizenship, a concept they called *politeia*. Let us now unpack this idea and understand why the Athenian notion of citizenship was intimately the same as a culture of learning.

Politeia

Like all rich concepts, *politeia* is not simply translated. We call it "citizenship," but in today's world that tends to imply a sort of passive legal status – having the right to carry a passport, having the obligation to pay taxes. For the ancient Athenians, the word meant many things at the same time, including for example, "membership in the city-state," "a constitution," even "a way of life." Ultimately, however, the term carried much more meaning than a single phrase can communicate. Looking more deeply at the concepts and traditions behind *politeia* will be a more fruitful approach.

Athenian citizenship in the democratic age was an organic and dynamic combination of three dimensions: values, structures, and practices. We will look at each of these in turn and in each case also see how knowledge and learning were deeply ingrained in the essence of these dimensions. Taken together, the three dimensions represented a vital and living system of self-governance that was inseparable from both individual and collective learning and growth.

Communal values

Let us begin with the values of *politeia*. Here again the dissection is difficult because of the complexity and interconnectedness of many of the ideas. For convenience, we might call them "communal values" because they embodied everything important that the community, and membership in it, stood for. They represented three sets of overlapping beliefs. There were communal values of the individual – every citizen's right to self-determination, to freedom, to equality of opportunity, and to security against harm. Every citizen was believed to have some spark of goodness, something to contribute to the public welfare.

Every citizen was at the same time free to – and expected to – engage in public debate and deliberations that directly affected him; but he was also free to pursue private interests and usually not obliged to participate, particularly when his skills or needs did not dictate. On the other hand – and here lies one of the many deliberate paradoxes of the culture – the citizen was always expected to engage and band together with others when some kind of risk or harm was present, when any citizen was threatened, either internally or externally, or when the security of the entire community was in danger.

This notion of security bleeds into a second piece of the value set – the values of community *per se*. As we have already mentioned, the core concept here was that the "citizens were the state" or, to use a more contemporary phrase, "the people are the organization." The Athenians did not imagine an abstract entity separate and separable from themselves; there was no eternal "corporate center," no brand name distinct from those who lived it. Symbolically, "Athens" was only the name of a particular place; the political community was always called in Greek "the Athenians." Thus the historian Thucydides famously quotes one general with the eternal phrase, "Not ships, not walls, but men make our city."[8] The Athenian city-state was simultaneously all about the individual and all about the community: the personal was communal and the communal was personal.

The key to this fundamental paradox was a third set of communal values, and it is here where learning shines forth in the essence of what

---

[8] Thucydides, *The Peloponnesian War*, 7.77. Translation adapted from Penguin edition, tr. R. Warner (New York: Viking-Penguin, 1972); used by permission.

the Athenians stood for. We call this third set of communal values "moral reciprocity" – the all-important link between "what's in it for me" and "what's in it for us." Moral reciprocity was a set of mutual expectations between individual and community: the individual owed allegiance and participation to the community if he were developed and made better through that participation; and similarly the community could expect to be made better by the collective growth of all who engaged. Stated otherwise, and more simply, *politeia* was education for one and for all simultaneously, and learning was the win-win of both citizenship and state.

It is important to distinguish the Athenian value of "moral reciprocity" from what today is called "the employability contract"; that is, when the employer promises to develop the employee during his tenure as long as the employee promises to perform at the highest possible level. Note, however, some critical differences between modern employability and ancient moral reciprocity: the former fosters no long-term loyalty, whereas the latter takes much of its power from a long-standing commitment to membership. And similarly, employability is simply a quid pro quo transaction agreed to by those in power, whereas moral reciprocity emerges from the members themselves, who are steering their own destiny. In its values, ancient Athens was a study of balanced paradox, made possible by heartfelt and enduring commitment on the part of both the individual and the community to make each other better.

Participative structures

The second dimension of *politeia* was the participative structures of decision-making; the organization was about as "flat" as it could be. Laws were made by all citizens, who deliberated and voted as a governing assembly that met regularly and who also took turns serving as jurors in popular courts to judge one another in matters of conflict or transgression. Leadership positions numbered in the hundreds, ranging from the council that steered the deliberative assembly, to the generals who led in battle, to the functionaries who administered things like the treasury, the outfitting of ships, and the organization of public festivals. Turnover in all executive roles was regular, and selection was made either by election or lot or some combination of the two. Demographic analysis tells us that during his lifetime, every citizen must have served in some leadership capacity in the community at least once, and that does not include the leadership roles that Athenians often played in local neighbor organizations. Indeed, one of the ingenious dimensions of the overall design was to establish central institutions that drew from the memberships of regional and local ones. Rotation through roles in the central institutions had the effect of reinforcing knowledge-sharing relationships and building "networks of networks" across the city-state.

The democratic structure and institutions treated knowledge in a special way. Expertise brought forward by relevant citizens in deliberations or executive roles was always welcome – indeed expected – but institutionalized professionalism had no place in the system. The Athenians preferred a broadly amateur approach to governance, valuing the participative engagement by all more than the privileged knowledge of a few. Courts had no professional lawyers, assembly delegates were only as permanent as those who chose to attend, and generals had to give up their commands to others in the regular rotation of positions.

These participative structures – assembly, courts, councils, executive positions – represented the tangible mechanisms of democratic decision-making and citizen engagement, but they also had a profoundly educational purpose. By design, it was through these mechanisms that citizens practiced the values of *politeia* and had reinforced to them the meaning of membership in the community. Because of the way the assembly was constructed and run, and the way courts were designed and managed, every citizen every day saw and acted out the values of equality, freedom, and security; the choices they made every day in those institutions played out the tension between individual and community, and helped create a "both/and" mindset of managing that paradox. The shoulder-to-shoulder debates, decision-making, and shared accountability built deep trust in the notion of collective and mutual respect for one's fellow citizens.

Practices of engagement

If values and structures provided the overall framework for *politeia*, practices of engagement, the last of the three dimensions, are what gave it life. The values played out in institutional settings and processes must be finally expressed in action: "doing citizenship" in a very particular way, in the same way that it has been said that "organizational culture" is "how we do business around here." Once again, it is difficult to separate this dimension from the others, and indeed values, structures, and practices are intimately interwoven. Think of values as more abstract and general, structures as tangible and operational. The practices of citizenship are somewhere in between; they are the daily assumptions, behaviors, and ways of engaging that reflect a way of thinking and being (at the same time) a citizen.

We can identify different groups of practices, each of which exemplified and contributed to this culture of citizenship: practices of access, reflecting free and equal opportunity for participation in self-governance for all Athenians; practices of process, reflecting a bias for well-intentioned deliberation, fair play, transparency, timely execution, and collective support in all deliberations and decisions; practices of consequence, reflecting a focus on merit as the ultimate criterion, the need to achieve results, the right to challenge, and the need to be accountable – good or bad – for all outcomes. The Athenians also practiced what we can call jurisdiction – ensuring that whenever a decision was made (sometimes locally, sometimes centrally, often in some combination of the two), it was made closest to those with the most knowledge and with the greatest stake in the outcome. In every case, practices were part of the overall framework of "public teaching" – reinforcing a way of acting consistent with the spirit of *politeia*.

Citizenship and the learning organization

Taken together, these values, structures, and practices of citizenship represented a holistic organizational system – and indeed a deep culture of learning. Even in ancient times, the great Athenian general and statesman Pericles echoed that idea, proclaiming that the city and *politeia* were "an education to all of Greece," even as he had implied they were an education to each and every citizen himself. Having described *politeia* in its constituent (though admittedly interrelated) dimensions, let me now step back and summarize why this system was such a powerful learning organization. Let us understand how it generated so much creativity, power, and wealth in the course of two centuries.

First, this system and culture created an unprecedented "marketplace of ideas." The freedom and equality reflected in its values, the forums for public debate and deliberation, the networks of networks, the idea of constant rotation among leadership roles, the processes to encourage challenges but also focus action – all these together created an environment that engaged thousands of people in collective problem-solving, fostered innovation, and ensured that if knowledge was had by someone and needed by another, it would flow freely and quickly between "buyers and sellers," horizontally, vertically, from region to region.

Second, the system created intense collective focus and ongoing alignment – in both the development and deployment of ideas. The culture and practices of *politeia* encouraged every person to pursue individual excellence zealously and at the same time, through the shared values and processes of governance, to pursue passionately the common good. The "both/and" thinking of individual and community meant that every problem for the city was the problem for the citizen, and vice versa.

Third, the culture inspired high motivation – the passion for excellence and achievement coupled with the knowledge that one was steering one's own destiny. This created an enormous pull – instead of push – for learning. Unlike modern knowledge-management or learning programs, there was no need to provide incentives for people to share information or sign up for training – learning was everyone's business, because knowledge was how you got ahead and how your city got ahead with you. Furthermore, learning was not just about success; Athenians had their own share of failures, and these were played out, discussed, and debated – vigorously and transparently – in the public forums of assemblies, councils, and courts. From failures came greater wisdom, which, coupled with the pursuit of excellence, also resulted in great organizational resilience – the ability to come back from defeat and reinvent oneself on the strength and determination of the collective citizenship.

Fourth, the culture made no real distinction between learning and work. Learning was coded into the civic culture, both in the practices that taught and reinforced ways of thinking and behaving, and in the institutions that shaped and formed the people who participated in them. Learning was part of citizenship, and citizenship always meant learning for both your own and everyone's sake. Learning was both doing and talking, just as doing and talking were learning.

This culture of learning embodied by the Athenian *politeia* was an unprecedented form of political and social organization in the ancient world. Never before had such military power been wielded without the power and riches of a monarch; nor had previous empires ever achieved the cultural and scientific innovations that Athens also displayed. As boastful and proud as the Athenians themselves could be about their achievements, they were not alone in admiring their peculiarly entrepreneurial "learning culture." In a famous speech preserved by Thucydides, we hear the Corinthians speaking enviously and even somewhat fearfully about the Athenians, hoping to inflame the Spartans to go to war in 431 BC. The Corinthian rhetoric enshrined the manifestations of this very special *politeia*:

An Athenian is always an innovator, quick to form a resolution and quick to carry it out . . . their daring will outrun its own resources; they will take risks against their better judgments, but in the midst of danger, remain confident . . . While you [Spartans] are hanging back, they never hesitate; while you stay at home, they are always abroad; for they think that the farther they go, the more they will get . . . If they win a victory, they follow it up at once, and if they suffer a defeat, they scarcely fall back at all . . . They regard [their bodies] as expendable for their city's sake, as though they were not their own; but each man cultivates his own intelligence, again with a view for doing something notable for his city. If they aim at something and do not get it, they think that they have been deprived of what belonged to them already; whereas if their enterprise is successful, they regard that success as nothing compared to what they will do next . . . Of them alone, it may be said that they possess a thing almost as soon as they have begun to desire it, so quickly with them does action follow upon decision.[9]

Building a company of citizens

The question that inevitably comes next in looking at this unusual learning culture is how the Athenians came to create it. That, alas, is a subject for a separate essay; space does not allow any kind of real treatment here. Suffice it to say, however, that the process was not

[9] Thucydides, *Peloponnesian War*, 1.70–71.

accomplished overnight; that it reflected hundreds of years of experiment, failure, and re-experiment; that it was indeed achieved with lots of help from visionary leaders but ultimately succeeded only because the people themselves – the citizens – made the commitment to find a better and more effective way to organize, a way that gave every member of the community a heartfelt and honest stake in governing the organization, whose success depended on each and every person's knowledge, skills, and even, finally, his life. This community, as history shows, was no elephant made to dance; it was a fierce lion that taught itself to run, jump, and leap with all its own self-discovered agility.

Well, "Good for them!" you might say – and then very reasonably ask, "What about us?" Supposing we are stuck with elephants, and supposing we do not have, say, a couple of hundred years of experimentation to reinvent – or rediscover – the glory that was Greece? Remember that this chapter was not intended as a handbook but as a "thought experiment." But even a mere thought experiment can point to some practical implications once we start to imagine an entirely different way of thinking about a problem. Let me conclude with a few suggestions about bringing the world of this very special learning organization into a modern context – understanding that every enterprise is its own unique case and that there is never a blueprint that can be imposed unilaterally with guaranteed success. None the less, for those who would go boldly forward, I offer the following suggestions.

Reconceive the idea of a "learning organization" around self-governance. That is, rethink the usual notion that training, development, and sharing knowledge are independent goals for organizational design. Instead, see them as dependent variables that flow from an overarching identity of citizenship – an organization made up of members whose individual and collective success are grounded in the continual betterment of all and the life of "public engagement" and decision-making for one's own future.

Build the culture with the "citizens" themselves. The Athenian lesson is the ur-chapter of what every good organizational consultant has always known: change cannot be imposed from above; it must be invented and owned by those who must live the new order. Leadership and facilitation can obviously play important roles – but without bottom-up design and development of key values, structures, and practices, self-governance will be but a false shadow. Understand who is a member, who is not, and then work together to invent the organization that is the people themselves and only the people.

Begin where there is organizational readiness and the greatest need for enhanced performance. The history of the Athenians shows that the revolution that produced their democracy grew in patches at first and then expanded to scale through a process of "networking networks"; it also shows that a steep performance challenge – which required faster learning and deeper collaboration – drove positive change. A citizen-style learning culture might begin at a team level, or a business unit, or within a virtual community – the proposition need not encompass an entire enterprise, especially at first. And similarly, some contexts might make more sense for this approach than others; groups or units of relatively autonomous knowledge workers are perhaps an easier place to develop a citizen model than an existing hierarchy of, say, industrial production (though the latter might be appropriate, depending on its business objectives and challenges).

Pursue the triad of values, structures, and practices. Learning cultures are complex and organic systems, never admitting a silver-bullet approach to development. The Athenian model demonstrates the subtle and mutually reinforcing strands of beliefs such as liberty, equality, and reciprocity; the institutions and processes for engagement and conflict resolution; and the constellation of behaviors and beliefs such as participation, meritocracy, transparency, and deliberation. No learning culture, and especially this citizen model, is built by a single process, or technology, or leader.

Be – and work only with those – willing "to both rule and be ruled." This simple phrase of Aristotle lies at the heart of democratic citizenship for any organization and opposes so many of our modern workplace assumptions. Leadership must be both embraced by everyone and limited for everyone; taking turns builds knowledge and experience, both bottom up and top down. As the Athenians first showed, doing is learning and learning is doing; and so is debating, voting, and teaching one another for the public good. The experience of making decisions and living with the consequences among one's peers is as powerful a learning strategy as has ever been invented. How many of today's CEOs would really step up to that challenge?

Blend revolution with evolution. Building a citizen learning culture will shatter many traditional assumptions and break many standard molds – but for all the blood and glory, Athens was not built in a day. Know that for every transformative advance, there will also be failures and slippage; and forward motion will always be punctuated by doubts and digressions. Keep your courage, and remember – you are not leading a project; you are creating a new way of work-life. And that takes time, not to mention an inevitable share of false starts and bumps along the road. *Politeia* is not for the one-minute manager but for hardy organizational adventurers who take the long view. And who else but an ancient historian could tell you that?

14 | *Individual competencies and partnerships: the primary cultural influencers*

BRENDA WILKINS

ORGANIZATIONAL culture is a lot like the weather, and then not. Weather and culture have distinct characteristics, unanticipated variations, destructive tendencies, and refreshing respites. They are understandable with extended exposure, but never a sure thing. Sometimes we get so caught up in organizational strategies, systems, and structures that we forget the crucial way in which culture is not like the weather. No matter how much we learn, no matter how many meteorological tools and techniques we have at our disposal, we cannot influence weather. However, no matter how little we know or how limited our resources, we can influence organizational culture.

Because influencing culture is so important for increasing productivity, market position, and the bottom line, it has become the subject of much research and debate. Many leaders turn to the latest theories, techniques, and technologies in the quest for the competitive edge – the "right culture." But, in reality, successful cultures depend on inspired individuals who, through their learning and leadership abilities, motivate and influence others. Some may think this is an idealistic view; instead, it is a heavy burden, because to change culture, each of us must face, improve, and capitalize on our strengths and limitations.

It is the premise that the individual is the primary cultural catalyst which immediately separates this text from so many, and I know it may be viewed with skepticism. But years of organizational and leadership research, and professional forays into many other disciplines have compelled me to assert that much of our thinking about culture is misdirected. Specifically, we give far too much credence to organizational systems, designs, and processes, and far too little credit to the role of the individual leader.

Experience tells me that the individual is the primary cultural catalyst. Therefore, when it comes to influencing culture, the focus must not be the organization's systems or resources, or the balance between those systems and the individual. Rather, the focus should be the individual's ability, alone and in partnership, that shapes organizational culture. By developing the competencies and partnering processes described here, you can directly influence the chaotic and continuous culture in your organization.

Developing individual competencies in the area of assessment, action, and adaptation are critical for individuals to influence culture. Further, committing to the development of individual skills enhances the power that emerges from collaborative partnerships like mentoring and coaching. The combination of individual competencies and partnering processes can be unstoppable when deployed by a focused, visionary, and resilient individual.

Individual processes

Every leader and every employee must ask, "How am I influencing or contributing to the company's culture?" The question demonstrates a fundamental understanding of the power individuals have over culture. For the leader the question is critical because no matter what is going on in the organization, no matter what organizational designs and processes are in place, no matter what the external market, the leader has the capacity to affect culture every day.

No anecdote demonstrates this better than the story of Carol. In the late 1990s, I was working with a human services organization in Montana, coaching county directors and their employees through very difficult stages of state welfare reform. The organizational designs were mandated and rigid, process and procedure set, and money scarce, all thanks to legislative action. The majority of the leaders and employees I worked with felt powerless – victimized – and it was palpable in the culture. However, it quickly became evident that one group of employees stood apart – Carol's. Carol, the county director in her region, had created a culture separate from that of the other counties. In her county, the focus was not on limitations but on the opportunities to serve the constituency; not on the lack of resources but on the infinite opportunities to treat clients with dignity and facilitate change; not on the numbers of people who would fall through the cracks but on the numbers who could be lifted out of dependence. To maintain the positive foci of her county seemed like a Herculean effort from an outsider's perspective, and to watch her employees experience and sustain this culture of hope and action was remarkable. Equally noteworthy was the mastery with which Carol created this amazingly positive culture in her own county when she and her colleagues suffered in a statewide department whose culture was predominantly negative and angry. This is a powerful example, because leaders often argue that their unique limitations prevent them from creating the culture they envision. Yet Carol was one leader in a group of thirty-seven who proved how much influence one individual has in creating culture.

The primary characteristic that set Carol apart from her colleagues was her capacity to engage in constant change. During my association with her, I recognized a pattern of success. Each time a need, question, challenge, or crisis was presented to her, she cycled through carefully assessing the situation, deciding on her actions, and then adapting at every turn, if necessary. She applied this process to everything: communicating a new policy or budget cuts to her staff, providing performance appraisals, helping draft legislative bills, and implementing the destructive or heroic outcomes of welfare reform.

Assessment, action, and adaptation are age-old processes for learning and change, yet they are as fresh and useful today as they were a hundred years ago. Their uses range from scientific research and development to artistic exploration, but nowhere are they more powerful than in the hands of a leader. These three individual processes form the foundation for a learning culture in which leaders and employees are constantly learning and changing.

Assessment

To learn continually, people must be able to assess themselves. This requires two skills that are in direct conflict with human experience: the ability to view oneself objectively and the ability to open oneself to criticism for the purpose of change. Both require an openness and vulnerability that most people resist.

Recently, I worked with a CEO in California who espoused learning as his organization's central value. Full of energy and vision at the height of the dot-com revolution, he lost his company for one reason: he could not assess himself as a leader. Not only could he not view his own behavior objectively, but also he rejected any feedback from his executive team about his leadership style, his strategy, his decision-making, and his vision. As a result, the executive team slowly disregarded his direction and ultimately disintegrated, leaving the company a casualty in what looked like a typical dot-com failure. The reality, however, was that the company's concept was strong, the momentum in the market-place was well paced, and the company had talented employees and substantial financial resources. The CEO's inability to engage in assessment stifled learning, change, and the partnership between him and his executive team.

Conversely, I had the privilege in the early 1990s of working with a midsize publishing company in Washington state whose three executive-team members were committed to self-assessment for the purposes of understanding how they could be better leaders and increase their effectiveness as a team. When I began working with the organization, the executives had tremendous capabilities to lead the company, and the CEO had abdicated all operational functioning to them, giving them both formal and informal power. However, they were not working well as a team, primarily because of differences in leadership style and a lack of trust among them. As a result, the entire organizational culture was one of suspicion and distrust.

One executive was an extroverted maverick who made decisions quickly, took big risks, and communicated often and spontaneously but ineffectively and inaccurately, often leaving his peers and employees confused and suspicious. His employees were both inspired and irritated by their boss, riding a roller-coaster of productivity and focus. The second executive was an introverted and thoughtful person who researched thoroughly before making decisions, communicated precisely, and was a caring mentor to her employees. She struggled with her two extroverted and exuberant peers on the executive team and often withdrew from them. As a result, her peers were distrustful of her, but her employees were dedicated and loyal – willing to take the sword for their leader. The third executive was the peacemaker, working to negotiate the relationship between her extroverted and introverted peers. Her employees liked her – she was an excellent conversationalist and a nurturing boss – but they failed to respect her as a leader because she spent more time negotiating than she did accepting her role as a decision-maker. Not surprisingly, she was continually frustrated by her inability to maintain credibility with her employees and exhausted by the futile efforts to bring her peers together.

Learning to assess their leadership and communication styles was a monumental challenge for all three executives. It required many uncomfortable realizations and a commitment to individual accountability, learning, and change. The very act of rigorous self-assessment became the first step in creating an organizational learning culture. In the case of this publishing company, assessment came in several forms. Some formal assessment tools such as temperament testing, multi-rater feedback, performance management, and goal-setting were used, but informal processes of self-reflection, perception checking with others, soliciting advice and input from team members and colleagues, and personal assessment were equally powerful.

After six months of continual assessment, action, and adaptation, each leader was more effective and accountable in the organization. The executive team began to function smoothly and collaboratively. Two years later, thanks to the executive team and the employees, the company had quadrupled its revenues. Employees of the three executives openly communicated their trust in the team and worked to support its vision. The cultural stories were no longer ones of criticism and distrust but instead focused on the company's potential in the marketplace and employees' confidence that goals could be achieved. Another executive joined the team along with other employees as growth continued. Through growth, the culture of the organization remained steadfast as the executive team continued to assess, act, and adapt. Today, the company is the most recognizable name in its marketplace and has spawned additional profitable businesses. The three original executives appreciate their capacity to influence culture, and they consider the company's culture its greatest competitive asset.

Action

To create change, people must be willing to transcend assessment and act. Self-assessment is critical to moving leaders forward but futile if they do not move; that is, if they do not act on what an assessment reveals. Action requires risk-taking on the part of leaders, and often organizations. However, without action, assessment is wasted, and the rewards of risk are unrealized.

In the late 1980s and 1990s, I worked with two sets of leaders who all suffered from the inability to act on assessment. One company was a leading US aircraft manufacturer; the other was a state government office. Worlds apart in their bureaucracy and mission, they both failed at successful and sustainable culture change. The first organization invested hundreds of thousands of dollars in assessment and action planning. The second invested hundreds of hours in federal and statewide research, as well as internal workforce assessment. When it came time to act, however, both sets of leaders stalled, paralyzed by the fear of change.

In the case of the aircraft manufacturer, thousands of employees had been promised leadership change that would create a "world-class company." When the individual leaders became paralyzed by their personal requirements for learning and change, their lack of action reduced the commitment and morale of the entire company. Years later, the company is still battling the debilitating impact of a wounded culture. The word most often used to describe the company and the workforce by both internal and external sources? Mediocre. It is no surprise that it has never regained its market position of a decade ago or that the workforce is significantly smaller.

The state government office stalled for two and a half years while its leader summoned the courage to act. During this time, the organization met its basic obligations but otherwise did not move forward. Even the leader acknowledged that without action on her part, the organization's culture would remain unprofessional and outdated. But act she did, first changing her communication and leadership behavior, then redefining her relationship with state legislatures and politicians, and finally restructuring the leadership of her department. In less time than it had taken her to decide to act, she was able to transform the entire organization into the best-run agency in her state. For the next ten years, she continued to advance in state government by continually assessing, acting, and adapting. Her impact has increased exponentially. Recently retired, she now develops new not-for-profit organizations to serve the underserved. Her national reputation is as an exceptional leader, lifelong learner, and social advocate.

I am often asked how to deploy the action stage of developing individual competencies. Usually the asker is looking for a step-by-step process, and there are hundreds I could recommend. I refuse to give one. Part of the responsibility and accountability of developing individual competencies is to determine the "how" for ourselves. Plenty of processes can serve as excellent tools, but each leader, each individual, must accept, internalize, and finally externalize his or her own actions for learning and change.

Adaptation

To continue the learning process, people must commit to ongoing adaptation. Experimenting with new behaviors and processes requires constant adaptation on the path to mastery and success. In my experience, this is the most frustrating and neglected component of the learning process, primarily because people are tired by the time they have gone through the assessment and action stages. They do not want to begin the cyclical process of adaptation, which requires still more assessment and action. Instead, they want to think and act linearly with the satisfaction that they have assessed, acted, and are now *done*. Common sense tells us this is a fallacy, but human nature resists the pressure to continue the learning cycle.

Adaptation is the process of assessing effectiveness – being accountable to change – and then adjusting behavior to increase effectiveness. Having engaged in assessment and action, leaders must then determine what adaptations are needed. The very nature of adaptation strengthens the assessment and action steps in the individual's learning cycle because both are required for successful adaptation. When we look at our competencies, our work, and our organizations with the perspective that adaptation is necessary, we are forced to continue changing and learning.

Because change is unavoidable, adaptation provides us with the conceptual structure to manage change by taking a focused approach to assessing effectiveness and adapting our behaviors as needed. And the goal of all of this is to increase our effectiveness and competencies as learning individuals who have the power to create learning cultures, improve business function and individual competencies, and, therefore, boost the bottom line.

After a decade of working with organizations, my careful assessment revealed an important distinction between culture interventions that succeeded and those that did not. The successful interventions occurred because there was an individual, or individuals, somewhere in the organization who possessed the motivation and the competencies to champion the cultural work. All the processes and bags of tricks, whether they are handed down from the top or implemented at the grass roots, have no lasting traction without people.

Therefore, it is self-evident that one of the primary ways to empower individuals is to give them the support to succeed, the tools. Most often leaders consider "tools" to be new processes, strategies, products, designs, or even new organizational structures. However, one of the most valuable tools can be partnerships that support and advance the leader and the organization together. These partnerships require, support, and challenge the individual processes of assessment, action, and adaptation. The outcome is that the partnership accelerates and advances changes in culture.

Partnership processes

The two partnership processes discussed here, mentoring and coaching, are available to every individual at any stage of life, in any organization, with limited or limitless resources. They are powerful culture catalysts because they not only support individuals' (leaders' or others') efforts to influence culture, but they push them beyond the original goals born from individual assessment, action, and adaptation.

Mentoring and coaching are similar in that both usually involve an "expert" working with an individual. Both support the goals and interests of the individual. Both challenge and push the individual to achieve more and support that person in the process of achievement. Both mentoring and coaching are dependent on the quality of the relationship with the individual and on the individual's dedication to learning and change.

Where they differ is in expertise and derived benefit. Mentors typically bring the wisdom and experience of a sage who has traveled a road similar to the individual's (protégé's) goal, and they usually expect something in return, ranging from the satisfaction of helping another succeed to direct access to the protégé's own resources and expertise. Coaches, on the other hand, bring the wisdom and experience of facilitating learning and behavioral change for the purpose of the individual's goal achievement, rather than expertise in a specific content area or field of business. In return, coaches expect the individual to focus on and be accountable for setting and achieving specific goals. While it is expected that mentoring will be an equally beneficial relationship for both parties, coaching exists only to benefit the coaching client. Either way, both relationships are useful partnerships to support individuals in crafting culture.

Mentoring

Mentoring is a common term, often understood simply as a relationship in which an expert, the mentor, gives advice to another who is less experienced, the protégé. Historically, mentors have been helpful in both personal and professional contexts because of the unique capacity of the relationship to promote learning and change.

A mentoring relationship meets the following criteria: the mentor has specific knowledge and experience to share with the protégé; there is a synergy between the mentor and the protégé; and the relationship is clearly defined. Given these criteria, the goal of the relationship is for the mentor to make available his or her wisdom, experience, influence, resources, and knowledge for the explicit purpose of helping the protégé reach defined goals.

Mentoring focuses on the interpersonal relationship between the mentor and protégé, which requires mutual collaboration and reflection about the process and results of learning.[1] In this way, mentoring supports the individual competency strategies discussed above: assessment, action, and adaptation.

For example, a significant amount of challenge for the protégé comes from a willingness to examine beliefs, skills, and practices – a partnership requirement of mentoring that supports the individual work of assessment.[2] Therefore, in order to facilitate learning, the mentor must be committed to supporting the protégé while also challenging him or her to rethink assumptions, step outside his or her comfort zone, and ultimately advance and learn in a secure environment.[3] For this learning to occur, the protégé must enter into the mentoring relationship prepared to experiment with assessment, action, and adaptation.

[1] N. H. Cohen, *Mentoring Adult Learners: A Guide for Educators and Trainers* (Malabar, Fla.: Krieger, 1995).

[2] K. Yamamoto, "To See Life Grow: The Meaning of Mentorship," *Theory into Practice* (1988), pp. 183–189.

[3] L. A. Daloz, *Effective Teaching and Mentoring: Realizing the Transformational Power of Adult Learning Experiences* (San Francisco: Jossey-Bass, 1986).

The mentor's responsibility is to commit to a relationship in which he or she is willing to share stories of success and failure, resources and relationships, and strategies for achieving goals.[4] This responsibility is often described as three types of giving.[5]

(1) *Awakening.* Through an assessment of the protégé's life and work, the mentor awakens the protégé to a new vision and then provides the tangible support to realize the vision.

(2) *Sharing.* The mentor shares wisdom, knowledge, and resources that enable the protégé to learn and grow on a steady path toward the accomplishment of goals.

(3) *Continuing.* The mentor, upon helping the protégé achieve goals, suggests or inspires a commitment on the part of the protégé to be a mentor for someone else, continuing the cycle of learning, change, and support.

A couple of years ago, I had the privilege of mentoring the executive director of a nonprofit organization for severely disabled adults – the largest organization of its kind in the state. The director was not accustomed to being in a leadership position, and she faced many challenges in her new job. The most monumental one was the culture of victimization and unprofessional conduct in an organization restricted by the bureaucracy and regulation inherent in a government-funded agency.

She wanted the organization to turn itself around, but she could not see past the systemic problems. After struggling for five years, she found that the best way to change the culture was to change herself. As her mentor, I helped her assess her strengths and weaknesses as a leader, her professional goals, and her goals for changing the culture of the organization. She envisioned a culture of strategic collaborators whose professional focus was growing the organization and continually adapting in the face of state and federal changes in the disability industry. In effect, she envisioned a learning organization.

The mentoring process was difficult, and at times, despite clear and specific advice from me, she turned away from needed change. However, as the process continued she learned to accept her leadership role, take responsibility, and change behaviors that did not support the

---

[4] B. Kaye and B. Jacobson. "Reframing Mentoring," *Training and Development* 50 (1996), pp. 44–47.

[5] N. J. Gehrke, "Toward a Definition of Mentoring," *Theory into Practice* (1988), pp. 190–194.

culture she envisioned. She stopped minimizing organizational conflicts, set clear goals and expectations, communicated assertively, and stopped using or allowing the language of victimization. She fired some of her management team and recruited a new staff that supported the mission she had outlined. She changed the organization's communication systems, implemented policies, and modeled her personal changes for her staff. Through the mentoring process, not only did she emerge as a strong and compassionate leader, but also she single-handedly created a learning culture. The process took about three years.

Today she leads a team of executives in a newly designed organization destined to become one of the most influential nonprofits in the industry. The culture is energized by the prospect, challenges, and opportunities of constant change. The mindset of the organization has changed, and with it a learning culture has emerged and stabilized. For her part, the leader is hooked on change and learning, and she recently began her master's work in organizational development and leadership.

I like to share this story because it shows how mentoring can support the individual work of assessment, action, and adaptation to create a learning culture. The mentoring relationship is a powerful partnership for creating learning organizations because it conceptually and practically positions the individual at the center of change and cultural influence. The organizational culture changes organically as individuals begin to change and model those changes to those around them. It is this simple but dramatic shift of focus away from organizational systems to individuals that makes mentoring useful in creating a learning culture. In the mentoring partnership, the protégé is in the lead, and all other resources in the department or organization support the changes the individual is making, rather than the individual supporting a new organizational system or process.

To create the ideal mentoring relationship – one that can be valuable across organizational contexts – certain criteria should be established. The ideal mentoring relationship has several important characteristics:

- *Power is limited to the relationship.* A mentor should have no direct authority over the protégé, so that guidance, feedback, or even suggestions are not perceived as performance-related conversations. It is important that the mentor does not have any direct impact on or decision-making authority over the protégé's career or organizational role.

- *Rules must be clear.* The mentor and protégé should decide how formal or informal they want their relationship to be. Some organizations or individuals that use mentoring like to have specific commitments; for example, the mentor and protégé meet for two hours every week. Others prefer more spontaneous arrangements. While it is important to develop the relationship that best suits the individuals involved, research suggests that formal agreements are most successful.[6]
- *Resources must be assessed.* The mentor should possess the knowledge, resources, and expertise that enable the protégé to achieve his or her goals. Before agreeing to a mentoring relationship, the protégé must clearly communicate his or her goals and the mentor must examine his or her ability to help the protégé achieve them.
- *Communication and expectations must be clear.* Communication must be clear, and the expectations for *each interaction* must be explicitly stated. As in all relationships, this is perhaps the most difficult quality to sustain, but given the goal-focused nature of mentoring, clarity is essential.

Having established these ideal characteristics, it must be said that there are many situations in which these characteristics are *not* present, yet a valuable mentoring relationship can emerge. Such relationships should not be discounted, but it is important to acknowledge that the full power of the partnership will be somewhat diminished. When a power dynamic exists in the mentor–protégé relationship, the individuals are not free from previous conditions or expectations. A classic example is succession mentoring, which occurs when an organization's founder identifies an individual to replace him or her as the next organizational leader.

I have a client, a founder of a business, who is passing the business to his son. The relationship is complicated not only by the fact that a father, who naturally holds power over his son, is attempting to be a mentor, but also by the dynamics that existed between the two long before they became colleagues. Furthermore, the father has rigid ways of conducting business, while the son is a change agent, schooled

[6] K. E. Kram, "Phases of the Mentor Relationship," *Academy of Management Journal* 26 (1983), pp. 608–625, and *Mentoring at Work* (Lanham, Md.: University Press of America, 1988); S. B. Merriam, "Mentors and Protégés: A Critical Review of the Literature," *Adult Education Quarterly* 33 (1983), pp. 161–173.

in the science of chaos. Despite these hurdles, which are common in succession stories, the exceptional communication skills of both men have allowed them to craft a successful mentoring relationship.

They have done this by establishing clear rules and practices: they communicate expectations, determine what resources and expertise the father must make available for the son, decide who is the leader on any given project – requiring the nonleader to forgo power, allow the son to make changes unless the father provides a compelling reason not to do so, and use a coach to keep them focused on their goals and accountable to their relationship. With these agreements, the two have worked together successfully since the son joined the business seven years ago. The transition of the large, multinational family business is almost complete. Very soon the father will no longer play a role in the organization, but both he and his son will benefit as their relationship makes the transition to one that truly meets the criteria of a pure mentoring relationship.

Not surprisingly, the organization has changed under the father-and-son partnership. As I said earlier, anytime someone new enters an organization, the culture is affected. Certainly in the case of a succession, the impact is significant. The organization has maintained its compassionate, customer-focused, and personal qualities but has added new qualities of learning and change. In the last few years, business revenue and employees have doubled as the learning culture has taken root and the son has inspired confidence in his ability to lead, learn, and chart the organization's future.

Whether mentoring relationships meet the ideal criteria or some realistic version, there is no doubt that mentoring supports the individual work of assessment, action, and adaptation. For the purpose of creating a learning culture, it has been well documented that individuals, under the influence and support of mentors, are powerful culture creators. Part of this is because the nature of the relationship requires constant learning, but mentoring relationships are also powerful because the focus of learning and change is where it belongs – on the individual.

Coaching

Coaching is a second partnership for change that requires even more from the individual than mentoring. It also has the potential to offer the individual and the organization a significant return on the individual's efforts. Coaching is very different from mentoring, although the two are often confused. While mentoring relies on the mentor's expertise and resources as the primary assets to advance the protégé, coaching relies on the communication and intuition skills of the coach to catalyze action and accountability on the part of the client.[7] The "client" is typically the organizational individual or leader, while the "coach" may be a member of the organization who performs the coaching function or an external coach. Both coach and client focus on achieving the client's goals by means of a supportive and challenging relationship. In coaching, the resources for learning, change, and success must come primarily from the client. There is no mentor in the wings with expertise, knowledge, and resources to advance the client's goals. It is all up to the client. Therefore, the client becomes his or her own source of influence and expertise in the creation of personal leadership attributes and ultimately of culture.

Coaches use specific communication skills that require the client to engage in assessment, action, and adaptation. Through the communication skills of questioning, feedback, restating, checking perspectives, asking for commitment to action, and checking on achieved actions, the coach pushes the client along the path to learning and change. Much as in the mentor relationship, trust, clear communication, and clear agreements are critical. Unlike a malleable mentoring relationship, coaching requires rigorous accountability and action from the client.

The coach's responsibility is both to challenge and to support the client, and to hold the client accountable to his or her goals through a process of "checking-up" on the client, identifying obstacles to the client's progress and learning, and celebrating the client's success. The coach manages the relationship and agrees strategies with the client to ensure continual progress. The client is responsible for actively participating in the assessment, action, and adaptation that are required in the pursuit of goals. The relationship is characterized by strong expectations of accountability and action to move the client toward goal achievement.

Future-focused learning and goal accomplishment are the hallmark outcomes of coaching. Where a mentor relationship may allow for

---

[7] For this section I have drawn on material from my doctoral dissertation, "Personal Coaching: A Grounded Theory Study," University of Montana, Missoula, 2000.

passive learning and reflection in an amicable low-key relationship, the coaching relationship demands rigorous and visible reflection, learning, and change. Both quantitative and qualitative studies support learning and change as the primary returns on the coach and client's investment of time and energy. IBM provides an ideal example of how profound the impact of coaching can be in organizations. Several years ago, Jane Creswell was renowned for creating a coaching culture at IBM. Because learning is the central characteristic of coaching, Creswell's efforts translated to the creation and ongoing support of a learning culture for IBM.

According to Creswell, the biggest benefit of using coaching to manage culture is that "coaching strategies can be consistently employed in any venue of the organization, creating such a frequency and volume of coaching experiences that the culture shifts, often seamlessly." At IBM, Creswell experienced firsthand the return on investment of coaching. Coaching not only transformed the culture of her division into one of the most committed and energized learning and leadership environments in the world, but, as Creswell attests, "The entire organization saw revenues double each quarter, five quarters in a row."

The premises of Creswell's and others' approaches to coaching are simple. As people gain competency in learning and leadership, they model those personal changes to others. This modeling triggers large and small changes in the policies, procedures, and processes of the organization, which, all totaled, equal a deep and substantive transformation. In essence, changes resulting from coaching often grow roots in the organization, stimulating organic change where other cultural initiatives fail to remain steadfast.

Coaching can also have a dramatic impact on leaders who are promoted because of their technical competencies rather than their leadership skills. Such was the case with a former client whose tremendous technical capacity eventually landed him in a department-head position. A proclaimed perfectionist, his early managerial experiences were frustrating to him and those around him. Today he attributes a new leadership style and a new learning culture in his division to extensive coaching. His journey was, at times, agonizing. But his team now enjoys the leadership of a supportive, rigorous, and rewarding leader, and they describe their culture as fun and collaborative. This learning culture exists because the leader learned and changed, and in modeling and managing those changes, he created a learning culture.

Regardless of the personal or organizational issues or goals that bring a coach and client together, the learning is ideally anchored in three characteristics: purpose, people, and process. These are the central components of the coaching model I have developed. As individuals seek to create optimal coaching relationships, these characteristics should be carefully assessed and nurtured.

Purpose. Clients experience coaching as an assessment and discovery process in which their purpose is clarified and defined with specifics that can be measured and optimized through planning and action. This is assessment at its most difficult – reaching to the depths of a leader's contribution to the organization and its people.

People. Coaching is anchored in a relationship focused exclusively on supporting the client's learning and goals and in which the coach has no formal or informal power over the client. Further, the dynamics of the coaching relationship are unlike any other relationship because there is absolutely no expectation of relational benefits for the coach – the entire benefits of the relationship are constructed to create learning and change for the client. (Certainly, coaches do attest to the emotional satisfaction of being in service to a client's growth.)

Process. Coaching is a process that combines communication skills and goal-directed strategies to create a rigorous standard for the client's goal-setting, action, accountability, and achievement. Forward momentum and commitment to learning are not optional. If a client is not ready to work hard, coaching is not a useful partnership. The combination of these elements allows clients to develop their potential as learners and as leaders.

As clients engage in coaching, their learning and leadership capabilities are catalyzed, sometimes unknowingly. They become cultural mavericks. And as the principles of coaching are applied to organizational procedures and best practices, the effect on culture is synergistic. Learning is inevitable and spontaneous for many clients, and learning cultures emerge as both planned and organic outgrowths of the coaching partnership.

Two organizations come to mind for their success in applying coaching across the organization to effect change. One is a large utilities company and the other a global medical device company; both, in different parts of the world, have strategically used coaching to create deep, organic culture change. In both cases approximately thirty-five high-potential leaders across the organizations, and across divisions, were identified by the CEOs and provided with two years of intensive executive coaching. The utility company used two executive coaches throughout the organization to coach all thirty-five leaders. The medical device company used a team of twenty coaches for thirty-five leaders. Both organizations rated coaching as the most effective leadership development tool they had used, and noted dramatic shifts in culture. Both organizations are in their fifth year using coaching as a partnership to facilitate learning, change, and culture creation.

A call to change

History has shown us time and time again that only individuals can change their systems and societies. Ultimately, each person must be willing to do the work to create change – personally or professionally. By focusing on the model of assessment, action, and adaptation, people have a template for constantly evaluating the degree to which they are increasing their competencies and meeting their goals.

The influence of the individual can be catalyzed through partnerships whose sole focus is helping an individual. While partnerships and alliances are common in organizations, rarely is the focus the attainment of another's goals. Mentoring and coaching are unique: whether it is the protégé or the client, the sages in these relationships focus on the other person and his or her goals. The compounded effect of such relationships is learning and change that are visible, tangible, and replicable.

This thinking is a far cry from the early paradigms of culture change in which we managed organizational systems, processes, messaging, and more as the first or primary course of culture creation. The new paradigm requires acknowledging that individuals are primarily responsible and accountable for influencing culture, and everything else only supports or undermines their efforts. If our organizations are not learning cultures, then you and I need to get to work. Change awaits.

Appendix: The Wilkins Coaching Model

The Wilkins Coaching Model emerged from grounded theory research distinguishing coaching as a verifiable learning process and presenting a theory of coaching. The key to the model is not only the individual components of purpose, process, and people but also the inseparable

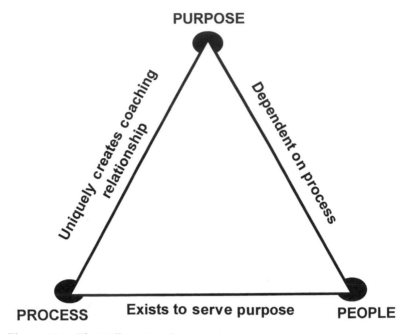

Figure 14.1. The Wilkins Coaching Model.

and synergistic relationship among them. If any component is absent, coaching ceases to exist in its pure form. As Figure 14.1 illustrates, purpose and process combine to create the relationship between people: the coach and the client. Similarly, the purpose of coaching and the people involved (client and coach) are completely dependent on the coaching process. And finally, the process and the people engage solely to serve the purpose of coaching. To integrate coaching into an organization, all three components, and their interdependent relationships, must be present.

Consider what happens when managers attempt to be coaches. Managers cannot meet the "people" component of the model because they are in an inequitable relationship with employees. They influence employees' performance reviews, raises, job security, opportunities for advancement, and other measures of success. Managers can, however, apply coaching skills with their subordinates.

Given the compounding effect of the three components, it is not surprising that 100 percent of the people surveyed said that learning and change are the key outcomes of coaching. Coaching is a viable and systematic partnership for individuals and organizations striving to integrate learning into their culture. Whether managers use coaching skills or deploy a coach, coaching can help align the challenges of human-capital management, the processes of learning, and the goals of the organization.

15 | Learning culture in a global context

GUNNAR BRÜCKNER

IN these times of hyper-globalization, many of us work each day with people of other nationalities and from different cultures. Diversity and cross-cultural complexity are not lofty concepts anymore; they have become synonymous with the frequent challenges that run counter to the efficiency of business operations, and they can be quite aggravating. That frustration can make it impossible for us to learn from one another and ultimately to build a truly global organization.

I felt this frustration firsthand during my twelve years at what is arguably the world's largest global development operation, an organization with an almost unrivaled level of complexity and diversity – the United Nations Development Programme (UNDP). At UNDP, I also experienced the utter satisfaction of working in an intercultural environment of fine ideas and creative solutions.

The UNDP is the United Nation's global development network, advocating change and connecting countries around the world to knowledge, experience, and resources so that their citizens can build better lives. Working with a wide range of partners, the UNDP serves more than 166 countries and territories, striving to help fulfill the goals of the United Nations. Chief among its objectives is the achievement of the UN's Millennium Development Goals, which aim to cut world poverty in half by 2015. Other priorities include achieving universal primary education and environmental sustainability. For the UNDP, "development" means helping people help themselves. This is also known in UNDP circles as "building capacity for sustainable human development," a mantra that extends to the UNDP's own staff.

Today, the UNDP is a results-oriented, knowledge-driven, outward-looking organization, accountable in its relationship with development partners and program countries and committed to improving staff capacities as a basis for improving overall performance. The organization's mission is credible and sharply defined, and the speed with which the UNDP has responded to post-conflict situations, such as in Afghanistan and East Timor, and to development challenges in Africa and elsewhere, reflects the organization's agility.

The UNDP's position was not always so secure, however. In the past decade, the rapidly declining availability of multilateral grant resources for Third World development was mirrored by a shrinking confidence in UNDP's ability to deliver its projects and programs efficiently. This further decreased the availability of funds. In order to halt the downward spiral, which threatened UNDP with extinction, the organization had to demonstrate that it was going to deliver better programs using fewer resources in a shorter time. But consider the magnitude of that challenge: UNDP is dispersed around the world, working in the face of war and many varieties of governance shortcoming. UNDP staff, by virtue of the organization's design, do not stay in one job for more than a few years. It became essential for the UNDP to learn to become a networked, practice-based, results-oriented organization.

Responsibility for catalyzing a learning culture rested on the shoulders of the Learning Resources Centre (LRC), UNDP's formal education and learning department. The Learning Resources Centre operates out of the New York headquarters of UNDP and is responsible for stimulating and guiding the learning of more than 5,000 staff members of various cultural backgrounds who work in and move among offices in about 140 countries. The Learning Resources Centre, during the past decade, was the engine that drove the UNDP's new emphasis on learning as the critical tool to ensure an effective repositioning of the organization within the larger global-development community. Only after aligning human resources and organizational strategies more effectively could the Learning Resources Centre even begin to link the learning agenda directly to UNDP's goals and to the ongoing change process.

Along with the overall sharpening of mission and operational focus came the need for a more rigorously prepared and agile professional staff. As most large organizations have discovered, clarity of mission is the first step; the capacity of the staff is the second. The hallmark of this new, improved staff had to be its ability to respond immediately to an incredible array of local needs, in new ways and on short notice. We found that we could influence staff knowledge (what people know and how quickly and responsibly they put that knowledge to use) and staff interactions (how they communicate, especially when the communication is being modulated by and through a variety of cultural lenses). Taken together, these variables determine the speed and clarity with which every organization can respond to change. Developing and nurturing a learning culture may be the most effective way of influencing these elements in a positive way.

The need to align overall corporate strategy with staff development to produce a fast, flexible, results-oriented organizational culture was first expressed by the corporate pledge of "Learning for All Staff" that became the core message of UNDP's learning framework in 1998. This major shift in the internal development strategy of UNDP was an important signal to the entire UNDP community. It suggested new ways of doing business other than the prescriptive, curriculum-based training program delivered through a series of centrally planned events, which had been the operational strategy for decades. We needed to make this shift for a very simple reason: previous strategy had produced limited and short-sighted results, served only a small percentage of UNDP staff, promoted a reliance on a small cadre of experts, and did not stimulate innovation or creative thinking. Besides, it was costly. In essence, we knew that a shift was absolutely necessary, but to what – and where to begin?

Entry points: where learning occurs

Very early on in UNDP's learning culture initiative, the Learning Resources Centre began to distinguish at least three levels we could expect to influence: individual, group, and organizational. There is also a fourth level that comes into play in organizations like UNDP: the society at large.

With UNDP's mandate for global capacity-building, this fourth level is in fact central to our culture because it motivates the day-to-day work of most staff members. The local focus of UNDP's programs, whether the goal is poverty alleviation, creating good governance, or protecting the environment, is evidenced by the fact that all programs are negotiated between each country office and the government of the host country. Local ownership of the object of work and a locally rooted development program are essential for successful UNDP interventions. The same is true for learning and staff development.

Our approach was to focus as much as possible and as directly as possible on the individual learners who make up UNDP's workforce.

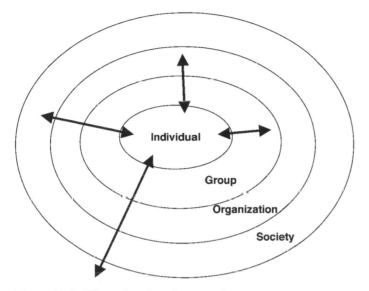

Figure 15.1. Where does learning occur?

This is best done by accommodating a variety of learning styles and affirming a core principle of adult learning: adults learn best when *they* are in control of their learning.

My colleagues and I, previously responsible for formal training, turned our attention to the problem of creating an organizational culture that at its heart values informal learning and personal growth while honoring intercultural complexity.

Individual learning: informal and local

Transforming an organization is hard. Creating a learning culture across two kinds of cultures – that of our organization as a whole and of UNDP's locations around the world – is even harder. We were aware of the difficulties when we set out, and we were mindful of costs, resources, and internal politics. So we decided to focus our attention on individual learning and change, which would then help the entire organization learn and would span both of our culture issues (organizational and local). Our intuitive goal was to promote the concept of individual learning as a prerequisite for stimulating sustainable organizational learning.

For this to happen across the globe, we needed to understand and embrace the complexity of our collective task. We also had to remember that there was no one right learning culture and, thus, no blueprint for creating one. Out of respect for local cultures, for example, we could not possibly introduce a one-size-fits-all solution for management development, even at the risk of alienating some well-meaning "friends" of the Learning Resources Centre. A senior Italian manager who submitted pages of sharp thinking on how to bring about management development in UNDP comes to mind as someone who failed to see the limitations of his (incidentally) US-centric approach. He became increasingly frustrated as he realized that his ideas would not be rolled out on a global scale, although in his view he had sufficiently field-tested them in Mexico.

Individual learning and staff development can be the result of informal – but intentional – activities. Consider one of the most culturally sensitive learning activities I know: the Annual Central American United Nations Soccer Tournament, which is hosted by a different country in the region each year. During what appears to be a weekend of sports and parties for busloads of staff and family from all over the region, senior managers talk strategy, meet peers from other UN agencies, and share best practices – as do operational and program staff with their respective peers.

The same appreciation for personal interaction between office staff is evidenced in El Salvador, where large groups of employees meet up for a daily lunch hour, just to keep in touch and keep information flowing. From a professional perspective, this lunch meeting represents a powerful informal learning activity, which we would have wanted to instigate had it not emerged quite naturally.

In retrospect, I can see why Japanese junior managers assigned to the El Salvador office would complain about the difficulty of integrating with the local and national staff. They were operating with fundamentally different workplace assumptions, such as strict hierarchical boundaries and a need to separate work issues and private life, so that activities (like meeting and chatting over lunch) considered necessary by the locals were almost unthinkable for these expatriates. A better informal activity for them would have been to pair them with a local senior staff member in order to help bridge intercultural differences.

On a global scale, think of it this way: a result of placing such a high premium on social interaction and a low one on hierarchies is that certain interventions work very well in one location and flop in another, or are perceived so differently that they raise confusion rather than promote bonding or attachment. It is conceivable, for example, that a number of outdoor, experiential learning activities successfully tested in the Costa Rica office might enhance team productivity and motivation in El Salvador, while the same approach might lead to utter confusion in the North Korea office, where any private interaction with and among the local staff is not common and is even discouraged for political reasons.

In practical terms, it was confirmed again and again that the essence of transformative change and learning in our organization (and probably any other) is the degree to which individual behavior is changed. So our question became: how do we create organizational programs that support individuals' needs, both those they perceive and those the organization perceives on their behalf? In deciding what to do and what not to do, we had to continuously challenge our own assumptions, operate with maximum flexibility, be aware of our own intentions, and remind ourselves that good decisions come out of reflective processes. The global rollout of a 360-degree feedback program for all managers, with an integral element of coaching support for each participant following the results, is an example of refocusing our resources on changing individual behaviors, one staff member at a time, as a prerequisite for large-scale organizational change. Not surprisingly, even the 360 program bumped into local obstacles, such as the hesitation of local staff in Asia to provide open and honest feedback to senior managers. On the whole, local managers were able to take actions such as lengthy briefing sessions and sharing of best practices from elsewhere in the UNDP world so that the feedback could have the fullest impact on their individual learning.

The most striking example for supporting individual learning as the starting point for broader learning is the way coaching is modeled for newly appointed learning managers as they are trained to become learning coaches in their respective countries. During an induction workshop, learning managers (the concept will be addressed later in more detail) develop an appreciation for the coaching approach through hands-on experience of one-on-one, group, and team coaching. In my opinion, a coaching approach, which emphasizes listening and respect and focuses on empowering rather than advising, is the best learning tool to stimulate intercultural interaction in a complex organizational environment.

Adult learning theory indicates that adults need to be treated as capable of self-direction and put in a position to be able to take on new challenges.[1] For as much as we wanted to influence, shape, and decide, we learned – sometimes the hard way – that this potential cannot be realized in a control-driven environment. Accordingly, without abdicating our corporate responsibilities, we had to become learning coaches or learning facilitators instead of training providers.

Letting go: the paradox of managing learning

The dilemma between letting go and actively creating change describes the paradox of managing learning. We often talk of learning as a spontaneous process triggered differently in different people. We think of learning as the result of a wide variety of circumstances and settings, some orchestrated and some not. When we reflect on our own deepest learning, we know that it has often been triggered by unexpected situations and facts. So, with this kind of context, the idea of "managing" learning creates some confusion and tension, and raises hard philosophical issues.

Consider this metaphor: creating a learning culture in a global organization is a bit like asking musicians from around the world to improvise a fine tune together. Apart from a general confusion as to what constitutes a fine tune, there would be all manner of instruments, the harmonies would range from five- to seven- to twelve-tone, and even the tastes and skill levels of the musicians would vary widely. So how could anyone possibly expect the tunes to sound like the classical works of either Beethoven or Wei Changsheng? We could reasonably expect that the musicians would have fun together, have a powerful sharing experience, learn some things from one another, and create something – perhaps even provocative, musical, and memorable – from their collaboration. But we would not want to have an overly prescriptive view

---

[1] M. S. Knowles, E. F. Holton III, and R. A. Swanson, *The Adult Learner: The Definitive Classic in Adult Education and Human Resource Development*, 5th edn. (Houston: Gulf Publishing, 1998).

of what they would accomplish, how they would go about it, or what they would learn in the process.

Stay with the metaphor for a moment longer. Our uncertainties would not mean that we could not try to minimize the chaos or that we could not create a setting and process for their collaboration, or even that we could not suggest a tangible goal toward which they could work collectively. We could do a variety of things to support the musicians – while still challenging them to be musicians. In this sense we could call what we were doing "managing the creation of music."

Letting go and expecting accountability are not contradictory. In the Learning Resources Centre we found that the trick was to establish a highly conceptual framework for the overall organization but leave the implementation to local and even personal discretion. In other words, we provided the structure and let others fill in the details. By being "just" a framework, the strategy document mentioned earlier was quickly endorsed by top management and within months became the *de facto* learning policy and road map for implementing learning interventions in UNDP.

For instance, once the framework was erected, a simple letter to all staff from the head of UNDP announced the recommendation to spend 5 percent of staff time on learning. As with the learning framework itself, implementation of this new concept was deliberately left to the local level – no guidelines were issued.

The immediate reaction to what many perceived as a new policy was an outcry from many offices, demanding that the recommendation be followed by a detailed set of guidelines (which was precisely the way the old UNDP culture worked and how the new one was determined not to). Because we were prepared for this reaction, the Learning Resources Centre resisted the pressure to publish guidelines and instead started collecting and publicly sharing ideas from countries such as Brazil, Cuba, and Peru, which were quickly generating positive responses to the new opportunity. In all those places, the launch of the concept had resulted in creative chaos and the testing of widely different approaches to a new emphasis on learning – from fixed hours for individual learning, to whole office learning through presentations of resident experts, to additional time off for participation in professional events, to mandatory field visits.

Not surprisingly, the reactions differed region by region and in some cases country by country. For example, several African country offices appeared to have frozen all learning activities for fear of breaking the rules, even though there *were* no rules. Some Asian countries, India and China for example, tried out the concept and then volunteered to write guidelines for the Learning Resources Centre.

Gradually, and with the significant assistance of UNDP's emerging Learning Manager Network, the majority of our offices began to accept the 5 percent as an opportunity rather than a compliance issue, though I admit it helps that the 5 percent has found its way onto the Organizational Scorecard. I predict that most UNDP staff will eventually devote 5 percent of their time – and perhaps much more – to learning as a matter of principle, and the 5 percent concept will become an institutional memory, a reminder of how modestly parts of the learning agenda started.

Rather than managing budgets alone, the Learning Resources Centre had now begun to influence, but never control, the way people spent their time. Our decentralized, country-office approach, which did not emphasize or demand "control of the learning process," proved to be an excellent way to generate an increase in local staff knowledge, a precondition for effectiveness in the global setting.

Our conclusion: there simply is no empowerment without some degree of letting go. We needed to trust the processes we created and our people, both individually and as groups of peers. I always found it intriguing that the value of our admittedly hypothetical time-spent-on-learning budget calculated in monetary terms quickly exceeded the annual Learning Resources Centre learning budget of approximately US $5 million by many millions of dollars. Combined with senior management support, this leverage helped us build more and more trust into the business value of the learning function and, over time, position ourselves solidly within the UNDP's larger change-management strategy, a tactic that gave us a badly needed element of stability in an otherwise complex and volatile situation.

High-impact learning interventions

The UNDP now devotes a great deal of resources to the development of the individual and the support of informal learning. Early on in the process we argued strongly for this, knowing (especially in a global setting) that this is the only way to deliver effectively on the promise to facilitate learning for *all* staff. It was our firm belief that the inclusion of all staff in learning activities is an essential characteristic of an exemplary learning culture. The following interventions were designed to promote this individual engagement of learning – and in turn help us create a learning culture.

The Electronic Platform for Learning

One of the big promises of UNDP's learning initiative was "Learning for All," and technology made that possible. The Internet and newly available products allowed us to create an easy-to-use and leading-edge online learning and communication environment accessible to all UNDP staff worldwide through their computers. The Electronic Platform for Learning was not going to be a learning management system; the credibility gap faced by the corporate learning function was not going to be addressed by more control but by making more learning resources available. The learning platform was launched in June 2000.[2] It puts thousands of free learning resources, including documents, web pages, online courses, video clips, and materials from CD-ROMs, within reach of every staff member, just a few clicks away. A visually appealing presentation of these resources, rather than an exclusively text-based format, like UNDP's Learning Resources Catalog, added some badly needed energy and context to the learning journey of each self-motivated and self-directed visitor to the site.

Individual learner awareness is an integral part of the Learning Resources Centre's approach. So, as a critical part of this e-learning environment, all staff members are invited to take a free online learning-style assessment to help them understand as individuals how they prefer to learn, what kinds of resources will facilitate their learning process, and how their learning style may differ from their colleagues'. Taken as a whole, the learning platform resources collection, individualized tools, and contextual interface acknowledge the diversity of learning-style preferences embedded within the many cultural communities linked through the site.

Integral to the platform and essential for supporting informal learning is the availability of a UNDP-branded online collaborative tool, with which users can create virtual spaces, on the fly, for information-sharing and communication. Complementing about ten moderated

[2] See the Electronic Platform for Learning at http://learning.undp.org.

corporate listserv discussions and with close to 4,000 individually registered subscribers, MyLearningPlace provides a learning environment – outside the corporate firewall and the confines of the UNDP intranet – in which not only staff but also external participants can freely manage their relationships by creating or joining topics for discussion, by storing and exchanging knowledge, by taking online courses, and by chatting.[3] The application helps transcend geographical borders as well as the borders between individual, group, and organizational learning.

In essence, the learning platform provides a refreshing view of learning for UNDP managers and staff around the world, particularly in country offices, where learning resources are otherwise difficult to access. This fact is critical, because dedication and motivation are not problems within UNDP. Staff need the right support, at the right time, using the right method. By providing this and so moving from a limited focus on training to the provision of continuous learning and career development, the Learning Resources Centre was able to meet staff energy with real tools and support. And when Learning Resources Centre staff or learning managers – the power users of the learning platform – are able to point to resources that are available to all their colleagues, they enhance their credibility and the desired learning culture starts to take root. This is an in-house example of UNDP's core mission, sustainable human development, which is all about providing choices within a knowledge context that supports smart decisions.

The Learning Manager Network

The UNDP's Learning Manager Network, which was launched in October 1999, is a group of change agents. It comprises volunteers from all hierarchical levels and sectors of the organization who promote continuous learning and staff development in their respective offices. The network has more than 140 active members, representing all of the UNDP's regional bureaux and most of the country offices.

Working locally and independently, with support from the Learning Resources Centre and a global network of peers, a learning manager's responsibilities include encouraging and if possible coaching staff to use the time UNDP allots for intentional learning; promoting learning opportunities and resources; and supporting the learning components

---

[3] MyLearningPlace is at http://eltree.undp.org.

of the UNDP's new annual Results and Competency Assessment process. Increasingly, learning managers are asked to intervene at the interface of knowledge management and staff development and learning.

Learning managers are also championing the use of the learning platform. They connect with one another online, using MyLearningPlace, the learning platform's collaboration software. Although the virtual communities that emerge on the learning platform benefit from worldwide access to peer support as well as a wide array of learning resources, learning managers are an indispensable element in the learning process. They catalyze thinking about learning and help facilitate the development of local solutions to local problems.

Some learning managers have begun to initiate regional meetings with their peers. Organized with little or no support from the central learning function, these meetings create additional opportunities for peer learning, networking, and sharing best practices as they emerge around the globe. Because of this propensity for self-organization and ongoing regeneration, the Learning Manager Network has become an ideal breeding ground for champions of learning – people who can help the UNDP reach a tipping point in creating and mainstreaming a culture of learning.

The Virtual Development Academy

The Virtual Development Academy is a curriculum-based, primarily online learning initiative that was established to support the professionalization of potentially 1,400 UNDP staff.[4]

The academy has become a successful and highly visible operation – as well as a signal of the emerging organizational support for learning. It helps create cutting-edge development professionals by providing top-quality content through a combination of face-to-face meetings, an asynchronous delivery mechanism with threaded discussions using Internet technologies, facilitators, and work-related assignments.

In its first year, the academy successfully supported 87 mid-level UNDP staff members from 57 countries as they improved their management skills, consulting-for-development skills, information technology abilities, and knowledge in UNDP's practice areas. The academy is now in its second year, with 129 participants from 79 countries. It is positioned as one of the flagship learning products that each UNDP staff

[4] See the Virtual Development Academy at http://vda.undp.org.

member can access, because it is increasingly democratized, through the provision of self-paced modules that will be available for all staff.

The Educational Assistance Program

Immediately after the approval of the learning framework, the Learning Resources Center modified some of its individual learning programs so that they could offer more impact with the same amount of financial resources. The UNDP's Educational Assistance Program is an example of such a changed initiative. The program was originally built around a closely controlled and lengthy administrative process, through which financial support for academic activities could be obtained only if the area of learning fit into a predetermined and narrow set of corporate priorities. The modified program contributes to the creation of the UNDP learning culture by offering targeted, concrete support to each requesting staff member.

It has been both administratively streamlined and decentralized and now supports staff initiatives, provided they are listed in the employee's individual learning plan, by giving help (50 percent financial assistance) with expenses for virtually all learning activities, such as buying a CD-ROM or book, attending a workshop, taking part in distance learning, or joining a professional organization. Travel, hotel, and cost of living expenses are not eligible for reimbursement.

The underlying idea is that an objective listed in the learning plan invariably leads to a discussion between the staff member and supervisor, which is often a natural place for the local learning manager to engage. As a result, the objective is honed and strengthened. Although 50 percent of costs must be borne by the beneficiary, the Educational Assistance Program reaches people who had previously not received support for their development. A learning manager or office manager can now approve the application at the local level. Consequently, more employees, especially women in country offices, have been receiving the benefit. UNDP's learning function has been a major beneficiary of this program, improving its credibility by reaching out with tangible support to otherwise marginalized groups.

Coaching and mentoring

Coaching is an expensive way to support individual learning, but it is particularly effective. Giving and receiving coaching are core activities in the action-learning-based induction workshop for newly appointed learning managers. To date, nearly 200 people have trained to be learning coaches within UNDP. Mentoring arrangements have also been made for more than 200 participants in the Virtual Development Academy, for some 40 mid-career staff new to UNDP, for participants in our emerging leaders program, and for junior professionals joining the UNDP on a one- to two-year contract.

The list above illustrates that coaching and mentoring are gradually making their way into the organization, which I see as a strong indication of positive cultural change. The UNDP is moving from a hierarchical command-and-order culture toward a collaborative environment where respect builds the basis for sharing information and learning from each other. Coaching, with its emphasis on listening and its focus on the needs of the coaching client, is one of the best-suited learning activities in such a culturally complex environment.

Be aware that coaching, while preferable from an organizational standpoint, is often strongly resisted, especially among employees who are used to getting quick answers. But making the client happy is not always the best solution, especially when your goal is to create a learning culture – and not just get the client off your back. Another potential pitfall is that there are so many different approaches to coaching and mentoring that it's often difficult for a large, complex organization to evaluate them all. Insisting on a clearly defined coaching or mentoring standard as a precondition for corporate support may mean that these sorts of learning experiences never gain a foothold. The best practice, as UNDP found, is to support a variety of promising approaches to coaching and mentoring simultaneously.

Intentionality: how good decisions are made

From a practitioner's perspective, it all boils down to this question: How do we determine which learning intervention is most appropriate at a given time? The answer is *intentionality*. Intentionality implies the act of creating something, of deciding where to go next. At some point, and in light of strategy, professional knowledge, and common sense, somebody must make decisions.

I often used the following question to illustrate my personal dilemma as a learning professional in a global setting: If the process of learning were an ailing patient, what kind of a medical professional would you need? A Western-style surgeon? A Vietnamese acupuncturist? A

Ugandan healer? A Mexican shaman? The list is potentially very long. In each case, how much time would be needed to diagnose the patient before taking action? What would this action look like and what remedies would be used? If the patient happened to be in the antiseptic environment of a modern hospital, would you allow a traditional healer to use incense?

It is not at all surprising that different people in different environments give different answers. Creating a learning culture in a global context requires organizations to develop an awareness of what R. Roosevelt Thomas Jr. described as the "diversity mixtures" in the organizations and cultures where we live and work. Some elements of the diversity mixture are race, gender, geographical origin, color, style of working together, religious background, cultural norms, tenure, work-life balance, and time orientation. Then, only then, can organizations determine the most appropriate course of action.[5]

Deciding what is most appropriate must involve a degree of pragmatism. Let me share with you a phrase I have often heard in Latin America, one that helped me make more pragmatic decisions: "Lo perfecto es el inimigo de lo bueno!" This means, "The perfect is the enemy of the good!"

I remember one complex decision we faced about whether UNDP staff worldwide should be given access, free of charge, to a set of thirty online courses for self-paced learning even though the courses were built around biased US-centric content. The question was whether to offer what was available then or wait until the courses were available in all the official UN languages and in culturally adapted versions. Well, the pragmatist in me wrote a general disclaimer, acknowledging the shortfalls and almost apologizing for publishing the courses. I promised that all efforts would be made to improve the offering, and then I went ahead. This decision generated thousands of learning hours at a wonderful price, with virtually no complaints about the cultural limitations of the content.

In other words, when it comes to making decisions, the real question is not how can we be perfect, but how good can we get? We must be intentional about that, too. It would be easy for us to lose sight of the fact that a certain solution may get us farther along on our desired

---

[5] R. R. Thomas, Jr., *Redefining Diversity* (New York: American Management Association, 1996).

path than waiting until we have the best solution. Many companies that place a premium on solid data and scientific approaches may find this difficult to accept.

Often, I had to challenge my assumptions about what was the "best way" to proceed and what, under local circumstances, was the better or even right way to proceed in a specific situation. Decisions were often influenced, if not biased, by political considerations outside my area of responsibility. Just before I left UNDP, for example, I do not know how much longer I could have resisted the pressure to create a two-day staff orientation program to be delivered three times a year, which for whatever reasons seemed to be high on the senior management team's agenda.

My plea to take a little more time in order to work on a blended solution using multiple learning channels based on materials of other UN agencies, which I already had in my possession, was simply not going to win the day. I was confronted by the probability that I would have to deliver a program, quite different from – and in my mind weaker than – what I wanted and thought possible.

When resources like people, money, and time are scarce, it helps to have a quick way to evaluate the potential of various learning activities or methods and pick the ones destined to have the greatest impact. What helped me was a grid that categorized all learning interventions in four dimensions according to their learning relationships and their expected impact: one provider to one recipient (coaching), one provider to many recipients (classroom), many providers to one recipient (expert panel), and, for highest impact, many providers to many recipients (communities of practice) (Figure 15.2).

One-to-one learning, as in giving advice or coaching, is often very gratifying. But if many-to-many learning can generate the highest possible impact without necessarily requiring the highest amount of management, it becomes a much better bet for most organizations.

Figure 15.3 shows how selected UNDP activities fit into this grid. Those are the activities to pursue with vigor, mindful that it is still difficult to meet the needs of a globally distributed staff with a wide range of expectations. For example, the merits of an empowerment-based approach with lots of free-flowing ideas and collaboration between staff of different positions, like our whole-office training, are generally an easy sell to a staff member from the United States. But someone from the Philippines, a country with a great respect for hierarchies and

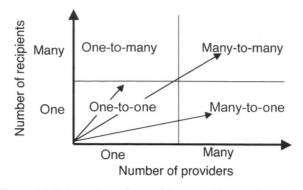

Figure 15.2. Learning relationships: providers and recipients.

age-related positional power, would almost inevitably prefer to receive direct answers to learning challenges, from an experienced staff member or a trainer, for example. Likewise, staffers from Greece or Belgium, places with high levels of uncertainty avoidance, are quite comfortable in structured learning situations and fully expect the learning professional or subject-matter experts to have all the answers. People from countries with low uncertainty avoidance, such as Singapore and Argentina, are more comfortable with unstructured learning situations, open-ended questions, discussions, and coaching.

Some of UNDP's most successful programs are positioned in the many-to-many category, including the Electronic Platform for Learning, the Learning Manager Network, and the Virtual Development Academy – all of which offer peer-learning experiences and promote self-directed learning.

If learning from many to many can be combined with just a minimum of central control mechanisms and a constant flow of information among all the actors (informally and locally relevant), the chances are that organizational learning will be nurtured. For example, global collaboration would look something like this. The learning team in India talks with the team from China about how to implement the 5 percent recommendation as outlined in our learning framework. The teams from India and China hear about the experience of the learning manager in Vietnam and explore that. This is communicated on the network, giving the learning manager from Brazil a head start as she prepares to explain the new performance-appraisal system to staff in her office. Her presentation in Portuguese stands to benefit staff in Angola

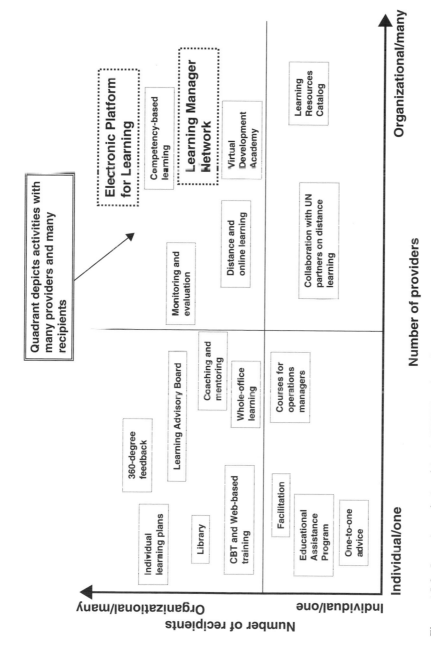

Figure 15.3. Learning relationships in UNDP: selected activities.

and Mozambique right away. The job of the Learning Resources Centre in this scenario is not to micromanage such exchanges but to facilitate discussion by, for example, offering assistance with the use of an online collaboration tool that would enhance the interaction.

Conclusion

Has learning taken root in the UNDP? Of course, this question cannot be answered conclusively, although the trend is very positive. It is significant that staff development and performance is now one of four corporate goals, right next to the achievement of the UN's Millennium Development Goals. Accordingly, the UNDP's learning function is now focusing entirely on the organization's strategic needs and helping UNDP staff innovate, network, and update and monitor their skills. All non-essential logistical and administrative tasks related to supporting learning are now outsourced to a company that specializes in the transactional aspects of learning such as scheduling and administering training and learning programs.

As evidence that some of our more specific goals have been met, I am happy to report that by the end of 2002, 53 percent of UNDP staff confirmed that they spent at least 5 percent of their work time on learning. A respectable 81 percent indicated they are developing their knowledge and skill levels (up from 73 percent in 2000). In addition, 62 percent agreed with the statement, "My supervisor encourages me to take advantage of learning opportunities," as compared with 50 percent in 2000.

There are very few shortcuts to creating a learning culture – it does not happen overnight and best practices cannot be easily replicated. It takes cunning, time, and courage to keep pushing ahead. I should reiterate that achieving significant change in the UNDP's learning culture took years. This may serve as a reminder to set realistic goals and manage what you can actually influence – namely, your own expectations – as you create a time-frame for change in your organization.

We are now left with the confusing realization that there is no single best learning culture and, therefore, no single correct approach to creating one. But we also know that respect for local culture and the willingness to let go rather than to control all activities are indispensable drivers for the creation of a learning culture in a global context. Ultimately, it does not matter whether you are dealing with individuals, a community of practice, a peer group, a network, or an entire organization. It is a matter of trusting the people you work with (individually and as groups of peers) and trusting the processes they will inevitably find to create learning. These people and those processes have to be at the heart of your strategy to create a learning culture. Respect for local knowledge can only be expressed through a decentralized management of groups of learners, and respect for learners can only be expressed through the empowerment of the individual and through massive support for informal learning.

A corporate learning function that becomes complacent or succumbs too easily to other organizational dynamics fails to do its job and short-changes the organization in the process. Failure of the learning function to be assertive and creative (whether the result of low hierarchical position within the organization or the personality of its leader or some other set of circumstances) diminishes the potential for sustained, positive change throughout the organization.

Remembering the early days reminds me just how long this transformation takes and how it is a cultural journey rather than a geographical destination or a state of being. In other words, the goal is not to reach a point where someone can proclaim to have successfully created a learning organization but to foster and nurture individual and organizational learning in an ongoing, ever changing manner.

16 | *Learning in the company of maniacs*

GARRY O. RIDGE

I N 1996, the WD-40 Company had annual sales of $108 million. At that point, we were a single-product company focused on doing one thing. We had done that one thing magnificently for forty-three years, and that was to build a brand around WD-40, a product that became an icon around the world.

In 2003, our sales were more than $216 million, and we had some of the highest profitability ratios in any industry. What happened? First, we tried implementing a number of traditional growth-oriented strategies, things like acquiring complementary product lines and developing our distribution and sales network worldwide. Then, we created a culture of learning within our company. This culture quickly grew into an environment in which our best employees see themselves as learning maniacs, and mistakes are known as learning opportunities. These changes have enabled the WD-40 Company to look beyond its historically narrow focus into a future of virtually unlimited growth opportunities.

But getting there was not easy. In 1997, I started serving as CEO at the WD-40 Company after working with the brand since 1987 in various capacities. Throughout the late 1990s, we were faced with a number of challenges, from sluggish sales to stagnating stock prices. We knew that we would have to make some big changes if we wanted to thrive past the company's fiftieth anniversary. And while we could clearly see the need to move the company into a new era, it was not clear to me at the outset exactly what the WD-40 Company would or should look like once that transformation was complete. Consequently, the late 1990s marked a period of soul-searching and learning, for the company and for me.

A simple beginning

The WD-40 Company's namesake product was created in 1953 by the Rocket Chemical Company as a water displacement fluid meant to prevent rust. Initially, the product was sold only to industrial customers in aircraft and missile manufacturing, but after staffers at the fledgling company discovered a myriad of uses at home for the new product, WD-40 was introduced to the consumer market. Almost immediately after its launch in 1958, WD-40 was a hit, and by 1968, the company had dropped its other rust-resister and rust-removal products and renamed itself the WD-40 Company. The company went public in 1973 with virtually no competitors in its market niche.

My personal history with WD-40 began in the 1980s, when I worked for a WD-40 licensee in Australia. In 1987, the company decided to open a wholly owned subsidiary in Australia to explore the Asian market, and they asked me to lead the new division. When I went to my father, an engineer, to ask whether I should accept the offer, he said, "I can't live without that product, son," and he gave me his blessing. Eventually I moved to the company's headquarters in San Diego, California, where I served as vice-president of international operations. When the president of the company retired just three years later, I threw my hat into the ring. I got the job, I believe, because I knew the old way of doing things and I also had an interest in creating something new.

And create something new we did. The WD-40 Company was in a bit of a jam, partly by virtue of its own success. We had saturated the US market and were having difficulty growing our sales domestically with just one brand, which in turn caused our stock price to stagnate. The most obvious way we could see to expand was to take on new products that complemented our signature product. And so the WD-40 Company began to acquire other brands, beginning with 3-in-One Oil in 1995, which provided the firm with a well-established distribution network in seventeen countries. The company then launched a new product in 1996, a synthetic lubricant called TAL 5, and continued its strategy of growth by acquisition into the new century, purchasing the Lava brand of industrial hand cleaners in 1999; Australia's Solvol brand of heavy-duty hand cleaners in 2000; Global Household Brands' X-14, 2000 Flushes, and Carpet Fresh in 2001; and Spot Shot Instant Carpet Stain Remover in 2002.

At the same time, we were expanding our overseas endeavors. From our European headquarters in London we opened new sales and marketing operations in Germany, France, Spain, and Italy. We also expanded our San Diego operations, adding new competency in marketing, supply-chain management, and financial reporting. We continued to grow in Canada, and our Australian operation expanded with a new facility in Malaysia to manage our growing Asian markets.

After two decades as a publicly traded corporation, WD-40 Company was a success story in many regards: investors were happy overall, receiving annual yields that well exceeded market averages; consumer acceptance was high, with 83 percent of households in the United States owning at least one can of our original product; and the company had a great line of complementary products and a solid set of distribution channels.

Yet, despite our aggressive product strategy and steady stock prices, our persistently sluggish sales indicated that something was still not right. Growth by acquisition was not enough. We could not look just at the end result; we had to look at how we got there. The changes we had implemented to that point, as helpful as they were in many respects, had failed to address some core issues that had grown up around the company, issues that affected our ability to encourage innovation, foster learning, encourage accountability, and spur on leadership among the company's employees worldwide.

Tomorrow from today

As a leader, I have always intuitively understood that it is not my job to make people comfortable. And I do not like being entirely comfortable myself, because that means I am not moving forward.

Several years ago at a gathering of the International Mass Retailers Association, I met Don Soderquist, who was at that time vice-chairman at Wal-Mart. My take-away from his presentation was this: "You have to separate those responsible for today from those responsible for tomorrow." A flash went through my mind as I realized the implications for WD-40. The company had gotten where it was with a team of people responsible for today. The company had done the same thing for more than forty years – and its culture, management style, and leadership were deeply embedded in maintaining the status quo. If we wanted to develop a culture that could take us into tomorrow, we would have to expand our tolerance for risk, devote more energy to learning, and actively court change.

I accepted this vision totally and started looking at the company not only from the perspective of "What do we have to do?" but "Where can this take us?" With my senior management team, I began the process of articulating our corporate vision. We realized that WD-40 had become a brand fortress – a brand that was very well accepted in the consumer's mind. The WD-40 product was bought over and over again, and, because of that, it created sales, revenues, and profits with which few could compete. What would happen, we wondered, if we extended that concept to our entire line of current and future products? After having been a brand fortress for many years, we had to become a fortress of brands.

Then came the hard part: making sure that our senior management team was united with me in this vision. Lip service would not do – I had to see in their everyday behavior that they were committed to building the WD-40 Company into a bigger, better company and making more money with more opportunities for our employees.

During our discussions, it became very clear who was going to buy into making changes and who was not. Some of those in our executive tier who advocated against making dramatic changes may have done so out of love for the company (why not be loyal to the vision that has worked for the company for more than forty years?) and some undoubtedly did so out of fear (what will happen to *me* if things change?). But there is no room for ego in matters of leadership.

I recall one instance when I had sent everyone in our executive tier a copy of the book *The Leadership Engine* by Noel M. Tichy and asked them to read it in preparation for what I was calling our "gathering of the future." Well, some people took to the idea wholeheartedly and seemed genuinely excited to imagine what our future could hold. Others were less generous and grumbled about "New Age management crap."

Ultimately, as we went through the process of articulating where we could take the company, I was afraid that my detractors were seeing something that I was not. My biggest fear was that I would blaze down this path and ignore people along the way who were smarter than me. But in time I could see that with some of these people, their hearts just were not in it. Again, I brought them back and tried to coach them through what needed to happen. I wanted to give them every opportunity in the world to get on the winning side. Ultimately, those who did not buy into the plan had to find opportunities elsewhere. And sadly, we lost two very senior people and four or five others during this transition.

I am a big fan of embracing my enemies, actually. What I want to know when someone disagrees with me is this: "Where is this person coming from?" I believe that a person's point of view is influenced by his or her beliefs, feelings, and intentions. I realize that I probably cannot influence most people's feelings or intentions, but I can try to assess whether their beliefs are based on fact. And if their beliefs are based on fiction, perhaps I can influence their point of view by sharing more accurate information with them. Likewise, I can change my point of view when I have access to new and better information.

That's why getting on board, to me, is not the same thing as becoming a "yes man." You can spot someone with bad intentions a mile off. But I recall one meeting in particular that involved a lot of hand-wringing but was productive none the less. We were in the initial stages of developing our "fortress of brands" concept and not everyone agreed that we should significantly expand our product offering. One person in particular was very persistent in questioning the concept. He kept asking, "How many brands should there be in a brand fortress? What should each of those brands be worth, at minimum?" Afterward, one of my close colleagues came up to me and said, "I don't know how you put up with that." I said, "You know what, I *learned* something in there. I hadn't thought of those issues before that meeting, and if I had tuned him out or shut him down, I wouldn't have heard what he said."

Solid sense of values

Next came the task of identifying the underlying values that had built our original brand and could be carried with us into the future. These values had never been collected, communicated, explored, or considered in depth. We decided to express our vision through a set of five value statements that anyone in the company could easily understand.

Value 1: Increase the value our fortress delivers. To incorporate this value, we started letting people make their own decisions. We needed to create an environment in which people could make decisions that increased the value of our fortress, the value of the brand to the consumer, without fear and within the context of doing good business. An example: Nancy in the mailroom can now make a decision on almost anything as long as it jibes with our values. If a customer asks for a replacement cap for a can of WD-40, she does not need to ask anybody – she can send the cap, no problem, because it is clear that doing so will increase the value our fortress delivers to our customers.

Value 2: Make it better than it is today. This value was my way of communicating a healthy discomfort with the status quo. We had arrived at this place where we were successful, but employees had never been asked to do anything differently. If you get to the top and you do not start to resurrect the company, it can stall and die. In practical terms, appreciation for this value is what caused us to redesign the cap on WD-40. Customers had told us their number-one gripe was losing the distinctive red straw that helps them spray WD-40 neatly in small places. We redesigned the cap so that the straw can now snap into a recessed slot on the top of the cap, simultaneously making our can better than it was and improving our relationship with customers.

Value 3: Own it and act on it. This value is about taking action. Our employees had learned they did not have to be accountable, because the old leadership would take responsibility. I wanted our people to have their own sense of responsibility instead. For example, previously, corporate headquarters had insisted that our sales representatives around the world doggedly follow established procedure on every transaction. In fact, many years ago our sales managers were informed that if they ever asked for an exception to the rules, they would be fired on the spot. Accordingly, our sales managers became very rigid in their approach, a tactic that did not always go over well with our customers, who would prefer that we customized our approach to address *their* needs more often. These days, our sales managers have greater influence over the decisions in their domain, though it was not easy for them to integrate and feel safe with the new approach. "You take a little step at a time and look both ways. It was an eye-opener for me," one manager said. But ultimately, because employees are more empowered now than ever

before, the imperative is for them to find approaches that will work –
even if that means taking a risk.

Value 4: Our actions reflect our commitment. This is my favorite value
because it speaks to what I believe is one of the most important ingredients in life and business: doing what you say you are going to do.
Today trust and accountability must be deep in the culture of business.
It is not good enough to commit to something and not follow through.
We will never help people if we fail them with shallow commitments
and false promises.

Value 5: Drive faster, more profitable growth. Some people ask why
this value is not number one. It is because if we do the other four, the
fifth one will happen automatically.

In 2002, we added one more value: "The perfect transaction." We
put this at number two in our list of values. This one is about making a commitment to meet the agreed-upon expectations of all parties
involved in a transaction. That could be a transaction between the
WD-40 Company and consumers, customers, or shareholders, or it
could be a transaction between people in our organization. For example, we delivered 98 percent of our product on time and in full to our
customers. That is a perfect transaction. When two people sit down
and each of them says, "Here is my expectation of the outcome," it is
possible to learn and then meet expectations. And there are no opportunities for finger-pointing.

With regard to all of our values, I think one of our core successes
is that we have kept things simple. If someone asks, "What business
are you in?", I answer, "I'm in the squeak, smell, and dirt business."
They get it. If someone asks, "What sort of products do you think you
will have in the future?" I say, "We'll have products that live under the
sinks, in the toolboxes, and in the garages of the world." Very simple.
Easy to learn.

Simplicity is so important, but too many people get caught up in
their egos and their intelligence. They are trying so hard to prove how
smart they are that they complicate things. True leadership is about
being as humble as you possibly can be, keeping it simple, being out
in front, cheering your people on, and never letting go of the vision.

Genuine learning never lets go of the idea that no matter how much you know, there is always something new to learn.

Framework for learning

From the abstract process of naming our values, we moved to the nitty-gritty of creating specific programs that overtly support learning at the WD-40 Company. First of all, we have started what we call the Leadership Academy, a lunchtime forum in which we train people on issues that not only help them do their jobs better but also are relevant to other aspects of their lives. The first Leadership Academy was on giving and receiving feedback. We have also done one on investing, and in another session, we helped employees create personal profiles to help them understand more about what makes them tick.

One week, our Leadership Academy focused on negotiations. A guest speaker came in for a one-hour session, and we gave employees a book to take home. They left with an overview of how negotiations work. It is great to think of people going home and saying, "You know what I learned at work today?" I am happy if someone saves $200 on his or her next car because of this workshop. That person will have seen the intrinsic value of working at this company, of working in a learning culture.

We have also created a library in our lunchroom with lots of leadership and learning books available to anyone who wants to read them. One of the women in our customer service department had the idea for it. Now you hear people talking in the lunchroom about what they have learned from this book or that.

Several years ago, I finished the master's degree program in leadership at the University of San Diego. Afterward, I created the President's Path to Leadership so that key employees, people who would be most influential as leaders, could also study at an advanced level. At this point, seven of our senior executives are either taking that course or about to graduate from the program, and two more are set to begin. The company foots the bill for their study – an investment of $40,000 per person.

Then there are what I call "functional learning opportunities". Every two years, an outside consulting firm conducts an anonymous employee-opinion survey for us. The firm asks employees to rate the company on a number of factors, including communication and ethics. The first time we conducted the survey, employees gave the company an 80 percent approval rating. We just did the survey again, and we went up to 83 percent. What we learned from this survey is that employees feel we need to improve our IT training.

So we developed a program to improve our IT training. Within two years, we hope to have 80 percent of our employees earning an IT certificate that would demonstrate competency in various areas, depending on the job. For example, a receptionist might need to be an expert in areas regarding communication, such as the e-mail program and the phone system, but would probably need only basic skills on using our sales tracking system.

The plan is that we will identify which level of certification is required for every position in the company. Then, after everyone is certified, we will make sure that employees get re-accredited every year or so by doing a certain amount of update training through our IT department.

All of this happens without a formal training department – we have only three people in our human resources department. Anybody can schedule training courses. New courses are developed by the leader of an operating unit, a boon for us because courses are developed by those most familiar with the concepts being taught.

Finding the maniacs

Perhaps because I am from Australia, I am partial to the Great White Shark, which sometimes feeds maniacally off the shores of my native country – wildly attacking its food and anything else in the area in a frenzy of activity. I want WD-40 Company employees to feast on knowledge in much the same way that Great White Sharks feed on a school of fish, and I want them to let nothing get in the way of supporting our company's values.

Because it has been difficult at times to inculcate in our employees a strong sense of our corporate values, we have developed a fun but serious tactic. We ask everyone to take a Maniac Pledge, which states, "I am responsible for taking action, asking questions, getting answers, and making decisions. I won't wait for someone to tell me. If I need to know, I'm responsible for asking. I have no right to be upset that I didn't get this sooner. And if I'm doing something that I shouldn't, that others should know about, I'm responsible for telling them."

If I have capital, I can set up the best warehouse, the best distribution system, the best whatever, but it is the people who can make a company magnificent. It was my firm belief that in order for us to unlock the value of this company, we had to have all of our employees performing their personal magnificence on a daily basis. It is my job as a leader to cheer them on as best I can and dispense tough love only when necessary. In other words, I am not here to mark your paper, I am here to help you get an A. That's where the magnificence comes in.

Not only that, but we encourage employees to recognize magnificence in one another. One year, we created a Maniac Program to recognize people who go out of their way to help others in the company. Each employee was issued a checkbook filled with maniac bucks. You could give someone a maniac buck each time you saw that person do something for someone else, help someone learn something, or make a contribution to his or her part of the business. If you had 100 maniac bucks in your wallet at the end of the month, you could buy something from a catalog. And at the end of the year, we named a grand maniac from all the monthly winners. The grand maniac could pick from two prizes: a company car for a year or free groceries for his or her family for a year.

When we first began charting our course, we spent a considerable amount of time with our employees so that we could figure out where our competency gaps might be. Not only did we want to know whom else we might need to hire, but we also wanted to identify our training needs. Likewise, we became concerned at that time with hiring employees who could show us that they genuinely wanted to learn. Know-it-alls are not as interesting to us as people who are always prepared to learn more.

Likewise, we look for people who know how to celebrate their successes as well as their failures. The great former Miami Dolphins coach Don Shula created a "24-hour" rule for his team that allowed players to celebrate their victories and mourn their defeats – but only for 24 hours. Once the time was up, everyone was expected to move on to the next challenge, without looking back. I love that approach, because in this business, you are only as good as your last sale. That is why I have a sign on my door at the moment that reads, "'We are no worse than anyone else' does not apply here." Because we are not everyone else – we have a chance to be magnificent.

I sometimes say my job here is a bit like that of an orchestra conductor. I do not make any music – I just make sure everyone has the best instrument, the best training, and the best seating to play the sweetest music they can. That's my job. If they are not capable of playing magnificently, or they choose not to be magnificent here, we ask them to go be magnificent somewhere else.

Learning never stops

Once upon a time, decision-making at the WD-40 Company went pretty much in a straight line. People could easily pass the monkey onto someone else's back. The only way I could see to change that environment was to help people become more comfortable with making mistakes. But, of course, most people are afraid to make mistakes. What we needed to do at the WD-40 Company was to change our mindset from simply making mistakes to having "learning moments."

A learning moment is when you recognize either a positive or negative outcome of an action. And you recognize it in a public forum. By calling it a learning moment, you take away the fear of saying, "I made a mistake." What you say at the WD-40 Company is, "Hey, I just had a learning moment." Under your breath you might really be saying, "You know, I made a mistake. But I'm OK. By sharing, I know that someone here will also learn from my mistake."

That is not to say it is easy to admit your mistakes, no matter what you call them. Accordingly, it is all the more important that I, as a leader in this company, try to model this behavior myself, even though it is a scary prospect for most executives, myself included. Yet I stick my neck out as often as possible.

I have been encouraged by many glimmers of hope that suggest we are benefiting from the hard-won changes we have made. A future is taking shape in which we can move forward freely, unburdened by the tendencies that had grown up like weeds around us.

About two years ago, I received an e-mail from one of the senior marketing guys attending a global brand managers meeting in Ireland. He wrote, "You would have been so pleased today. Everyone opened their presentations with their learning moments from the past year." I said to myself, "We have arrived." In the past, people would have been hiding those mistakes deep down in the bellies of their souls. We had to get people cheerleading each other's learning. We had to start rewarding people for telling us that they had screwed up. Not that they had screwed up in a negative way, but that they had screwed up in a positive way, and that they had learned something from it.

Even I had a learning moment recently, and though I was very irritated when I first found out about it, by the time I walked out of the office that night I was smiling, saying to myself, "Aren't I glad that happened? Next time, I'm going to do that so much better."

17 | *Trust, identity, reputation, and learning in organizations*

CLIFF FIGALLO

Y OU would think that today's organizations would find the learning process much easier than it used to be. Given the ability to communicate and collaborate across an office, between offices, and with people and information resources around the world, knowledge-sharing should be fast and easy, right?

In fact, it seems that the organizational learning process is ridden with more pitfalls than ever. In many organizations, the more executives promote companywide learning practices, the more employees resist sharing their knowledge, skills, and the secrets of their successes and failures. And with the greater access to people and resources that the Internet gives us come greater responsibilities for evaluating their credibility.

At the center of these learning challenges is the challenge of *trust*. Can we trust our co-workers enough to share with them what we know? Can we trust those we meet on the Internet enough to learn from them?

Until about fifty years ago, when information was first stored on computers, learning was a matter of finding the right books or mentors. That was, in itself, a complex operation, perhaps even requiring a university education. Today, with literally billions of web pages and vast amounts of information available on the Internet, learning is about understanding how to extract relevant knowledge out of a swirling sea of news, opinion, entertainment, and propaganda. The bombardment of stimuli – inside and outside of the office – is far more intense than at any time in history. And this age of information is also an age of networked interpersonal communications in which anyone with access to the Internet can be in contact with many individuals at once – individuals who are becoming necessary elements in our modern learning process.

The information age is not, however, the truth age. In our complex and highly networked environment, trust is particularly difficult and crucial. Any search for truth and knowledge today is an exercise in distinguishing trusted sources from spurious ones.

This chapter is about how trust works in the networked business world and the importance of trusted sources within learning organizations. It is also about the two components of trust on which we all rely – identity and reputation – and the ways they can be managed to promote the trusting relationships that are crucial for learning.

Identifying trusted sources

To save us the time and effort of researching the backgrounds of people we meet or are assigned to work with, we can instead try to establish a person's identity. Is the person who he says he is? And who is that? What has he done in his life or in your company that verifies the value of his knowledge? What has he experienced that can help him relate to your needs? How many years has he been alive and accumulating experience?

I learn more about the identities of my friends and close working associates by talking with them, collaborating with them, watching them in action, going through experiences with them. But in the networked world, and even in our own organizations, we tend to associate with many more people than we can get to know in those ways. So, even before I have interacted with people, I often rely on their reputations to guide me. I may learn of those reputations through projects they have worked on, articles and books they have written, public statements they have made, companies they have led or worked for, people they have associated with, or simply what other people tell me about them. On the basis of reputations, I may choose to contact people directly, believe or disbelieve what they say, question them deeply before committing to a relationship with them, or invite them to speak as experts in my projects.

In the world of real-time, face-to-face interactions, we may extend trust to people about whose identities and reputation we know nothing, if they make a positive first impression. On the Internet, we may trust anyone who shows up in an online community devoted to one of our hobbies or belief systems. Such a contact does, after all, satisfy the criterion of having shared interests or values – the very same criterion we use to decide whether to join a club or association in our face-to-face life. We each have an internal mechanism that helps us decide when someone is worthy of trust, and even when we do not have the face-to-face dimension to validate our trust, we can now fall back on various forms of online evidence.

In a modern learning organization, where knowledge exchange is a crucial engine of innovation, the relationship of our trust to a person's identity and reputation is a critical variable. Trust is the lubricant for the collaborative engine. Considering that an increasing proportion of communication is virtual rather than face-to-face – via such technologies as telephone, e-mail, instant messaging, and online discussion – some creative means of establishing and maintaining trust have been and are being developed. These will be described later in the chapter.

Relying on virtual communications for trusted learning challenges the belief systems that we have established in the world of face-to-face interaction at home, in school, and on the job. We are raised to believe that conversation, eye contact, and handshakes form the foundations for a trusted exchange of information. So, it may be unfair for management to throw employees into a situation where all of these clues are lacking without helping them through the acculturation process that must take place before the virtual environment itself can be trusted. To illustrate the importance of knowing the people you work with and learn from, let me share my own early experience with a community of people who met each other through an electronic network.

Identity and The WELL

My first exposure to a precursor of the Internet took place in 1985. Stewart Brand, the founder and creator of the counterculture resource the *Whole Earth Catalog*, had applied his visionary entrepreneurship to the new and burgeoning use of personal computers. He saw these technical instruments as more than calculating devices; he recognized their potential as communications tools for individuals outside of the workplace. With some meager funding, he set up a system through which people could pay to communicate with one another in large groups, naming the system the Whole Earth 'Lectronic Link, making the convenient acronym, WELL.

The shared interests that attracted The WELL's first users were their allegiance to the *Whole Earth Catalog* and the supplemental magazine *Co-Evolution Quarterly*, the collection of product reviews in the *Whole Earth Software Catalog*, and their attendance at the Whole

Earth-sponsored conference of hackers, which attracted many of the pioneers in the development of the Internet and personal computers. The mix was, thus, one of counterculture veterans, new technical enthusiasts, and vanguard technical experts.

The social interaction of The WELL, arguably the first online community, was conducted through telephones, modems, and computers, and I remember my first experience of it as entering a dark cave where only voices could be heard, except that the "voices" were in the form of words sent through keyboards miles away.[1]

My small, black-screened monitor showed the glowing green words and sentences scrolling past like a fast-motion extravaganza of pen-pal correspondence. The experience was like reading the script of a play but without stage directions. And at the end of each string of messages, I was invited to write a response.

Occasionally, an expression was added to a message to convey or affirm an emotion. "Ha Ha," or "<grin>" would follow a statement that I suspected was weighted with subtle sarcasm. It was at first difficult for me to relate to these people I did not know, even if they were paying subscriptions to support my job as The WELL's director. This collection of remote writers was far removed from the close-knit communities I had previously inhabited. Now, after almost twenty years working in the field of online community, I know that everyone has a similar experience when first encountering social interaction on electronic networks.

The written conversations I found on The WELL were spontaneous, often profound, sometimes silly, and occasionally filled with conflict and frustration. Some people seemed to communicate with confidence and an open, curious attitude. Most seemed more tentative, testing the technical and social waters. A few appeared willing to abandon all civility in their comments to selected individuals, as if in this new faceless realm they could practice behaviors that might get them punched in the nose in the "real world." Most WELL subscribers spent the greater part of their time online "lurking," a derogatory term used to describe the practice of reading others' conversations without participating in them.

I could easily distinguish the facilitators and the agitators in a conversation, but I soon discovered that some members exhibited different

---

[1] See the WELL at http://www.well.com.

personae and moods depending on the topic. They might be combative
in a political discussion but receptive and compassionate in a discussion about health or raising their kids. Based on such a sampling of
a person's online interactions, I could decide whether I was willing to
trust his or her opinions and assertions completely, circumstantially, or
not at all.

Up to that point, I had not met any of these people in person, but at
least I could identify them by a verifiable name. On The WELL, a real
name was required for registration. The WELL was (and still is) a comparatively closed system, accessible through the Web but with "walls"
and a "gate" that can be passed through only with a login name and
password. Real names have always been a part of its culture because
subscribing has meant giving The WELL a credit card number or a
personal check. And though members are known mostly by the login
name that appears above each posted response, a member's real name
can be retrieved – via the software – by every other WELL member.

Real names were not just a fortunate byproduct of the billing system;
the founders of The WELL had social reasons for requiring them. They
posited that speaking under one's real name would raise the integrity
of the members' interrelations and that under those conditions self-
governance would lead to a smarter, more collaborative community.
People, the founders assumed, would be less inclined to misbehave
under their real names than under pseudonyms.

The founders were at least partially prescient. The WELL attracted
a populace that created many interesting and insightful conversations
anticipating the social and technical future that evolved into the Internet. *Wired* magazine once labeled it "the world's most influential online
community." But speaking under one's real name did not eliminate all
dysfunctional behavior. On numerous occasions, a single member was
able to damage the communitywide trust simply by being obnoxious,
obstinate, and omnipresent.

As WELL managers, our first tendency was to let the community heal
itself organically rather than through our top-down intervention, but
we eventually learned that the community needed to define some limits
and consequences for antisocial behavior in order to maintain the trust
that made the community worthwhile. If the uncivil were allowed to
run rampant, the civil were likely to abandon The WELL.

A culture is a shared social perspective that includes a group's
reactions to different kinds of stimuli. A group can acculturate to a

challenging environment such as a jungle, a desert, or the Internet. It can also acculturate to survive typical dysfunctional behaviors that occur in its environment, but it takes time and collective learning to do so.

It took The WELL – which is acknowledged to be one of the most stable (though some would say inbred and provincial) of all online communities – about five years to learn how to absorb the efforts of social saboteurs whose goals were to poison the growing bonds of trust among members. It took five years of experience in the online environment for members to understand the interwoven importance of free speech, accountability for one's words, privacy, and intellectual property. These issues all rose to prominence as the Internet expanded to include hundreds of millions of global citizens, and today they are much better anticipated and understood, though far from resolved.

Perhaps the most significant lesson The WELL's members learned was that real names are not the same as identity. Its members learned that their identities were formed by the record of their interactions in a variety of circumstances. They would witness each other responding to and conversing about a wide range of topics, from current events, to sports, to politics, to parenting, to the technology and policies of The WELL. Their personalities might appear to be very different across these dissimilar topics. And over time, they would often change in response to events in their lives, in the world outside The WELL, and in their growing experience within it. As time passed, we all learned that some people were experts in their field, and that some only acted like experts. We learned that some members were generous with their knowledge while others gave little but expected a lot in return.

Vetting trusted people on the Internet

From my experience with The WELL, I have learned that identity in the virtual world goes much deeper than a name and a résumé posted on a website. Depending on your learning goals, identifying someone as a trusted source may require more than a verifiable name and an online profile detailing his or her professional history, titles, and associations. It may require that you interact with the person and develop some perspective over time.

The WELL was a comparatively small community, reaching a peak population of several thousand active members. It took, literally, years to build its trusted relationships. The Internet is magnitudes larger than The WELL, hosting a population of hundreds of millions, and learning organizations simply do not have years to spend building the trust required to make interactive progress.

With only so much time in our lives, how can you interact with all of the potential trusted sources from whom you might learn? One practical shortcut is to build "networks of trust," which means that you trust people whose identity has been vetted by people with whom you have already established trusted relationships. You should also apply this method to impersonal information sources, of which millions now exist on the Web.

The networked world has already uploaded, translated, created, and invented a practically infinite supply of information, and the process continues to accelerate, even in the aftermath of the dot-com bust. The Internet builds on itself every second of every day as new conversations take place, new articles are written, and new virtual citizens enter the databases. Through e-mail, message boards, instant messenger interfaces, and even newer collaborative interfaces, we meet people and are exposed to their opinions and ideas. Everyone is now a potential publisher to an audience of millions, and huge media companies struggle constantly to figure out how to insinuate themselves into the attention of the Internet population. Spam and pop-up advertisements now assault us during every online session.

I search for answers to my questions through Google and in the conversations found in online communities composed of people who, I assume, share my interests. I am often captivated by the generosity of strangers who give their knowledge and advice to the world for free. "This is a miraculous boon to mankind," I think. I can learn almost anything from people who are willing to reveal their expertise to me.

That is the collective ideal of the Web. As David Weinberger describes it in his blog (more about these later): "The Web, built on top of the Internet, brought us pages, browsers and links. Of these, links are the most important because without them you only have a set of disconnected pages, not a Web."[2] The Web is the interconnections, while the Internet is the technical conduit that accurately and non-judgmentally passes information between the nodes of the network. As Weinberger

---

[2] See http://www.hyperorg.com/blogger/, January 16, 2003.

writes, "The Internet is about truth and the Web is about morality." Whether the users pass true information to one another is up to them; they are not programmed in hard code. Their decisions about what to pass along to others constitute the morality of the Web. Which is to say that you cannot necessarily trust everything you hear from other people on the Web; they may be lying, they may have ulterior motives, or their "truth" may not be the truth you are looking for.

Conflicting with our tendencies to accept and believe information we read in newspapers, hear on the radio, and access through various Web-based media, many of us go into disembodied online interactions with some skepticism. Through the course of our lives, we develop a strong instinct for disbelieving things which seem too good to be true and people who proclaim their "authoritative" views on a subject.

An excess of wariness can deny us valuable knowledge. If we are too cynical, too reluctant to engage, we fail to create any social chemistry on the Web. We withhold the magic ingredient from spontaneous or emergent socially ignited activity. We withhold our trust and thus miss what could be a productive learning experience. To help us balance our reticence and enthusiasm, technical tools are being developed to reinforce our instinctual "BS meters" by providing wider evidence of the trustworthiness of online sources.

Reputation management

The Internet and its constantly developing suite of tools not only allow people to collaborate through online conversations using e-mail, message boards, chat rooms, and instant messaging systems; they also let them share their discoveries about the reliability of other people and information sources. This is called "collaborative filtering," and it appears in many guises. This section will describe some of the means through which sophisticated Web users can verify the trustworthiness of online information.

Of course, the need for trust and identity was not born with the introduction of computer networking or even with the invention of the telephone. For most of human history, people had no way of proving that they were who they claimed to be. Their words, mannerisms, and actions had to engender trust with strangers unless there was a trusted person who could vouch for them. "Any friend of Joe is a friend of mine," as they say, or from another viewpoint, "The enemy of my enemy is my friend." This passed-along identity is what constitutes reputation.

The concept of online reputation management was born with the first web pages, which amounted to a vanity press through which early users introduced themselves to the world and provided services to new arrivals. There was as yet no commercial use of the Internet, so each new page was posted as a complimentary guide to others – a free service from altruistic early adopters. If the service was helpful, the provider's reputation was enhanced. And using the linking property of the Web, users could refer others – that is, "point to" – web pages that would meet their criteria for usefulness.

Today, of course, the commercial use of web pages has made such reputation enhancement more difficult, but we can still rely on the links provided by a site that has already earned our trust. Weblogs (known popularly as "blogs") are the quintessential example of communities of reputation on the Web. Though the term "weblog" was not used until recently, the first blog was actually the first web page, created by the inventor of the World Wide Web protocol, Tim Berners-Lee. His first page was meant to describe the contents and purposes of other web pages and track the addition of new ones. He was the original trusted source, for who could mistrust the person who invented the very environment being used to report on its own growth?

The Web grew exponentially, as we all know, until its use became so commercialized that individual voices seemed to be drowned out by those of business and advertising. Sites that published a changing daily menu of content required expensive software platforms to do so. Then, sometime in the late 1990s, in a quintessentially Web-like collaborative process, a simple publishing approach to posting a daily log or journal on the Web was invented. The simplicity of its use guaranteed that the weblog would be adopted by thousands of people, just as the use of HTML to create web pages had been.

Using the inexpensive (often free) and relatively simple software, blogs are an easy way to publish running commentary on a variety of topics. Most blogs have an editor or host who has established a trusted reputation among a community of interested readers and correspondents. David Weinberger, cited earlier, is a well-known pundit in the world of Internet policy and social practice. He attracts people who agree with his philosophy and are entertained by his writing. His blog also attracts those who are interested in the information and links he provides. Like most good bloggers, he includes a list of links to recommended blogs on his web page. The authors of those blogs often comment on the contents of Weinberger's blog just as he comments on theirs. Together, they perform an information dance called "blogrolling," which comprises an extended and overlapping conversation. Reputations of other bloggers are enhanced by association with trusted blogger Weinberger. And trusting readers of other bloggers who point to Weinberger's site will also tend to attribute more trust to Weinberger. This is an example of reputation management by association.

Commercial sites on the Internet have also discovered that reputation management is the key to survival. Consider eBay, the online auction site that stands as the exemplar of business success on the Web. In its early days, participants realized that cheating in such an arrangement – where buyers and sellers knew each other only by pseudonyms and e-mail addresses – was too easy. Dishonest buyers or sellers could fleece vendors and customers numerous times before developing bad reputations. Pioneering subscribers helped eBay's software designers create what is today called the Feedback Forum, where buyers and sellers are encouraged to post ratings for their experience with the other party in each transaction. These "reputations" are then easily accessible by potential bidders and vendors.

What eBay provides – and what ultimately makes its business plan feasible – is a system for managing reputations. "Is this seller trustworthy? Have others had problems with the goods she sells or her promptness of delivery? Will this buyer pay me with a valid check?" Easing doubts and reinforcing trust make commerce possible on eBay to the tune of $14.9 billion in merchandise sold during 2002.

Reputation management can be as straightforward and mechanical as eBay's system. And in a more sophisticated form, reputations can be associative, as they are in "blogrolling," when bloggers point to other blogs they regularly visit and implicitly approve of, even if they disagree with the politics or views expressed there. Other forms of reputation management are being developed for the use of organizations and businesses with more closed memberships. In these cases, workers' expertise or follow-through performance may be evaluated or rated by co-workers as a service to other workers. Clearly, this presents some liabilities, but the best system designs attempt to include safeguards against reputation sabotage.

People who have proven to provide accurate, timely, and useful information and who are known to be interesting, entertaining, or even controversial can be noted as such in group e-mail exchanges or in systems installed within the collaborative online environments known as corporate portals or intranets. Such personal "profiles" allow members of organizations to seek and find appropriate knowledge sources who may not otherwise be visible.

Many state-of-the-art portal software developers now include powerful modules for displaying users' personal profiles. These have been used primarily to verify identity and search for people within the organization who have the skills and experience to contribute in learning situations. The features of profiles are now being expanded to include qualitative evaluation that can tell searchers not only who knows what but also how useful that person's knowledge is when tapped.

Reputation management systems are now the cutting edge in portal development, with modules that allow people to rate their experiences with others or to assign ratings to messages posted in online conversations. For each message, participants might be asked, "Was this response helpful?" And ratings might range from Very to Not at All. A manager – or all participants, depending on the configuration of the software – might be able to see that employee Joe posts many messages that get a Very Helpful rating while employee Bob does not earn many points for being helpful.

Does this mean that Bob's reputation is shot? Hopefully not, but it might lead managers to coach Bob in the more effective use of learning tools so that his contributions can be more supportive of the overall learning effort.

Of course, any such system is only as valid as the information entered into it. An enemy might unfairly try to put a black mark on a person's online reputation. But the more participation there is in an organization's systems for vetting identity and reputation, the more likely that the trust that validates all information in the system will develop. New software systems may simplify identity management and reputation management, but the human managers in an organization must always stay in touch with the human relationships that ultimately determine the level of trust and the quality of learning.

Facilitating learning in a virtual workplace

Organizations learn through the exchange of knowledge, and trust can ensure that what is taken for knowledge is indeed knowledge rather than unverified information. Years of grassroots experimentation have occurred in online communities through the Internet and its Web-based interface. This has helped define and establish the process of forming trusted relationships in electronic environments while creating proven evaluative tools and techniques for finding trusted information across that environment. Ultimately, what is being learned and practiced on the Internet has its application in our daily face-to-face lives – in the office, in the classroom, and in our homes and associations.

As more of our human interaction moves to the Internet and other electronic networks, establishing and proving one's identity in the online environment becomes more crucial. And once that identity is established, some form of reputation must assign value to each identity so that we do not have to prove our trustworthiness over and over again. Reputation management, facilitated through technology, will help us sort the gold from the dross without having to vet each individual source through individual experience. The Internet will allow us to share the knowledge born of others' experiences. But in such an intermediated world, we must remain vigilant. We are already aware of the increase in "identity theft" and erroneous credit reporting. These products of a systematized identity system demonstrate the capacity for reputation sabotage that could undermine trusted learning environments.

Any learning organization wishing to leverage the technologies and practices being developed to vet online identity and reputation must proceed with caution. At the same time, organizations must encourage participation in such systems and practices to gain their full advantage for learning. In the end, people will continue to rely on face-to-face interpersonal relationships to confirm what automated systems tell them and for their most effective learning. Only with this human-to-human verification process can we ultimately trust the improvements that networked relationships bring to our learning process.

Afterword

MARCIA L. CONNER AND
JAMES G. CLAWSON

I F organizations can sense and respond to emerging opportunities, there is a good chance they will endure. If they can embrace each new opportunity with greater ingenuity and speed – that is, if they can get better at getting better – there is a good chance they will bloom. Bruce Henderson, an early writer on business strategy, noted that strategy and its implementation are related to the natural system of evolution and survival of the fittest. His argument – that organizations, like organisms, must adapt or die – is perhaps even more poignant now.

Today it seems that organizations need to be able to do more than just adapt; they must become agile in the face of constantly changing conditions. And if organizations are to respond intelligently, they must make learning a central part of their strategy for survival and growth. If they do not, the future looks more and more bleak; it will just be a matter of time. If, however, leaders and the people within the organization are learning all the time, faster than competitors, and applying the right strategies at the right times, the organization has hope.

To create a climate in which all of that is possible, leaders must ask themselves, "How can I dramatically increase my organization's ability to learn?" As this volume has demonstrated, there are many answers to that question. Face-to-face in-person education has not disappeared and is not likely to anytime soon. The role of senior management in modeling, mentoring, and supporting learning principles is even more critical amid shorter product life cycles. Technology continues to provide intriguing new possibilities – some of them expensive blind alleys, others efficient levers for learning. The development of networks of learning and learning communities, and the emergence of a global value for learning also promises high returns, albeit at high costs. The central issue here for leaders is their own personal initiative and responsibility. If each leader is not learning, not coaching learning, and not building a learning organization, he or she is sowing the seeds of organizational demise.

In these early years of the information age, technophiles have made claims about technology's ability to accelerate organizational learning. In many cases, these claims have proven to be overstated and oversold. Technology has the ability to augment what active learners can learn. It can help each of us gather information and generate new insights. In a vibrant learning culture, in which people are responsible for their own learning and for helping one another learn, well-planned and well-delivered technology enhances everyone's experience. But technology can enhance a learning culture only if it helps answer such challenging questions as "How can we share critical performance-related information in a more interactive way in our organization?" "How can we make sure that customers' data are up-to-date and available?" "How can we best learn from one another's successes and mistakes?" "How can we extend our reach?"

In organizations where people hoard knowledge and resist new ideas, where leaders say things about learning that sound good and then relegate learning to the human resources or training department, technology only increases costs and drains resources. In this kind of culture or in a vibrant learning culture, technology accelerates what is already there. Let us repeat that: the incongruent injection of learning technology into a non-learning culture only confounds the organization; it does not save it. Technology is not the panacea for an organizational culture led by nonlearners.

A culture worth reflecting

An organization's culture is a complex thing. It includes the shared history, expectations, written and unwritten rules, values, relationships, and customs that affect everyone's behavior. Ed Schein in *Organizational Culture and Leadership* defines culture as the sum of solutions to yesterday's problems.[1] It may seem like an odd definition, but think about it: a tribe, a family, or an organization encounters a problem (earthquake, divorce, missed interest payments, for example). And the lessons that people learn from those problems (accurately or otherwise)

[1] E. H. Schein, *Organizational Culture and Leadership* (San Francisco: Jossey-Bass, 1991).

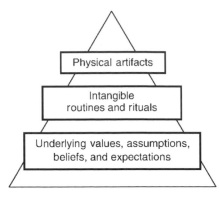

Figure A.1. Organizational culture appears on different levels.

and the way they solve them (obey the gods, stay away from the opposite sex, manage your expenses to the penny) become the cultural underpinnings of the next generation. Hence, an organization's culture is the sum of the distinctive behaviors, intentions, and values that people develop over time to make sense of the world.

Schein points out that organizational culture appears on different levels (see Figure A.1). At level one, there are the culture's physical artifacts: the buildings, the furniture, the manuals, the décor, the cars, the stone hand-tools. Physical artifacts can be very powerful. One company, for example, that was considering making a change from a top-down hierarchical organization toward a flatter, more egalitarian culture, had to deal with a strong artifact of its old culture: a headquarters building in the shape of a pyramid, with the CEO's office at the peak. You can imagine how difficult it would be to change the hierarchical nature of that organization's culture.

At level two are the intangible policies, rituals, procedures, and networks of relationships. Company parties, celebrations, bonus calculation methods, communication patterns, and methods for booking airline flights are all examples of these very real components of culture. And at level three are the values, assumptions, beliefs, and expectations that underlie levels one and two. "The boss knows best," "The only thing that counts is the bottom line," "It's okay to change a decision after you leave a meeting," "Meetings are only formalities for agreeing with management," and a host of other premises constitute this deeper foundation of an organization's culture. Sometimes these level three assumptions are clear, but often they are not – and many organizational members may be acting on them without realizing they are doing so.

One of the challenges of defining an organizational culture is to infer this third level, the underlying values and operating principles, which Chris Argyris calls the organization's "theories in use." If leaders within an organization publicly espouse one thing and model another, their actions speak louder than their words. Such leaders create confusion and sap the organization's energy. Leaders who close the gap between their talk and their behavior tend to create cultures that are more powerful because employees do not have to spend their time negotiating the distance between what is said and what is done.

When Jack Welch was leading General Electric, he often stated his belief that people should face reality "as it is," not as it was or as they wish it were. This value became evident in his management culture: he demanded the facts and pushed employees to know them as well. Welch's espoused theory in this instance matched his theory in use. Many managers champion a theory of truthfulness and then neglect to model it for employees. In such a culture, leaders may want to make changes but do not have the influence they think they do. This is especially true in the case of learning in a culture. If the executives in an organization do not have strong personal values for learning, it is unlikely that those around them will either – regardless of the official rhetoric.

Yet many leaders seem to believe that if they declare that the company must become a learning organization, it will. In fact, leaders do not directly influence organizational outcomes. Rather, they make decisions that shape the culture of the people working in the organization, who in turn influence outcomes. An organization's culture stands between the leader's intentions and the organization's results (see Figure A.2). The challenge then is for the executive group to design structures and systems that encourage the desired culture and then to monitor the impact of those structures and systems on the culture to make sure that in reality they do.

Learning cultures make a difference

The implication of this indirect influence of leaders on organizational outcomes is that they must concentrate less on trying to achieve specific business results and more on creating a self-sustaining culture that

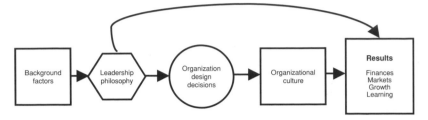

Figure A.2. The indirect road to results.

produces more energy than it consumes. The beautiful byproduct of an organization whose entire culture focuses on learning is that it inspires ordinary people to learn how to prosper in an increasingly turbulent world.

Learning cultures also offer a source of sustainable competitive advantage: they bring superior value from the customer's point of view, they are difficult for competitors to imitate, and they have built-in flexibility. Learning helps organizations get better at getting better – and that makes them more competitive and more likely to survive and thrive in the long run. That is because learning cultures are constantly discovering new ways to satisfy customers' needs, new ways to develop products and services, and new ways to deliver those products and services.

After twenty years, the annual survey by *Fortune* and the Hay Group still finds that the world's elite organizations share one thing: corporate cultures that value people and how they learn. These companies do not just claim people are their best asset; they behave that way. They offer intensive leadership-development programs that address individuals' needs and the organization's strategic goals. They emphasize the importance of people and recognize that this value must be balanced with financial results. And their leaders have such attributes as self-confidence and self-control, achievement orientation, empathy, and teamwork, yet they still manage expenses and pay attention to the bottom line.

The recruitment firm Robert Half International found similar results in a 1999 study. "For a growing number of workers, corporate culture is the key determinant in their choice to stay with an organization long term . . . While compensation will always be a strong motivator, today's professionals are placing greater emphasis on issues ranging from management style and degree of autonomy to intellectual challenge and relaxed dress code policies."[2]

The *Fortune*/Hay Group findings go even further, noting that as a society, we admire companies that successfully transform themselves, in good times and bad. "This ability to predict changes in the marketplace, adapt to them, and capitalize on them more quickly than the competition is what keeps a company on the list during difficult times."[3] People who are learning allow and even stimulate transformations. And the leaders of admirable companies recognize that connection.

The executive imperative

The decision to invest in learning is initiated by executive management. Whether or not leaders take that initiative depends on their values, expectations, and behaviors regarding organizational learning. Their orientation to learning sets the context for everything the organization does. All leaders can create a learning culture, and we hope we have convinced you that all leaders should – but how?

Get clear

Are you clear about how much you value learning? If you are not motivated by learning, you will not be able to inspire others to learn. As a leader, you set an example for everyone in the organization. We invite you to do a little self-assessment. What have you learned in the past year? What new concepts and principles are you using today that you were not using last year? How many nonfiction books have you read (not skimmed) in the past year? How often do you ask yourself, "What will I learn today?" If you open yourself up to learning, you will motivate others to do the same. And if this occurs, the value for learning will begin to spread throughout the organization like a virus – or, using the technical terminology, you will be spreading new learning

[2] Max Messmer, chairman and CEO of Robert Half International, Inc.
[3] The *Fortune*/Hay Group Annual Survey is published each year by *Fortune* magazine in the early spring.

memes.[4] We advise you to check your own core value set and add active
learning if it is not already there. Then, even if you are not certain how,
begin.

Get started

If you start by examining your own learning habits and trying new
things, you will find a way. It may be messy and unclear, but if you
lead yourself, others will follow. Learning is not necessarily a neatly
defined and well-controlled process. There will not be a moment when
the stars align and you will know it is time to start. In today's rapidly
changing world, real-world practice never presents itself as a collection of precise problems but as messy, indeterminate situations. It is
everyone's job to develop better ways to deal with the unstructured,
the undefined, and the unknown. Ralph Waldo Emerson once noted
that there are always two parties: the movement and the establishment.
Which one are you in? Unless you are an active learner, you are stuck
in the past and are likely stifling learning in ways you do not even
notice.

Get informed

Okay, you ask, what do I do? One way to begin the process of creating
a learning culture and to enroll others in the effort is to conduct a
learning culture audit. Although there may be no single best way to do
this, a simple diagnostic can help you assess your organization and your
management team's orientation to learning. An assessment describes
the characteristics of cultures that encourage learning and those that
block learning.

While our learning culture self-audit (Table A.1) is not exhaustive
and may not be in the form that will work best for your organization,
it may help you assess how you are doing as a leader of a learning
culture. We invite you to consider each question carefully and think
about your behavior and that of your colleagues. You might also want

---

[4] From the Greek *mimesis*, meaning "an action that is imitated," truncated
to approximate the meaning and sound of the biological term "gene."
Memes are to knowledge what genes are to DNA. These essences of ideas
have been shown to spread quickly in groups of people.

Table A.1. *Learning culture self-audit*

Rank your organization on each characteristic on a scale of 1 to 5, 5 being always yes and 1 being always no. At the bottom, tally your numbers to determine if your organization has more of a pro-learning or an anti-learning culture. Circle the items in each category that will require special attention from you in the coming days, weeks, and years.

Pro-learning culture	*1 – 5*	*Anti-learning culture*	*1 – 5*
People at all levels ask questions and share stories about successes, failures, and what they have learned.		Managers share information on a need-to-know basis. People keep secrets and don't describe how events really happened.	
Everyone creates, keeps, and propagates stories of individuals who have improved their own processes.		Everyone believes they know what to do, and they proceed on that assumption.	
People take at least some time to reflect on what has happened and what may happen.		Little time or attention is given to understanding lessons learned from projects.	
People are treated as complex individuals.		People are treated like objects or resources without attention to their individuality.	
Managers encourage continuous experimentation.		Employees proceed with work only when they feel certain of the outcome.	
People are hired and promoted on the basis of their capacity for learning and adapting to new situations.		People are hired and promoted on the basis of their technical expertise as demonstrated by credentials.	
Performance reviews include and pay attention to what people have learned.		Performance reviews focus almost exclusively on what people have done.	

Learning culture self-audit. (*continued*)

Pro-learning culture	1 – 5	Anti-learning culture	1 – 5
Senior managers participate in training programs designed for new or high-potential employees.		Senior managers appear only to "kick off" management training programs.	
Senior managers are willing to explore their underlying values, assumptions, beliefs, and expectations.		Senior managers are defensive and unwilling to explore their underlying values, assumptions, beliefs, and expectations.	
Conversations in management meetings constantly explore the values, assumptions, beliefs, and expectations underlying proposals and problems.		Conversations tend to move quickly to blaming and scapegoating with little attention to the process that led to a problem or how to avoid it in the future.	
Customer feedback is solicited, actively examined, and included in the next operational or planning cycle.		Customer feedback is not solicited and is often ignored when it comes in over the transom.	
Managers presume that energy comes in large part from learning and growing.		Managers presume that energy comes from "corporate success," meaning profits and senior management bonuses.	
Managers think about their learning quotient, that is, their interest in and capacity for learning new things, and the learning quotient of their employees.		Managers think that they know all they need to know and that their employees do not have the capacity to learn much.	
Total for pro-learning culture		**Total for anti-learning culture**	

employees to complete such a survey to get a sense of how they feel you and the entire organization are doing.

By taking organizations through this audit, leaders begin to demonstrate that they are willing to ask tough questions and are interested in hearing answers that are honest rather than reassuring.

Get practical

Learning theory and the study of organizational behavior over the last twenty years have clarified many principles about how adults learn in organizational settings. First, adults have a pragmatic approach: they are more likely to learn what they need to learn to do their jobs better. Second, they approach learning with a personal style or set of preferences – not everyone learns in the same way. Third, they learn at their own pace, no matter how much you rush them or unintentionally slow them down. Fourth, their interest in learning new things varies widely. Fifth, they want to be in charge of their learning rather than yielding to an instructor. Sixth, their learning occurs mostly in context, on the job, from day to day. And seventh, the transfer of learning in organizations is largely a function of the quality and strength of personal relationships.

Get together

The social component of learning means that one of the challenges of leadership is to foster relationships among people in the organization, particularly so that leaders can convey what and how they have learned. If leaders try to automate learning by replacing real-time human interaction with technological solutions, they lose the creative tension inherent in face-to-face encounters with instructors and peers. They also forgo the relationships that develop when people learn from one another.

It turns out that many people are social learners. They learn from people and in order to remain included among people. The Chinese have institutionalized this concept in *guanxi*, one's personal network. While technology can augment the development of a personal network, it cannot replace it. Recent research has shown that 85 percent of managers get information critical to project success from their personal networks – and that the strongest predictors of effective learning from a network of relationships include knowing another person's expertise and thus when to turn to him or her; being able to gain timely access to that person; the willingness of the person sought out to engage in problem-solving; and a degree of safety in the relationship.[5]

People need information to do their work, and they can get it only by working with others whom they respect. From this perspective, learning for adults is less about taking in new information than it is about connecting with people who help put that information in context and suggest new ways of understanding it. This social aspect of learning and influence is central to the way people learn at work. In fact, it is the central feature of a learning culture.

Have you ever wondered why college towns are consistently rated as the most livable and enjoyable even for people not affiliated with the institution? The answer lies in the community: the people who live there, who are willing to share their experiences and learn with those they spend time with each day. Adults learn and adjust their approaches not just by getting facts but also by getting relevant information *in situ* with all the nonverbal cues that real people's stories afford. From such information, we see patterns emerge and discover new ideas worth trying. Leaders who attempt to substitute technology for community isolate their high-potential employees from the very (human) system that will accelerate their learning. Presumably, these leaders believe that investing in technology is cheaper than funding training staffs and establishing facilities where employees can take classes. They may also believe that standardizing learning instead of delivering customized programs will help the organization achieve its goals faster.

Computers, the Internet, e-mail, cell phones, e-learning, and the myriad technologies that will be sold as "the next killer application" can enhance our learning, but in a culture that does not allow people to learn in context, technology adds nothing. Technology does not replace a learning culture; it is one tool to use in the community of learning. We prefer to think of technology and how it is used not as stimuli to more learning but as indications of how active a learning culture might be. In this way, distance-learning technology, for example, is not a stimulus

[5] R. Cross, A. Parker, L. Prusak, and S. P. Borgatti, "Knowing What We Know: Supporting Knowledge Creation and Sharing in Social Networks," *Organizational Dynamics* 30 (2001), pp. 100–120.

for reshaping an organization's learning culture but a mirror of that culture.

Get consistent

Suppose that you have assessed the learning climate in your organization and your own energy for learning more, and you have committed to getting started – however messy that may be – and have begun to do some of the things that truly successful companies are doing. At some point, you will want to spark a more profound cultural transformation in order to achieve the competitive advantage that learning offers. That requires a day-in and day-out shift in attention and practice.

As long as employees view learning as the latest fad you are introducing, your culture will not become a learning one. If you look to technology – distance-learning modules and Web-based technical courses, for instance – and assume you have done your job, you will be paying lip service to the idea of a learning culture rather than taking the lead in creating one. While technology can be a helpful tool, do not assume that once you have invested in computer-aided instruction you have done your job.

To cement the elements of learning into your organization's culture, you will need to ensure that new ways of asking questions, running meetings, conducting performance reviews (asking "what did you *learn* last year?" for instance) become your organization's new routine. Leaders who consistently and energetically reinforce the value of learning serve as the reactor core of an organization in which people learn. With that core energy source – your commitment to learning and to creating a learning culture – your organization will come to know that this is "just the way we do things around here." That is when learning will have become a part of your culture.

Leaders who seek to offload the responsibility for creating a learning culture onto technology are missing the point: learning cultures thrive on large, free, safe networks of experts. The role of technology is to assist in developing and maintaining those networks. Companies who misunderstand this will continue to pour millions of dollars into standardized technologies that may or may not help their people learn, share, grow, and produce. Companies who understand this will make wise investments in technology that accelerates their organizations' learning.

Every organization has the potential to develop a learning culture. It takes enlightened leadership and the application of the right technology to bring that potential to fruition. Consider the acorn. There is no giant oak inside an acorn, just the potential to become one. The realization of a large, growing, powerful oak tree from a tiny acorn requires a confluence of the proper genetic coding, a sustaining environment, nourishment, and time.

As the shapers of organizational culture, business leaders, educators, and technologists must examine the changing environment, put new tools into context, adapt to new environments, and be productive under a new reality. Adam Smith did not invent the division of labor and foist it on Europe. He described a fundamental social shift that he observed and then projected the implications of responding to that shift in different ways. Our task is to understand our situation, project the implications, and respond with new tools so that we continue to have a progressive impact on shaping society through our ability to learn.

We are indebted to the Batten Institute's Elizabeth O'Halloran and Steve Mendenhall, to Gretchen Lee, as well as to our exceptionally patient spouses. We also recognize outright that we could not have built such an extraordinary collection of chapters without the delicate work of our managing editor, Amy Halliday.

Index